From Quirky Case to Representing Space

Photo by Lauri Karttunen

Annie Zaenen (2001)

From Quirky Case
to
Representing Space
Papers in Honor of
Annie Zaenen

edited by
Tracy Holloway King and Valeria de Paiva

CSLI
online
PUBLICATIONS
Center for the Study of
Language and Information
Stanford, California

Copyright © 2013
CSLI Publications
Center for the Study of Language and Information
Leland Stanford Junior University
Printed in the United States
17 16 15 14 13   1 2 3 4 5

From Quirky Case to Representing Space: Papers in Honor of Annie
Zaenen

ISBN 978-1-57586-662-8 (paperback : alk. paper) –
ISBN 978-1-57586-663-5 (electronic)

∞ The acid-free paper used in this book meets the minimum requirements
of the American National Standard for Information Sciences—Permanence
of Paper for Printed Library Materials, ANSI Z39.48-1984.

CSLI was founded in 1983 by researchers from Stanford University, SRI
International, and Xerox PARC to further the research and development of
integrated theories of language, information, and computation. CSLI headquarters
and CSLI Publications are located on the campus of Stanford University.

CSLI Publications reports new developments in the study of language,
information, and computation. Please visit our web site at
http://cslipublications.stanford.edu/
for comments on this and other titles, as well as for changes
and corrections by the author and publisher.

Contents

Contributors

FARRELL ACKERMAN: University of California, San Diego
fackerman "at" ucsd "dot" edu

RAÚL ARANOVICH: University of California, Davis
raranovich "at" ucdavis "dot" edu

MARTIN HENK VAN DEN BERG: Microsoft Corp.
mhvdberg "at" gmail "dot" com

DANIEL BOBROW: PARC Inc. bobrow "at" parc "dot" com

JOAN BRESNAN: Stanford University and Center for the Study of
Language and Information (CSLI)
bresnan "at" stanford "dot" edu

AMY DAHLSTROM: University of Chicago
a-dahlstrom "at" uchicago "dot" edu

MARY DALRYMPLE: University of Oxford
mary "dot" dalrymple "at" ling-phil "dot" ox "dot" ac "dot" uk

MARILYN FORD: Griffith University
m "dot" ford "at" griffith "dot" edu "dot" au

ANETTE FRANK: Universität Heidelberg
frank "at" cl "dot" uni-heidelberg "dot" de

JASON GRAFMILLER: Stanford University
jasong1 "at" stanford "dot" edu

ONE-SOON HER: National Chengchi University
onesoon "at" gmail "dot" com

JENA D. HWANG: dhwang90 "at" gmail "dot" com

RONALD M KAPLAN: Nuance Inc.
Ronald "dot" Kaplan "at" nuance "dot" com

LAURI KARTTUNEN: Stanford University
laurik "at" stanford "dot" edu

TRACY HOLLOWAY KING: eBay Inc.
tracyhollowayking "at" gmail "dot" com

TIBOR LACZKÓ: University of Debrecen
laczko "dot" tibor "at" arts "dot" unideb "dot" hu

BETH LEVIN: Stanford University
beth "dot" levin "at" stanford "dot" edu

JOAN MALING: Brandeis University
maling "at" brandeis "dot" edu

JOHN MOORE: University of California, San Diego
moorej "at" ucsd "dot" edu

VALERIA DE PAIVA: valeria "dot" depaiva "at" gmail "dot" com

MARTHA PALMER: University of Colorado, Boulder
Martha "dot" Palmer "at" colorado "dot" edu

LIVIA POLANYI: livia "dot" polanyi "at" gmail "dot" com

GYÖRGY RÁKOSI: University of Debrecen
rakosi "dot" gyorgy "at" arts "dot" unideb "dot" hu

HINRICH SCHÜTZE: University of Munich
zaenenfestschrift "at" cislmu "dot" org

SIGRÍÐUR SIGURJÓNSDÓTTIR: University of Iceland
siggasig "at" hi "dot" is

ANNIE ZAENEN: Center for the Study of Language and Information
(CSLI) azaenen "at" gmail "dot" com

Acknowledgements

The vast range of topics dealt with in this volume do credit to the person who inspired them, namely Annie Zaenen. We would like to thank the authors and reviewers, without whom there would be no Festschrift, for all their work on the project. Authors are named in the Contributors section. Our dedicated reviewers include Alex Alsina, George Aaron Broadwell, Joan Bresnan, Cleo Condoravdi, Richard Crouch, Elisabet Engdahl, Martin Forst, Olga Gurevich, Ronald M. Kaplan, Lauri Karttunen, Carmen Kelling, Tracy Holloway King, Anubha Kothari, Beth Levin, Victoria Rosén, Peter Sells and Ida Toivonen. Lauri Karttunen compiled the detailed bibliography and curriculum vitae in Part IV.

We would like to thank Danny Bobrow and Ronald M. Kaplan for co-organizing the workshop which led to this Festschrift and for co-authoring the introduction. We are grateful to PARC Inc. which hosted and sponsored the workshop on From Quirky Case to Representing Space, An AnnieFest.

Finally, as always, our heart-felt thanks go to Dikran Karagueuzian for always being there and for giving us CSLI Publications.

1

Introduction

DANIEL G. BOBROW, RONALD M. KAPLAN, TRACY HOLLOWAY KING, AND VALERIA DE PAIVA

In 2011, Annie Zaenen retired from the Palo Alto Research Center where she had been a foundational member and leader of the Natural Language Theory and Technology group. To celebrate her long and distinguished career, a workshop in her honor was held at PARC. Six researchers, representing different areas of linguistics that she has profoundly influenced, presented at the event.

The workshop, held on October 5th, 2011 and hosted by PARC, featured speakers who collaborated closely with Annie at different times and on different topics, representing the broad sweep of her theoretical and practical contributions. The talks and discussion reflected on their collaborations with and influence by Annie and offer new perspectives on linguistic issues of current interest. The program included:

- **Joan Bresnan**, Stanford University and CSLI *The evolution of syntax in the time of Annie*
- **Anette Frank**, Heidelberg University *Diving into semantics – and getting hidden meanings out*
- **Joan Maling**, Brandeis University and U.S. National Science Foundation *Chapter 1. Iceland: Is Icelandic a natural language?*
- **Geoffrey Nunberg**, University of California at Berkeley *L'avis des mots*
- **Livia Polanyi**, Microsoft Corporation *Sentiment analysis and the linguistic structure of discourse*
- **Hans Uszkoreit**, DFKI and Saarland University *NLP is OOG?*

From Quirky Case to Representing Space: Papers in Honor of Annie Zaenen.
Tracy Holloway King and Valeria de Paiva.
Copyright © 2013, CSLI Publications.

We are grateful to the speakers not only for their perspectives on Annie's contributions to the field but also for the lively discussion that they engendered, reflecting the true spirit of academic research and exchange.

Fortunately for us, Annie's retirement from PARC has not meant a retirement from linguistics: She is now a senior researcher for Stanford University's Center for the Study of Language and Information and a consulting professor at Stanford University's Department of Linguistics.

Contributions to the Volume

The contributions in this volume represent the broad influence of Annie's research from details of lexical representation to the architecture of formal linguistic theories. The volume is divided into three major themes: Mapping from arguments to syntax; Views on syntax; Semantics and beyond. The papers speak for themselves and so in this introduction we provide only a brief overview. The papers all reflect Annie's academic rigor and honesty, which have inspired all of us: Linguistic research must involve an unerring devotion to the details of the languages themselves and to the theories which account for the phenomena that those details reveal.

Mapping from Arguments to Syntax

Lexical Mapping Theory, which governs the mapping from thematic roles to grammatical functions, is a cornerstone of Lexical Functional Grammar and has been a topic of active research for over twenty years. Annie's work has played a key role in both the evolution of Lexical Mapping Theory and in establishing the complexity of the data which must be accounted for.

Ackerman and Moore's paper *Proto-Properties in a Comprehensive Theory of Argument Realization* addresses the fundamental theory of mapping from arguments to syntax. They propose a new approach, termed Correspondence Theory, which uses aspects of Dowty's proto-property theory with LFG's Lexical Mapping Theory. They then demonstrate how it applies to morphosyntactic and morphosemantic operations, namely passives and applicatives, two phenomena that have been key in the development of mapping theories.

Levin and Grafmiller's paper *Do You Always Fear What Frightens You?* revisits the vexing issues of pairs of verbs which seem to be synonyms, but which have different argument realization, such as *fear* and *frighten*. They present results of a corpus study which supports the analysis whereby the stimulus argument of the verb *frighten* is a causer of the emotion, while that of the verb *fear* is an entity at which the emotion is directed.

Aranovich's paper *Mistmatched Spanish Unaccusativity Tests* harkens back to Annie's seminal paper on Dutch unaccusativity: The representation, and even existence, of unaccusative verbs has been at issue in LFG and other linguistic theories. In this paper, Aranovich argues for a semantic analysis of split intransitivity and uses proto-patient and proto-agent properties to capture the lexical entailments.

Her's paper *Lexical Mapping Theory Revisited* builds on Bresnan and Zaenen's work on Lexical Mapping Theory and proposes a revision which maintains the spirit of the theory but aims for greater simplicity. He proposes a revision to the markedness of grammatical features which in turn results in a stricter grammatical function hierarchy. The paper then demonstrates how this revision affects classic mapping phenomena such as passive, unaccusative, ergative, ditransitives, and their interactions.

Dahlstrom's paper *Argument Structure in Quirky Algonquian Verbs* pays homage to Annie's dedication to the detailed understanding of linguistic data as well as her work on Icelandic that brought the phenomenon of quirky case into mainstream linguistic theory. Dahlstrom argues that the patterns in Algonquian verbs reflect a mismatch between inflectional morphology and syntactic valence as opposed to quirky case.

In addition to the five papers in this section, several of the papers in the other two sections involve the representation of verbal semantics, which is crucially tied to the phenomena Lexical Mapping Theory strives to account for.

Views on Syntax

Annie's work on syntax covers a broad range of concerns from the fundamental role of syntax in the broader architecture of linguistic theory to the (non-)existence of traces and their role in word order constraints cross-linguistically.

Frank's paper *A Tour of Grammar Formalisms* examines four linguistic theories, namely LFG, HPSG, LTAG and CCG, comparing their strengths and weaknesses. The paper considers architectural implications for linguistic theory as well as for grammar engineering. She uses two notoriously difficult phenomena, complex predicates and asymmetric coordination, to demonstrate how formal fundamentals enable or restrict analyses in often unexpected ways.

Ford and Bresnan's paper *They Whispered me the Answer* addresses the core issue of grammaticality in linguistics and reports on a comparative study of Australian and US usage of different argument realizations in dative communication and transfer verbs. They show that there is more variation in pronominal recipient objects of communication verbs than of transfer verbs and tie this to the difference in possible syntactic realizations of the arguments.

Maling and Sigurjónsdóttir's paper *Nothing Personal? A System-internal Syntactic Change in Icelandic* analyzes an on-going syntactic change in Icelandic which allows for a transitive impersonal "passive". They use data from two nation-wide studies to untangle the situation and provide linguistic accounts for the different speakers' grammars, building on the existing data and analyses for passives and impersonals cross-linguistically.

Rákosi's paper *Down with Obliques?* takes on the issue of whether semantically marked prepositional phrases are adjuncts or arguments, supporting ideas put forward by Zaenen and Crouch in the context of computational grammars. His paper focuses on *with* instrumentals and comitatives. Using corpus data to differentiate potential linguistic analyses, he concludes that instrumentals are adjuncts as are most comitatives, but that reciprocal social verbs can take comitatives as arguments.

Dalrymple and King's paper *Nested and Crossed Dependencies and the Existence of Traces*, strongly influenced by Zaenen's work on unbounded dependencies, argues against the use of traces to account for nesting and crossing dependency constraints. They propose an account which combines f-structure and c-structure constraints with the Direct Association Hypothesis to anchor the apparent gaps.

Semantics and Beyond

Annie's early work on mapping between thematic role information and syntax grew into research on the semantic representation of verbs, their arguments, and the events which they comprise. This move resulted in fundamental research encompassing the lexicon, the syntax and then the semantics built upon the interaction of these key grammar components.

Underscoring Annie's dedication to the field, she is a co-author of the first paper in this part of the volume. Hwang, Palmer, and Zaenen's paper *Representing Paths of Motion in VerbNet* examines the existing representation of paths in VerbNet and argues for a new representation that captures the semantic information necessary for semantic reasoning over the resulting structures. In particular, they propose a PATH predicate with source, trajectory and destination roles and demonstrate its use within VerbNet.

Karttunen's paper *You Will Be Lucky To Break Even* examines the entailments and presuppositions of the linguistic construction *be lucky to* and its counterparts. He outlines a complex set of features that enable (or disable) the idiomatic reading of this construction and in doing so demonstrates the detailed linguistic analysis that is necessary to provide an accurate semantic analysis for seemingly simple constructions.

Laczkó's paper *On Presenting Something in English and Hungarian* compares English and Hungarian verbs of presentation and their nominal counterparts, showing how their syntactic realization reflects the perspective from which the event is viewed. Couched in terms of Lexical Mapping Theory, the analysis reflects larger concerns in cross-linguistic representations of event semantics.

Polanyi and van den Berg's paper *A Semantic Account of Contextual Valence Shifting* builds on Polanyi and Zaenen's work on sentiment analysis and the factors that can shift the valence of the sentiment. This paper argues that sentiment is a semantic scope phenomenon: In particular, discourse syntax encodes semantic scope and since sentiment is a semantic phenomenon its scope is governed by the discourse structure.

Schütze's paper *Two Maps of Manhattan* addresses the fundamental issue of what an adequate formal theory of the meaning of linguistic expressions should be. He argues that meaning is inherently heterogeneous and so semantic theory must consist of distinct modules which can capture and reflect this heterogeneity. As a concrete example of the information a theory would need to capture, he shows the difficulties in producing a unified semantic representation for simple facts about Manhattan.

Annie Zaenen: Career and Bibliography

The diversity of these contributions, including their varying focus on architecture and formalisms, linguistic phenomena, and specific theoretical analysis, only begins to reflect the broad range of contributions Annie has made to the field of linguistics, both theoretical and computational. Her resumé and bibliography are found at the end of this volume. Her teaching career spanned many institutions (from Université de Genève to Harvard University to numerous linguistic institutes in the United States and Europe) and numerous subjects (from ethics to French to the many linguistic topics reflected in her publications). Her research career included decades at Xerox research centers in Palo Alto and Grenoble, where she served as a Principal Scientist and managed teams of linguists and computational linguists. She has maintained a strong affiliation with Stanford University's Linguistics Department, Symbolic Systems Program, and Center for the Study of Language and Information.

The editors and authors of this volume are extremely grateful to have been able to work with and be inspired by her, and we look forward to a long, continued collaboration.

Part I

Mapping from Arguments to Syntax

2

Proto-Properties in a Comprehensive Theory of Argument Realization

FARRELL ACKERMAN AND JOHN MOORE

2.1 Introduction

ARGUMENT REALIZATION is of central importance in the syntax-semantics interface. Since Fillmore 1968, it has been recognized that aspects of lexical semantics determine how a predicate's arguments are grammatically encoded. Building on Zaenen 1993, we seek to integrate two proposals in this domain: Dowty's 1991 PROTO-PROPERTY approach to ARGUMENT SELECTION and the LFG LEXICAL MAPPING THEORY (LMT). Superficially, these two proposals appear to be incompatible competitors. Dowty's proposal is designed to predict lexical semantic/argument encoding alignments only for simple transitive predicates. Crucial to his approach is the deconstruction of atomic thematic roles. Furthermore, his approach is not PROJECTIVE (in the sense of Levin and Rappaport Hovav 2005); that is, it assumes that lexical representations contain both lexical semantic specifications for arguments as well as specifications for grammatical encodings. His principles govern their alignment, but do not derive, i.e., project, specific case or grammatical function encodings from their semantics. The Lexical Mapping Theory, on the other hand, applies to predicates of all valency types, assumes atomic thematic roles, and is projective.

Both theories have been subject to criticisms; some of these are summarized in Levin and Rappaport Hovav 2005. Most relevant for present purposes, however, are Davis and Koenig's 2000 critiques of both the Lexical Mapping Theory and Dowty's theory of argument selection.

From Quirky Case to Representing Space: Papers in Honor of Annie Zaenen.
Tracy Holloway King and Valeria de Paiva.
Copyright © 2013, CSLI Publications.

As suggested, each theory, on its own, has various limitations and potential liabilities. Davis and Koenig identify these failings and propose an alternative, multiple inheritance argument selection theory, which, they argue, avoids these shortcomings. We argue that once the proto-property proposal and Lexical Mapping Theory are integrated and appropriately extended, as outlined below, the force of the purported problems disappears and the need for an alternative is, consequently, diminished.

In this connection we argue that the LMT and Dowtian argument selection are designed to handle largely complementary phenomena; given a natural extension to the modest domain over which Argument Selection was originally formulated, the two theories can be integrated in a manner that addresses many of Davis and Koenig's challenges. Here, we limit discussion to passives and applicatives. A key aspect of this extension and integration involves a distinction between MORPHOSYNTACTIC and MORPHOSEMANTIC lexical operations. Briefly, we take the former to be the domain of the Lexical Mapping Theory and the latter to be handled by an appropriately augmented Argument Selection theory. Building on Zaenen 1993, Ackerman 1992, Ackerman and Moore 1999 and 2001, we develop some of the details of the integrated CORRESPONDENCE THEORY sketched in Ackerman and Moore 2001.

2.2 Correspondence Theory

A core element of our proposal is the taxonomy of lexical operations in (1):

(1) a. MORPHOSYNTACTIC RULES: Function-changing rules that do not correspond to a change in lexical semantics; they are often discourse related (e.g., PASSIVE and LOCATIVE INVERSION).

b. MORPHOSEMANTIC RULES: Rules that alter lexical semantics; this is formally associated with function and/or valence changes (e.g., CAUSATIVE and APPLICATIVE).

This type of distinction has been discussed by Simpson 1983, Ackerman 1990 and 1992, Joshi 1993, Markantonatou 1995, Dubinsky and Simango 1996, Sadler and Spencer 1998, among others.[1] Our essential hypotheses are that morphosyntactic rules are monotonic operations and are the natural domain of the LMT, while morphosemantic operations are non-monotonic, and more naturally handled in a Dowty-style proto-property framework, such as the Paradigmatic Argument Selection theory proposed in Ackerman and Moore 1999 and 2001. Once, the

---

[1] The terms MORPHOSYNTACTIC and MORPHOSEMANTIC are due to Sadler and Spencer.

morpho-syntactic/semantic distinction is taken into account, several of the criticisms of both Dowtian argument selection and LMT disappear — morphosemantic operations should not be within the scope of the Lexical Mapping Theory, nor should morphosyntactic operations be within the scope the Argument Selection proposal.

Under this arrangement, an augmented version of Dowtian argument selection connects sets of semantic entailments (proto-properties) with the intrinsic classifications of the LFG Mapping Theory ([±o], [±r]). Morphosemantic operations may alter these predicate entailments through the Paradigmatic Selection Principle argued for in Ackerman and Moore 1999 and 2001; these new proto-property sets are then related to intrinsic classifications via the normal Dowtian selection mechanism. Because morphosemantic operations yield different proto-property sets (which correspond to different semantics), these sets, in turn, can correspond to different intrinsic classifications, and, eventually, to different grammatical encodings. In this way, morphosemantic operations yield semantically-driven encoding alternations. While the proto-property sets represent aspects of the lexical semantics of predicators — the grammatically relevant entailments associated with valence slots — the intrinsic classifications consist of purely formal features that represent underspecified grammatical encodings. In order to cash out the intrinsic classifications in terms of grammatical encodings (e.g. grammatical relations/functions), the Mapping Principles come into play. Before the Mapping Principles, however, morphosyntactic operations can monotonically alter the intrinsic classifications, yielding the possibility of grammatical encoding alternations that are not semantically motivated.

2.2.1 Lexical Mapping Theory

The LFG LEXICAL MAPPING THEORY provides a means for determining grammatical function encodings from ARGUMENT STRUCTURE (L. Levin 1985, Bresnan and Kanerva 1989, Bresnan and Moshi 1990, Alsina and Mchombo 1993, Zaenen 1993, Alsina 1996, Butt, Dalrymple, and Frank 1997, among others). While specific details of the Mapping Theory differ from proposal to proposal, they usually include four crucial components:

(2)

i. A predicator's arguments are ordered according to the THEMATIC HIERARCHY: (ag > ben > exp/goal > instr > pat/th > loc)

ii. Each argument is intrinsically classified with the features drawn from [±o], [±r]. The thematic role of the argument determines this INTRINsic classification by principles like the following:

a. patients/themes are classified $[-r]$
b. secondary patients are classified $[+o]$
c. other roles are classified $[-o]$

iii. Monotonic operations may suppress arguments if features are added, but may not change existing ones.

vi. Arguments map to grammatical functions by simultaneously satisfying a series of principles. These include:

a. THE SUBJECT CONDITION: Every predicator has a SUBJ function.

b. FUNCTION-ARGUMENT BIUNIQUENESS: Every a-structure role must be associated with a unique grammatical function.

c. MAPPING PRINCIPLES: Map the highest argument onto the SUBJ function, other roles are mapped onto the lowest compatible grammatical function on the functional hierarchy (SUBJ > OBJ > OBL > OBJ$_\theta$), according to the functional decompositions:

SUBJ : $[-o, -r]$
OBJ : $[+o, -r]$
OBL : $[-o, +r]$
OBJ$_\theta$: $[+o, +r]$

The operation of the Mapping Theory is illustrated for simple transitive, unaccusative and unergative English predicates in (3):

(3) *hit* <ag, pt>   *fall* <pt>   *work* <ag>   a-structure

       $[-o]$ $[-r]$ $[-r]$ $[-o]$ intrinsic
                                                       classification

       SUBJ OBJ   SUBJ   SUBJ   grammatical
                                                       functions

2.2.2   Argument Selection

In order to render Dowtian argument selection compatible with the Lexical Mapping Theory, the Argument Selection Principle needs to be restated as a well-formedness condition on the alignments between proto-property entailments and intrinsic feature classifications. In addition, argument selection must be extended to account for the intrinsic feature classification of arguments of both transitive and intransitive predicates.

Zaenen 1993 proposed precisely this type of revision of Dowty's selection principle, thereby incorporating a proto-role theory of thematic relations into the Lexical Mapping Theory. We follow her proposal, in a slightly modified form, in formulating the argument selection principle below. Recall that Dowty's Argument Selection Principle constrains the association of grammatical functions and arguments of underived transitive predicates (i.e., transitive predicates that have not undergone morphosyntactic operations such as Passive). Under the Lexical Mapping Theory, such predicates are two-place, and have the intrinsic classifications [−o] and [−r], where the [−o] argument maps to the SUBJ function and the [−r] to OBJ. This permits restatement of the Argument Selection Principle in terms of [−o] and [−r] intrinsic classification.[2]

Before presenting the revised principles, however, it will be useful to make use of Dowty's 1998 notion of GRAMMATICAL STATUS LOADING:

(4) The GRAMMATICAL STATUS LOADING of an argument is the number of proto-agent properties minus the number of proto-patient properties.

The intuition behind Grammatical Status Loading is that proto-agentivity and proto-patientivity status is not based only on the relative number of proto-agent/patient entailments, but rather, on the relative degree of proto-agentivity/patientivity, where 'degree' is defined in terms of the number of proto-agent properties minus proto-patient properties (and vice versa).[3] Putting this new, more nuanced notion of Proto-Agent (argument with greatest grammatical status loading) and Proto-Patient (least loading) together with intrinsic classification features, we propose the revised Transitive Argument Selection Principle in (5):

(5) TRANSITIVE ARGUMENT SELECTION PRINCIPLE: In predicates with [−o] and [−r] arguments, the argument with the greatest grammatical status loading will have the intrinsic classification [−o]; the one with the least grammatical status loading will have the intrinsic classification [−r].[4]

Mapping principles derive the ultimate grammatical functions for basic transitive predicates. This is illustrated for the transitive predicate *build*, where one argument is associated with four proto-agent

---

[2]Because of space limitations, we only discuss transitives; Zaenen extends this to intransitive predicates, and accounts for differences between unaccusative and unergative predicates.

[3]Dowty 1991 and Ackerman and Moore 2001 suggest that the explanatory role of the counting mechanism itself may be mitigated in instances where the weighting of particular properties may play a determinative role for grammatical encoding in certain constructions.

[4]Following Dowty (1991:576), the Transitive Argument Selection Principle does not constrain encodings when the arguments have equal encodings. In this case, encodings are lexically determined.

properties (volitional, sentient, causer, independent existence) and no proto-patient properties. The other argument is entailed to have four proto-patient arguments (change of state, incremental theme, causally affected, no independent existence) and no proto-agent properties:

(6) build $<\text{arg}_1,$ $\text{arg}_2>$
$+4$ -4 – loading (from semantic entailments)
$[-o]$ $[-r]$ – intrinsic class. (Argument Selection)
SUBJ   OBJ – grammatical functions (derived
                via mapping principles)

It is important to emphasize that as in Dowty's 1991 Argument Selection Principle, we assume that lexical entries specify both proto-property sets and intrinsic classifications. That is, unlike the original Lexical Mapping Theory, we do not derive the intrinsic classifications from semantic roles. Rather, the Transitive Argument Selection Principle only serves as a well-formedness condition on the way proto-property sets and intrinsic classifications can be aligned. Such selection principles constrain the class of possible lexical entries. As formulated, the Transitive Argument Selection Principle constrains the alignment of $[-o]$ and $[-r]$ arguments for predicates that have both. Of course, it is possible that transitive predicates have three arguments. This is discussed in Dowty 1991; he notes that a corollary of his Argument Selection Principle is that a 'third' argument — that is, one that is neither the proto-agent nor the proto-patient — will be neither a subject nor an object (COROLLARY 2, Dowty 1991:576; see also Primus 1999 for discussion of PROTO-RECIPIENT). Within the LFG Mapping Theory, these third arguments will either be obliques or restricted objects.[5] There are a number of intrinsic classifications that can yield these encodings. While there are clearly lexical semantic generalizations guiding some of these, the intrinsic classification is, in general, not determined by any of the selection principles, and can vary from entry to entry.

2.2.3 Morphosyntactic Operations

Once Dowtian argument selection is keyed to intrinsic feature classifications, instead of grammatical functions, the LMT can apply monotonically to handle morphosyntactic function alternations. For example, passivization is analyzed as a morphosyntactic operation that suppresses the most prominent semantic argument (Bresnan and Kanerva

---

[5]See Ackerman and Moore 2011 for extensive discussion of the cross-linguistic and cross-theoretical status of these 'extra' arguments, as well arguments that may, in some cases, take the OBJ function. The proposal therein dispenses with aspects of the LMT, but is largely compatible with the proposals here.

1989:27). In this case, 'suppression' simply means that the argument cannot be associated with a grammatical function, and if realized at all, is realized as an adjunct. The basic entailments of the predicate remain unchanged, however. The most prominent semantic argument is defined as the argument that is highest on the thematic hierarchy in (2i). As stated, the thematic hierarchy relies on atomic thematic roles. However, as pointed out in Dowty 1991, it is a simple matter to derive a similar hierarchy as an emergent property of degrees of proto-agentivity. Dowty 1998 does this in terms of grammatical status loading:

(7) X outranks Y on the THEMATIC HIERARCHY iff, X's grammatical status loading is greater than that of Y.

Given this reinterpretation of the thematic hierarchy, Bresnan and Kanerva's LMT analysis of passive, a morphosyntactic operation, is restated in (8) and illustrated in (9):

(8) PASSIVE: Suppress the highest grammatical status loading argument.

(9)

	destroy		destroyed	
	$<$arg$_1$	arg$_2>$	$<$arg$_1$	arg$_2>$
properties:	PA	PP	PA	PP
loading:	+	−	+	−
Intrinsic Classification:	[−o]	[−r]	[−o]	[−r]
Passive:	n/a		$\emptyset$	
Functions:	SUBJ	OBJ	SUBJ	

Notice that in both the active and passive predicates, the Transitive Argument Selection Principle is satisfied — 'transitive' in this respect refers to intrinsic classifications (which are identical), and not grammatical function assignments. This result is the outcome of the interface between Dowtian argument selection and the LMT's intrinsic feature assignment.

2.2.4 Morphosemantic Operations

Morphosemantic alternations occur when predicators exhibit alternative grammatical realizations accompanied by a lexical semantic contrast. There are two sub-types of morphosemantic alternations: those where the alternants maintain a constant valence, but differ in grammatical encoding (often in terms of different grammatical functions), and those where the alternants differ in valence.[6] Limiting ourselves to

---

[6]Some morphosemantic alternations, such as many cases of productive causative formation, have alternants that differ in both valence and grammatical function encoding.

the first type, consider the morphosemantic alternation in (10), where the grammatical function contrast between direct and indirect object correlates with a semantic contrast with respect to the proto-patient property UNDERGOES CHANGE OF STATE:

(10) a. Los   perros **lo**   molestan. DO: undergoes
         the.PL dog.PL 3SG.ACC harass.3PL   change of state
         'The dogs harass him.'

   b. Los   perros **le**   molestan. IO: no change of state
         the.PL dog.PL 3SG.DAT harass.3PL
         'Dogs bother him.'

Ackerman and Moore 1999 and 2001 propose that morphosemantic alternations like these be subject to the PARADIGMATIC ARGUMENT SELECTION PRINCIPLE in (11):

(11) PARADIGMATIC ARGUMENT SELECTION PRINCIPLE:
    Let P $(\ldots, \text{arg}_i, \ldots)$ and P' $(\ldots, \text{arg}'_i \ldots)$ be related predicates, where arg_i and arg'_i are corresponding arguments. If arg_i and arg'_i exhibit different grammatical encodings and arg_i is more proto-typical with respect to a particular proto-role than arg'_i, then arg_i's encoding will be less oblique than arg'_i's encoding (Ackerman and Moore 2001:67).[7]

(11) is intended to explain the empirical observation that prototypical patients tend to be encoded as accusative objects, while mitigated patientivity is reflected in more oblique encoding (and similarly, for agents and nominative subject encoding). Ackerman and Moore interpret obliqueness through various grammatical function and case hierarchies. In the present system we would like to use the Paradigmatic Argument Selection Principle to constrain intrinsic classification; to this end, Zaenen's 1993 hierarchy in (12) defines an appropriate measure of obliqueness, which correctly predicts the two senses of *molestar* in (13).

(12) $[-o] < [-r] < [+o] < [+r]$ (Zaenen 1993:151)

(13) a. *molestar$_a$* $<\text{arg}_1,$ $\text{arg}_2>$
                    P-A   P-P + COS
                    $[-o]$ $[-r]$

   b. *molestar$_b$* $<\text{arg}_1,$ $\text{arg}_2>$
                    P-A   P-P
                    $[-o]$ $[+o]$
                              (or $[+r]$)[8]

---

[7]There are two possible interpretations of this principle: it could be viewed as a well-formedness condition on lexical semantic rules that relate predicates or as a well-formedness condition that constrains the structure of the lexicon.

2.2.5 Applicatives

Davis and Koenig argue that the Chicheŵa applicative examples in (14) pose conceptual problems for the Lexical Mapping Theory:

(14) a. Asodzi   a-ku-póny-ér-a   pa-tsîndwi myálá.
     fisherman 1s-PR-throw-AP-FV on.the.roof stones

   b. Asodzi   a-ku-póny-ér-a   myálá pa-tsîndwi.
     fisherman 1s-PR-throw-AP-FV stones on.the.roof
     'Fishermen are throwing stones on the roof.'

Alsina and Mchombo 1993 propose alternative intrinsic classifications for these examples:

(15)   *póny-ér* 'throw-on'
                     <ag   th   loc>   or   <ag   th   loc>
         Intrinsic
         Classification: [−o] [+o] [−r]   [−o] [−r] [+o]
         Functions: SUBJ OBJ$_\theta$ OBJ   SUBJ OBJ   OBJ$_\theta$

Alsina and Mchombo derive these intrinsic classifications from alternative intrinsic classification options for certain arguments (e.g., instrumentals, patients, themes, locatives). While this works for the case at hand, Davis and Koenig note that this would also, in principle, allow alternative intrinsic classifications in simple transitive predicates; i.e., a patient argument could be classified [−r] or [+o]:

(16)   *build*
                     <ag   pt>   or   <ag   pt>
         Intrinsic
         Classification: [−o] [−r]   [−o] [+o]
         Functions: SUBJ OBJ   SUBJ OBJ

As can be seen, this is largely a conceptual issue, given the absence of any evident empirical consequence — the function assignment ends up being the same. Nevertheless, under our approach, the alternative classifications in applicatives are likely to be a consequence of a morphosemantic rule that introduces the applicative argument. Even when there is no demonstrable semantic contrast associated with applicative

---

[8]LFG does not treat INDIRECT OBJECT as a grammatical function. Thus, the intrinsic classification ([+o] versus [+r]) depends on the analysis of Spanish dative arguments (OBJ$_\theta$ versus OBL$_\theta$). Alsina 1996 treats both Catalan accusative and dative arguments as OBJs, and distinguishes them in terms of case. The Paradigmatic Argument Selection Principle can accommodate this type of analysis by interpreting obliqueness in terms of a case hierarchy. See Ackerman and Moore 2001 for arguments that the Paradigmatic Argument Selection Principle constrains both grammatical function and case assignment.

alternations, it is worth noting that the Transitive Argument Selection Principle under-determines the intrinsic classification of 'third' arguments: this predicts that any classifications should be possible and yields a *de facto* lexical class based account, as is the case in a multiple inheritance account proposed by Davis and Koenig.[9]

Simple transitive predicates, on the other hand, if they do not participate in a morphosemantic alternation, will typically have only one lexical entry and will involve [−o] and [−r] arguments, which will be aligned with proto-property sets according to the Transitive Argument Selection Principle in (5).

2.3 Conclusion

Correspondence Theory adopts Zaenen's revision to the Lexical Mapping Theory that accommodates Dowty's 1991 insights regarding the proto-type nature of thematic roles. It also accommodates Ackerman and Moore's extension to Dowty's basic proposal to provide an account of morphosemantic alternations. In doing so, it addresses liabilities and limitations of both standard Lexical Mapping Theory and Dowty's proto-role proposal. It frees the Lexical Mapping Theory from its dependence on atomic thematic roles and the thematic hierarchy and it extends Dowty's proto-role account to a wider range of data. The Correspondence[10] Theory also makes what we believe to be the right cut between monotonic and non-monotonic operations. The Lexical Mapping Theory algorithm that determines grammatical functions is monotonic and is entirely dependent on classificatory features. In contrast, lexical semantic information is accessed only where it is necessary — that is in the process of argument selection (intrinsic classification): The Transitive Selection Principle and the Paradigmatic Argument Selection Principle uses proto-properties to regulate the intrinsic classification of related predicates. In as much as these are exactly the cases where lexical semantic information is crucial for the eventual functional encoding of arguments: any mapping theory needs to access semantics here, and, perhaps, only here.

This division of labor crucially addresses some problematic issues identified by Davis and Koenig. Once a theoretical distinction between

---

[9]See Ackerman and Moore 2011, and references cited therein, for a more in-depth discussion of the typology of applicative constructions. While cast in somewhat different terms, this work also suggests that function assignment needs to be idiosyncratic in some cases.

[10]We are using the term adjunct in the present context simply with respect to its syntactic optionality, recognizing that the "argument" versus "adjunct" status of these elements is a complex issue.

morphosyntactic and morphosemantic operations is made, it becomes clear that the respective domains of the Lexical Mapping Theory and Proto-Property Theory divide roughly along these lines. The static well-formedness nature of the selection principles and the emergence of the Thematic Hierarchy from the Proto-Roles achieve some of the predicate-class effects that Davis and Koenig attribute to multiple inheritance. Thus, the Correspondence Theory brings together aspects of Proto-Roles, with static argument selection, and the Lexical Mapping Theory, with its account of monotonic morphosyntactic operations, to account for the full range of lexical operations. This can be accomplished by providing a synthesis of these proposals based on the intuitions guiding Zaenen 1993.

References

Ackerman, Farrell. 1990. Locative alternation vs. locative inversion. In A. Halpern, ed., *The Proceeding of the Ninth West Coast Conference on Formal Linguistics*, pages 1–13. CSLI Publications.

Ackerman, Farrell. 1992. Complex predicates and morpholexical relatedness: Locative alternation in Hungarian. In I. Sag and A. Szabolsci, eds., *Lexical Matters*, pages 55–83. CSLI Publications.

Ackerman, Farrell and John Moore. 1999. Syntagmatic and paradigmatic dimensions of causee encodings. *Linguistics and Philosophy* 22:1–44.

Ackerman, Farrell and John Moore. 2001. *Proto-properties and Grammatical Encoding: A Correspondence Theory of Argument Selection*. CSLI Publications.

Ackerman, Farrell and John Moore. 2011. The Object* parameter and the functional expression Continuum: Evidence from Moro. Unpublished manuscript. University of California, San Diego.

Alsina, Alex. 1996. *The Role of Argument Structure in Grammar: Evidence from Romance*. CSLI Publications.

Alsina, Alex and Sam Mchombo. 1993. Object asymmetries and the Chicheŵa applicative construction. In S. Mchombo, ed., *Theoretical Aspects of Bantu Grammar*, pages 17–45. CSLI Publications.

Bresnan, Joan and Jonni Kanerva. 1989. Locative inversion in Chicheŵa: A case study of factorization in grammar. *Linguistic Inquiry* 20:1–50.

Bresnan, Joan and Lioba Moshi. 1990. Object asymmetries in comparative Bantu syntax. *Linguistic Inquiry* 21:147–185.

Butt, Miriam, Mary Dalrymple, and Anette Frank. 1997. An architecture for linking theory in LFG. In M. Butt and T. H. King, eds., *On-line Proceedings of the LFG97 Conference*. CSLI Publications.

Davis, Anthony and Jean-Pierre Koenig. 2000. Linking as constraints on word classes in a hierarchical lexicon. *Language* 76:56–91.

Dowty, David. 1991. Thematic roles and argument selection. *Language* 67:547–619.

Dowty, David. 1998. On the origin of Thematic Role types. Paper, The Lexicon in Focus Conference. Wuppertal, August 1998.

Dubinsky, Stan and Silvester Ron Simango. 1996. Passive and stative in Chicheŵa: Evidence for modular distinctions in grammar. *Language* 72:749–81.

Fillmore, Charles. 1968. The case for case. In E. Bach and R. Harms, eds., *Universals in Linguistic Theory*, pages 1–90. Holt.

Joshi, Smita. 1993. *Selection of Grammatical and Logical Functions in Marathi*. Ph.D. thesis, Stanford University.

Levin, Beth and Malka Rappaport-Hovav. 2005. *Argument Realization*. Cambridge University Press.

Levin, Lori. 1985. *Operations on Lexical Forms: Unaccusative Rules in Germanic Languages*. Ph.D. thesis, MIT.

Markantonatou, Stella. 1995. Modern Greek deverbal nominals: An LMT approach. *Journal of Linguistics* 31:267–299.

Primus, Beatrice. 1999. *Cases and Thematic Roles: Ergative, Accusative and Active*. Niemeyer.

Sadler, Louisa and Andrew Spencer. 1998. Morphology and argument structure. In A. Spencer and A. Zwicky, eds., *The Handbook of Morphology*, pages 206–235. Blackwells.

Simpson, Jane. 1983. *Aspects of Walpiri Morphology and Syntax*. Ph.D. thesis, MIT.

Zaenen, Annie. 1993. Unaccusativity in Dutch: Integrating syntax and lexical semantics. In J. Pustejovsky, ed., *Semantics and the Lexicon*, pages 129–161. Kluwer.

3

Do You Always Fear What Frightens You?

BETH LEVIN AND JASON GRAFMILLER

3.1 Introduction

English has a rich inventory of psychological verbs, or psych-verbs: verbs that describe the experiencing of some emotion. Of these, few are cited as frequently as *fear* and *frighten*, exemplified in (1).[1]

(1) a. Indiana Jones feared the snakes.

b. The snakes frightened Indiana Jones.

Most likely, this verb pair is often used because its members appear to refer to the same emotion and involve the same arguments — often referred to as the experiencer and the stimulus[2] — and yet they associate those arguments with different syntactic positions. The verb *fear* is representative of verbs whose experiencer argument is realized as the subject, so-called experiencer-subject psych-verbs. Conversely, *frighten* represents the experiencer-object psych-verbs, verbs which map their experiencer argument to direct object, as the name implies. The fact that doublets like the pair in (1) involve the same emotion, and os-

[1] We are pleased to dedicate this paper to Annie Zaenen, whose investigations of unaccusativity, psych-verbs, and impersonal passives have inspired us to think hard about agentivity and related notions, as we hope to have done in this paper. We also thank the reviewers for their comments on an earlier draft.

[2] We use the label 'stimulus' (Talmy 1985) only as a way of referring to that argument of a transitive psych-verb that is not the individual experiencing the mental state described by the verb. This use of the term should not be taken to indicate any particular theoretical position.

From Quirky Case to Representing Space: Papers in Honor of Annie Zaenen.
Tracy Holloway King and Valeria de Paiva.
Copyright © 2013, CSLI Publications.

tensibly refer to the same situation, has led many researchers to treat these verbs as selecting arguments with the same semantic roles. This common semantic role assignment presents a puzzle for theories that assume that a semantic role is mapped to a unique syntactic position, such as those adopting Baker's Uniformity of Theta Role Assignment (1988:46, 1997): Why should the experiencer (or stimulus) argument be mapped to the subject of one verb, and to the object of the other?

Some researchers have approached this puzzle from a syntactic perspective, positing a common syntactic analysis for both verbs despite the surface differences in argument realization. For instance, one verb's realization of these two arguments can be (at least partially) reduced to the other's (Belletti and Rizzi 1988, Postal 1971). Alternatively, other researchers have questioned whether the two verbs really have arguments sharing the same semantic roles; if they do not, then there may not be a mapping puzzle to begin with. These researchers have proposed that the situations described by the two verbs differ in their causal or aspectual structure (Arad 1998, Croft 1993, Grimshaw 1990, Klein and Kutscher 2002, Pesetsky 1995, Reinhart 2001). Zaenen (1993), among others, draws attention to the subject of *frighten* and other experiencer-object psych-verbs, arguing that it is no less a causer than the subject of regular transitive causative verbs such as *break* or *melt* — an analysis not incompatible with the label 'stimulus'.[3] She incorporates Dowty's (1991) proto-role approach into LFG's Lexical Mapping Theory framework (Bresnan and Kanerva 1989). Specifically, she argues that the proto-agent properties entailed by the meaning of *frighten* determine that the stimulus receives an 'intrinsic classification' which guarantees its mapping to grammatical subject. For her, and others utilizing such a proto-role approach (e.g. Davis and Koenig 2000, Klein and Kutscher 2002), causation is among the proto-agent properties entailed by the meaning of *frighten* to hold of its stimulus.

What has received less attention is the status of the object of *fear*, which despite the label 'stimulus', presumably does not qualify as a causer, since otherwise it would be a subject. Even if, as Zaenen (1993), Dowty (1991), and others note, causation is attributed to this argument, its actual semantic contribution has not received the attention that the stimulus of *frighten* has. The precise differences in the types

---

[3]These arguments have been based in large part on the syntactic behavior of *frighten* and other experiencer-object psych-verbs, which on closer examination does not parallel that of *fear* and other experiencer-subject psych-verbs (Bouchard 1995, Grimshaw 1990, Pesetsky 1995, Reinhart 2001). For example, experiencer-object verbs pattern with typical transitive causatives with respect to middle formation, resultative predication, and *−er* nominal formation (Chung 1998, Iwata 1995).

of 'stimulus' arguments psych-verbs take, and the part these argument types play in shaping the syntactic structures that their verbs are found in, therefore require further study. Building on the groundwork laid out by Zaenen and others, we investigate the nature of these arguments through a corpus study of the verbs *fear* and *frighten* and show that a better understanding of the semantics of so-called 'stimulus' arguments of *fear* and *frighten* further supports Zaenen's overall approach.

3.2 *Fear* and *frighten* are not converses

Before turning to the corpus study, we mention an additional clue that the subject of *frighten* and the object of *fear* are likely to be different despite the assignment of the label 'stimulus' to both: the paucity of doublets like *fear* and *frighten* in English. Although these verbs are frequently cited together in studies of psych-verbs, they are not representative of a general pattern in the language. Most experiencer-subject verbs lack experiencer-object counterparts referring to the same emotion and vice versa. The only other easily identifiable doublet of this type consists of *like* and *please*, and further doublets are more difficult to discern. Other possible candidates might include: *abhor* or *detest* vs. *disgust* or *revolt*; *dislike* vs. *bother*, *bug*, or *annoy*; and *love* or *enjoy* vs. *delight*.[4] If the stimulus truly bears the same semantic relation to psych-verbs of the two types, then such doublets should be found across the psych-verb inventory. That they are not suggests that the two types of verbs convey different kinds of psychological events, and the title of the paper was chosen to suggest precisely this.

The intuition that the so-called stimulus arguments of *fear* and *frighten* are not semantically quite the same is also supported by changes in acceptability and/or meaning when the two NPs in a sentence with one verb are 'flipped' around so they can occur with the other verb, i.e. when the sentence *X fears/feared Y* is changed to *Y frightens/frightened X*, or vice versa. In many instances, such as in (1), rephrasing a sentence involving one verb with the other verb does not affect acceptability. The (a) sentences in (2)-(5) are corpus examples which sound quite natural when switched with their hypothetical *fear* or *frighten* variants, as in the (b) sentences.

---

[4]Given the scarcity of doublets such as *fear* and *frighten*, it is not surprising that a single psych-verb does not show the two argument realization options that characterize these two verbs. In this respect, psych-verbs contrast with dative alternation verbs such as *give* or *send* and locative alternation verbs such as *spray* or *load*, which show argument alternations. Our proposal, that experiencer-subject and experiencer-object psych-verbs have fundamentally different meanings, explains the lack of psych-verbs showing these two argument realizations.

(2) a. The government fears the answers to these questions.

    b. The answers to these questions frighten the government.

(3) a. You have people in this country now saying that they fear the Japanese economy ...

    b. You have people in this country now saying that the Japanese economy frightens them ...

(4) a. The darkness and the black depths frightened me.

    b. I feared the darkness and the black depths.

(5) a. Extreme side effects frighten patients.

    b. Patients fear extreme side effects.

Although these examples suggest that sentences with one of the two verbs can often be rephrased with the other, it is not difficult to find examples with one verb that lack a counterpart with the other. The (b) sentences in (6)-(9), which are the 'flipped' counterparts of the naturally occurring (a) sentences, are distinctly odd.

(6) a. They dropped everything and ran when something frightened them.

    b. ??They dropped everything and ran when they feared something.

(7) a. "Sorry if I frightened you last night," she told me.

    b. ??"Sorry if you feared me last night," she told me.

(8) a. Did you fear a negative response from fans?

    b. ??Did a negative response from fans frighten you?

(9) a. He "hesitated fatally on the edge of his own political transformation... He feared the new."

    b. ??He "hesitated fatally on the edge of his own political transformation... The new frightened him."

These data suggest that far from being a simple 'flipped' doublet, the verbs *fear* and *frighten* have differential preferences for certain types of arguments. This is especially clear in (8): the *frighten* variant (8b) can only be understood as presupposing that a negative response has in fact happened, while the *fear* example (8a) carries no such presupposition. In (8a) the experiencer fears merely the possibility of something happening. That is, there was no specific event that happened to cause him or her to become afraid. In the next section we present further evidence that this example represents a general tendency for complements of *fear* to refer to abstractions, e.g. propositions, properties and concepts, and for subjects of *frighten* to refer to more concrete entities, e.g. humans, physical objects, and events. These differences, we argue, reflect the different semantic relations that the 'stimulus' bears to verbs of the two types.

3.3 Corpus study

We now present the results of a corpus study examining the verbs *fear* and *frighten*. Data were collected from the Corpus of Contemporary American English (COCA) containing approximately 425 million words of spoken and written varieties of standard American English from 1990 to the present day (Davies 2008-2011).

3.3.1 Notes on data collection and annotation

To construct our corpus, we initially collected 500 examples of each verb from COCA using lemma searches which return hits for all possible inflected forms of the verb (e.g. *fear, fears, feared, fearing*). Sentence tokens that did not include both an experiencer and a stimulus were excluded, e.g. *their intention was to frighten to the point where our nation would not act*, as were examples of *fear for* and *frighten off/away*, which have different semantic properties from their counterparts. Finally, we excluded fixed uses such as *nothing to fear* and *fear the worst*. After removing such tokens we were left with 711 examples (*fear* = 365, *frighten* = 346).

Since this study focused on the types of stimuli involved, coding and annotation was most detailed for these arguments. For each token, the stimulus was coded for properties known to influence argument realization: definiteness, number, syntactic category (pronoun vs. full NP vs. full clause), and most importantly animacy. The animacy categories along with examples from the corpus are provided in Table 1.

3.3.2 Results

The results of animacy coding are presented in Table 2. The most noticeable difference between the two verbs is that *frighten* exhibits a more even distribution of stimulus types, with a preference for more concrete entities (human, animate and physical objects) overall (53.3%). *Fear* in contrast, displays a very strong bias (73.2%) toward abstractions (abstract entities and propositions).[5] Events and activities, which occupy an intermediate position on scales of concreteness or 'world immanence', show a tendency to be treated conceptually and linguistically more like concrete objects than abstractions (Asher 2000, Hegarty 2003). In accordance with this tendency, we observe a slight bias toward

---

[5] These findings corroborate and extend those of Grimm (2007), who found a similar pattern in data from the British National Corpus.

Animacy Coding	Corpus Examples
Human	'Husbands and boyfriends', 'Afghan women', 'the police'
Animate (non-human)	'God', 'crocodilians', 'the bear'
Concrete Object	'chemical weapons', 'side effects', 'the sound of the wind', 'beds'
Event or Activity	'a direct assault on the city', 'an ambush', 'my father crying'
Abstract Entity	'the number 13', 'her need', 'disapproval', 'an impulse', 'disgrace'
Proposition	'that North Korea could collapse', 'I couldn't feel him breathing'

TABLE 1 Animacy categories with examples

event-referring stimuli with *frighten* over *fear*. The collapsed pattern of stimulus animacy is shown in Figure 1.

	Fear		*Frighten*		Total	
	N	%	N	%	N	%
Human	37	10.1	110	33.3	147	21.2
Animate	10	2.7	13	3.9	23	3.3
Concrete object	20	5.5	53	16.1	73	10.5
Event	31	8.5	49	14.8	80	11.5
Abstract entity	142	38.9	87	26.4	229	32.9
Proposition	125	34.3	18	5.5	143	20.6
Total	365	100	330	100	695	100

TABLE 2 Distribution of stimulus animacy types by verb

Our corpus investigation demonstrates that *fear* heavily favors abstract objects. This preference is reflected not only in the kinds of NP complements it tends to take as in (10), but also in its frequent use with sentential complements, most of which denote yet to be realized propositions as in (11).

(10) a. Do you fear a quagmire for the international community?

b. ... preceding the intervention, markets panicked, fearing an imminent Greek default.

c. The authorities fear a possible destabilization ...

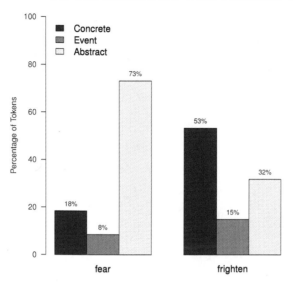

FIGURE 1 Distribution of stimulus animacy types by verb (collapsed)

(11) a. Space scientists fear that the manned space station ... will divert funds from space science in the '90s.

   b. They fear that Chinese state-owned enterprises will not hire their employers if they are openly critical.

The future-oriented nature of these uses highlights the evaluative nature of *fear*, which denotes an experiencer's disposition toward some (possibly non-existent) target. Such uses of *fear* are hard to reconcile with analyses of *fear* events that postulate a direct causal relation between the stimulus and the experiencer. Conversely, *frighten*'s frequent occurrence with concrete entities is entirely compatible with its usual treatment as a canonical causative verb.

The broader patterns of usage in Table 2 and Figure 1 are revealing on their own, but a closer look at the nominal stimuli found with the two verbs shows that the differences go even further than the aggregated numbers suggest. For example, a significantly larger proportion of *fear* uses involve indefinite stimuli than *frighten* uses do (Fisher Exact test: $p < 3.3e^{-10}$), as shown in Table 3.

A closer look at these indefinite examples reveals that even with apparent human referents, many objects of *fear* describe abstract conceptualizations of these human types, rather than discourse-new instances of actual individuals (cf. *I fear an earthquake* vs. *I felt an earthquake*).

(12) a. Most were initially skeptical of this political Euclid and feared

	Fear		*Frighten*	
	N	%	N	%
Definite	113	49.7	129	85.5
Indefinite	114	50.3	22	14.5

TABLE 3 Distribution of definite and indefinite NP stimuli by verb

    a conservative double agent in their midst.

    b. Everyone fears an Efficiency Ogre!

The same pattern also holds for *fear* complements referring to events.

(13) a. From all the grumbling, I feared an encounter with a giant Gerald Scarfe demon sitting on a throne ...

    b. He knew his troops were green and had families at home, and he feared a direct assault on the city ...

    c. Bill Miller said he feared an ambush.

In contrast to *fear*, indefinite stimuli for *frighten* are quite rare, and where found, they either refer to an existing entity that is simply new to the discourse as in (14), or they involve generic statements expressing a kind of episodic relation in which the stimulus typically causes fear (*Extreme side effects frighten patients*).

(14) a. Stories of the Holocaust drifted across to America and frightened him.

    b. "They probably dropped everything and ran when something frightened them," I said. "A bear, maybe."

    c. Frightened by a blistering barrage of bombs, Russian recruits ... are shot by their own superiors as they try to jump ship.

As shown in Table 2, the two verbs prefer different types of NPs for their stimulus, with *fear* showing a bias against concrete NPs. Another interesting subset of these stimuli is observed in the interpersonal uses of the two verbs — uses involving a human experiencer and a human stimulus. While there are many fewer instances of *fear* with human stimuli in the corpus data than *frighten*, the numbers do not tell the whole story. The relationship between a human stimulus and an experiencer with *fear* is often qualitatively different than with *frighten*: it frequently involves an imbalance of power between the two participants. In many instances, the stimulus constitutes an authority figure to the experiencer: it is higher than the experiencer on some scale of status, power or other comparable property. Further, this unequal relationship is inherent in the nature of the stimulus, such as when the stimulus is *God* or someone who holds a role that invests him or her with legal, political, or institutional power. It is not a temporary or accidental relationship that simply holds because of the immediate situation or context, but rather an inherent one that holds of the individuals across contexts.

(15) a. King Henry is feared by his enemies — and his family.

b. He admires yet fears his father.

c. It was always wise to fear a wizard whose lips had touched the Holy Grail.

In instances where this unequal relationship is not necessarily inferrable from common knowledge, the relation of authority is made clear in the context.

(16) I'd clawed to a position of respect as an accident reconstructionist. As a consultant, I was valued by law enforcement and insurance companies alike. As a professional witness, I was feared.

This asymmetric relation by no means holds across all uses of *fear*, but the large number of such examples makes sense given the nature of the emotion and the verb's overwhelming tendency to express experiencer dispositions or attitudes directed at some object.

Again, *frighten* contrasts with *fear*. Many of the interpersonal uses of *frighten* involve similar imbalances between participants — not surprisingly, as the verbs denote very similar emotions — but these relations hold due to particular circumstances, rather than being inherent in the relationship between the event participants. Although some human stimuli clearly have roles that put them in an authority relation over the experiencer, many of the examples make clear that the stimulus evokes an emotion in the experiencer by his or her actions, rather than as a consequence of a role invested in him or her, as in the following examples. For example, the bracketed phrases in (17) and (18) explicate the means by which the subject has managed to evoke fear in the experiencer in a particular situation, and represents a common strategy with experiencer-object verbs (Grafmiller in prep.).

(17) a. House Majority Leader Dick Armey complained that the president was trying to frighten the congressman's grandmother [by demagoguing the impact of Medicaid cuts on nursing-home care].

b. Another man looked thin and angry and frightened me [as though he carried a knife although he was full of easy compliments].

c. Most of the time she frightened me [because she was old]...

(18) a. Matt frightened me [with his intensity].

b. I frightened him [with stories about the missiles that entered buildings and shot up circular stairwells to find their target].

Providing such additional information is often necessary due to the context-specific, circumstantial nature of *frighten* events. In other instances, the stimulus is not truly a stimulus, but is better characterized as the causer of the emotion, and the emotion is directed at something else. For instance, in (19) what the experiencer is actually afraid of are grizzlies, not whoever the subject of the sentence, *they*, refers to. *They* are the cause of her fear only in that they brought to her attention the possibility of grizzlies, i.e. the 'subject matter' of her fear (Pesetsky 1995).

(19) They tried to frighten her with talk of grizzlies, but she just looked out the window at the low, treed terrain...

Such examples are not attested among the *fear* sentences and support the causative analysis of *frighten*. Given the causative nature of this verb, this difference in the stimulus–experiencer relationship is to be expected. In any given instance of 'frightening' it is possible that any individual could potentially frighten another under the appropriate circumstances.

3.4   Conclusion

In the introduction we reviewed the puzzle that doublets such as *fear* and *frighten* pose for theories of argument realization and argued that this puzzle resolves itself in light of claims by Zaenen (1993) and others that experiencer-object psych-verbs like *frighten* entail certain proto-agent properties of their stimuli, most importantly, causation. Conversely, experiencer-subject verbs like *fear* do not. Our corpus study reveals significant differences in the nature of the stimulus noun phrases found with these two verbs, which support these previous claims.

Our study shows that the stimuli found with *frighten* are truly causers of the emotion experienced, thus further supporting the analyses of Zaenen (1993) and Dowty (1991). This characterization receives support from the significantly greater tendency for these stimuli to refer to concrete entities or events in the immediate context. It is further substantiated by the arbitrary connections between stimulus and experiencer typical of many uses of *frighten*. These characteristics of *frighten* sentences reflect the circumstantial nature of the direct causation denoted by this verb.

In contrast, the stimuli found with *fear* represent entities at which a particular emotion can be directed, and the authority inherent in many of these stimuli simply reinforces this. Inherently fear-inducing entities, events, or abstract notions need not be present in the immediate context, or even exist at all, making a direct causal connection between the stimulus and experiencer difficult to establish. The low degree of causal efficacy possessed by these stimuli, along with the inherent imbalance of authority or power between the experiencer and the stimulus suggests that the experiencer's mental state should be conceptualized as a disposition directed toward something, rather than as a direct reaction to an immediate stimulus.

The question we chose as this paper's title, *Do you always fear what frightens you?*, plays on these fundamental, but distinct properties of *fear* and *frighten*, and was intended to evoke the long-standing controversy over the relation between *fear* and *frighten*: whether they are synonyms which take arguments with the same semantic roles, but expressed differently, as some work has suggested. The appropriate answer to the title question is *No*, precisely because the meanings of the two verbs are different in the way we have laid out. This answer suggests that synonymy analyses cannot be right, and our corpus study reveals not only the reasons why they cannot hold, but also why the question receives the answer it does. These two verbs have distinct meanings, so that you can indeed be frightened by things you do not fear.

References

Asher, Nicholas. 2000. Events, facts, propositions, and evolutive anaphora. In J. Higginbotham, F. Pianesi, and A. Varzi, eds., *Speaking of Events*, pages 123–150. Oxford University Press.

Baker, Mark. 1988. *Incorporation: A Theory of Grammatical Function Changing*. University of Chicago Press.

Baker, Mark. 1997. Thematic roles and syntactic structure. In L. Haegeman, ed., *Elements of Grammar*, pages 73–137. Kluwer.

Davies, Mark. 2008–. The Corpus of Contemporary American English (COCA): 425+ million words, 1990-present. Available online at http://www.americancorpus.org.

Davis, Anthony and Jean-Pierre Koenig. 2000. Linking as constraints on word classes in a hierarchical lexicon. *Language* 76:56–91.

Dowty, David. 1991. Thematic proto-roles and argument selection. *Language* 67:547–619.

Grafmiller, Jason. In prep. *Agentivity and Argument Realization in English Psychological Verbs*. PhD thesis, Stanford University.

Grimm, Scott. 2007. Flip verbs right side up. MS. Stanford University.

Hegarty, Michael. 2003. Semantic types of abstract entities. *Lingua* 113:891–927.

Talmy, Leonard. 1985. Lexicalization patterns: semantic structure in lexical forms. In T. Shopen, ed., *Language, Typology and Syntactic Description 3: Grammatical Categories and the Lexicon*, pages 57–149. Cambridge University Press.

Zaenen, Annie. 1993. Unaccusativity in Dutch: Integrating syntax and lexical semantics. In J. Pustejovsky, ed., *Semantics and the Lexicon*. Kluwer.

4

Mismatched Spanish Unaccusativity Tests

RAÚL ARANOVICH

4.1 Introduction

Mismatched unaccusativity tests offer strong evidence for a semantic analysis of split intransitivity.[1] In Spanish, two tests are said to distinguish unaccusatives from unergatives. First, unergatives, unlike unaccusatives, cannot be embedded in a causative construction with a generic null animate causee. Second, unaccusatives, unlike unergatives, can have postverbal bare plural subjects.[2] Mismatches arise with verbs like *heder* 'stink', for instance, which fail only one of the tests. I argue that mismatches like this one occur when a subject has mixed proto-patient and proto-agent properties, since different tests can be sensitive to different lexical entailment weightings.

I will also show that applying these tests to pronominal verbs in Spanish gives rise to analogous mismatches, offering additional support for the semantic analysis of split intransitivity. Pronominal verbs are de-

---

[1] An earlier version of this paper was presented at the 2000 LSA Annual Meeting in Chicago. I thank the participants in the session for useful comments and suggestions. Annie Zaenen's (1993) paper on Dutch unaccusativity tests prompted me to look beyond the syntax of unaccusativity in Romance. In that paper, Annie showed that seemingly untractable exceptions could be accounted for in lexical-semantic terms, with interesting theoretical consequences. Annie has been a source of inspiration and support over the years: I am glad that this paper is published in a volume to celebrate her work.

[2] In other Romance languages, perfect auxiliary selection (BE or HAVE) is often used as an unaccusativity test (Burzio 1986, Legendre 1989, Perlmutter 1989, among others). In Modern Spanish, however, the only perfect auxiliary is *haber* 'have'.

From Quirky Case to Representing Space: Papers in Honor of Annie Zaenen.
Tracy Holloway King and Valeria de Paiva.
Copyright © 2013, CSLI Publications.

rived intransitives marked by a reflexive clitic. In Spanish, a pronominal verb often occurs as the inchoative member of the causative alternation, as in (1a). The semantic range of pronominal verbs, however, extends beyond the class of change-of-state predicates, as shown in (1b).

(1) a. El espejo se rompió.
         the mirror SE broke
         'The mirror broke.'

     b. Los edificios se reflejan en la vidriera.
         the buildings SE reflect in the store.window
         'The buildings reflect in the store window.'

The semantic variation found among pronominal verbs, which will be central to the arguments developed in this article, contrasts with their syntactic homogeneity. The received view of pronominal verbs like *romperse* 'become broken' is that they are unaccusatives (Rosen 1988, Grimshaw 1990, Levin and Rappaport 1995).[3] The reflexive clitic indicates that the surface subject is an underlying object. All diagnostics for unaccusativity, then, should produce consistent results when applied to pronominal verbs. I will show that this is not the case, and that the mismatches that arise receive clear characterizations in semantic terms. These results, I will argue, support Zaenen's (1993) semantic approach to split intransitivity (see also Centineo 1986, 1996, Van Valin 1990, and Dowty 1991).

4.2 Two tests for unaccusativity in Spanish

As argued in Zubizarreta (1985), Burzio (1986), and Alsina (1996), the distribution of embedded verbs with null generic animate subjects in Romance causative constructions gives evidence for split intransitivity. Transitive verbs can appear in causatives with a generic null animate subject, as the example in (2a) shows, and so do unergatives, as shown in (2b) and (2c). Unaccusatives, on the other hand, cannot appear in the Generic Causee Construction (GCC), as the examples in (2d) and

---

[3]Several authors (Kayne 1975, Grimshaw 1982, Alsina 1996) have provided independent evidence for the valence-reducing nature of reflexive cliticization in Romance. I will assume with these authors that reflexive verbs are intransitive. The Spanish reflexive clitic serves many different functions. As in other Romance languages, it marks constructions in which the subject and object are coreferential (true reflexives), and also impersonal/passive constructions with an arbitrary human agent (see Mendikoetxea 2012 for an overview of the literature on the Spanish reflexive clitic and its functions). In this paper I limit the analysis to the different semantic classes of pronominal verbs, which I take to have only one semantic role to assign to their subjects (a different point of view is defended in Koontz-Garboden 2009).

(2e) illustrate.[4]

(2) a. El director del hospital hizo operar toda la noche.
the director of the hospital made operate all the night
'The director of the hospital made people operate all night long.'

b. El capataz hizo trabajar incesantemente.
the foreman made work without.pause
'The foreman made people work without pause.'

c. La película hizo llorar de emoción.
the movie made cry of sorrow
'The movie made people cry out of sorrow.'

d. *El mago hizo desaparecer misteriosamente.
the magician made disappear mysteriously
'The magician made people disappear mysteriously.'

e. *La directora hizo llegar a la escuela.
the principal made arrive to the school
'The principal made people arrive at school.'

Torrego (1989) and Alsina (1996) discuss another unaccusativity test in Spanish. They show that bare plural subjects can appear in postverbal position with unaccusatives, as in (3a) and (3b), but not with unergatives, as in (3c), (3d), and (3e).[5]

---

[4]The tense in the GCC must be controlled to avoid a generic reading of the causative construction itself, which licenses null objects normally. For this purpose, all the examples discussed here have a causative verb in the preterite.

[5]Many speakers reject Torrego's judgments, and some trained linguists have questioned the validity of the test. Postverbal plural subjects are ungrammatical with unergatives under a presentational reading. In my interpretation, sentences like (3c) and (3d) cannot mean 'there are stars shining intensely' or 'there are calves grazing'. Sentences like (3a) or (3b), on the other hand, can have this presentational interpretation. They can be used in a newspaper headline, for instance, to report an event. The reason why this test has become so controversial is that under certain conditions unergatives can have postverbal bare plural subjects. This happens if the sentence has a preposed locative phrase making reference to a definite location, as in (A), or if the bare plural NP is the focus of contrast, as in (B).

(A) Aquí pastan terneros.
here graze calves
'Calves graze here.'

(B) Pastan terneros, no cabras.
graze calves, not goats
'Calves graze, not goats'

In the first case, it can be argued that the bare plural noun denotes a property. As such it is part of the predicate. Sentence (A) is not about calves, but about the location: it specifies a property of the location designated by the adverb. In the second case, the sentence is not presenting a new event, or introducing a new

(3) a. Llegan trenes con retraso.
   arrive trains with delay
   'Trains arrive with delay.'

   b. Desaparecen periodistas todos los meses.
   disappear   journalists all   the months
   'Journalists disappear every month.'

   c. ??Brillan estrellas con   intensidad.
   shine   stars   with intensity
   'Stars shine intensely.'

   d. ??Pastan terneros por la   mañana.
   graze   calves   by the morning
   'Calves graze in the morning.'

   e. ??Trabajan prisioneros de   sol a sol.
   work   prisoners   from sun to sun
   'Prisoners work from dawn till dusk.'

In Torrego's analysis, an unaccusative like *llegar* 'arrive' can have a postverbal bare plural subject (PVBS) because its sole argument is an internal one. Bare plurals, she adds, can appear in object position (i.e. after the verb), as in (4a), but not in subject position, as (4b) shows. This shows that subjects of unaccusatives behave like objects, and subjects of unergatives behave like subjects of transitive verbs.

(4) a. Las ardillas   comen nueces.
   the squirrels eat   nuts
   'Squirrels eat nuts.'

   b. *Pediatras   vacunan a los niños.
   pediatricians vaccinate to the children
   'Pediatricians vaccinate children.'

4.3   Mismatches between the tests

When pronominal verbs are subject to the GCC test and the PVBS test, the results seem initially to support the unaccusative analysis of pronominal verbs. Verbs like *asfixiarse*, *arrepentirse*,[6] and *arrojarse*, for instance, are excluded from the GCC, as shown in (5a), (5b), and (5c).

---

participant, but rather correcting a statement that has been uttered previously or that is presupposed or salient in the consciousness of the speakers. In sum, there are valid objections to an indiscriminate use of the postverbal bare plural subject test, which disappear when the presentational sense of the construction is taken into account.

[6]*Arrepentirse* 'repent, feel remorse' is inherently pronominal. That is, there is no transitive counterpart *arrepentir*, meaning 'cause to feel remorse.' This is a not uncommon occurrence among pronominal verbs.

These data seem to indicate that the subjects of pronominal verbs, like the subjects of unaccusatives, passives, and true reflexives, are underlying objects at some level of representation.

(5) a. ??El   humo hizo asfixiarse   durante el   incendio.
       the smoke made suffocate.SE during the fire
       'Smoke made people suffocate during the fire.'

   b. ??El   director de la   escuela hizo   arrepentirse.
       the director of the school made repent.SE
       'The school principal made people repent.'

   c. ??Los bomberos hicieron arrojarse desde el   segundo piso.
       the firefighters made   throw.SE from the second   floor.
       'Firefighters made people jump off from the second floor.'

The PVBS test should give the opposite result since unaccusatives are allowed to have postverbal bare plural subjects. My own judgments are that verbs like *arrojarse* and *asfixiarse* can have postverbal bare plural subjects, as in (6a) and (6b).[7] This is expected under the assumption that all pronominal verbs are unaccusatives.

(6) a. Se arrojan inquilinos por desesperación.
       SE throw   tenants   by despair
       'Tenants jump out of despair.'

   b. Se asfixian   bomberos por descuido.
       SE suffocate firefighters by lack.of.care
       'Firefighters suffocate when they are careless.'

   c. Se derrumban edificios sin   aviso.
       SE fall.down   buildings without warning
       'Buildings fall down without warning.'

In the idealized model assumed by the standard syntactic analysis of unaccusativity, the GCC test and the PVBS test should divide all intransitives into two complementary classes. None of the intransitive verbs that appear in the GCC should be able to occur with postverbal bare plural subjects, and all the intransitive verbs that occur in the PVBS construction should be excluded from the GCC. Moreover, all pronominal verbs should behave as unaccusatives, passing the PVBS test but not the GCC test. There are, however, some critical examples that do not fit in this picture.

---

[7] There is considerable variation in acceptability across dialects and individuals about these examples. The data in this paper reflect my own dialect: River Plate Spanish. As an anonymous reviewer points out, it would be desirable to back up individual grammaticality judgments with corpus data. Even though that is outside the scope of this investigation, I hope the results I introduce here will guide further research in that direction.

First, there are some verbs that behave more like unergatives than like unaccusatives, in spite of being marked by a reflexive pronoun. Verbs like *revolcarse* 'roll on', *arrastrarse* 'crawl', and *menearse* 'swing', can occur in the GCC, as shown in (7a) to (7c).[8]

(7) a. El sargento hizo   revolcarse en el   barro.
the sergeant made roll.se   in the mud
'The sergeant made people roll in the mud.'

   b. Las balas   hicieron arrastrarse sobre el   pavimento.
the bullets made   drag.se   over the pavement
'Bullets made people crawl on the pavement.'

   c. La música hizo   menearse toda la   noche.
the music made swing.se all   the night
'The music made people swing all night.'

A second problem is that there is a mismatch not predicted by a syntactic theory of unaccusativity. A verb like *heder*, for instance, is excluded from the GCC, as in (8a). Therefore, it should be able to have a postverbal bare plural subject, but (8b) shows this is not the case. Moreover, the same mismatch between the PVBS and the GCC tests is observed for pronominal verbs. *Reflejarse* 'reflect' fails both tests, as shown by (9a) and (9b).

(8) a. *El   entrenador hizo   heder.
the coach   made stink
'The coach made people stink.'

   b. *Hieden atletas.
stink   athletes
'Athletes stink.'

(9) a. ??La vanidad hizo   reflejarse en las vidrieras.
the vanity   made reflect.se in the shop.windows
'Vanity made people reflect in the shop windows.'

   b. ??Se reflejan clientes   con   claridad.
se reflect   customers with clarity
'Customers reflect clearly.'

---

[8]There are many speakers of Spanish for whom infinitives embedded under causative constructions cannot have a reflexive pronoun under any circumstance (Moore 1996). For those speakers, the sentences in (7a) to (7c) will be ungrammatical. Care should be taken to test these sentences with speakers who may accept embedded reflexives in their dialect.

4.4   A semantic explanation of the mismatches

The mismatch between the PVBS test and the GCC test for unaccusatives can be accounted for in semantic terms. Postverbal bare plural subjects can appear with telic predicates like *regresar*, *desaparecer*, *arrojarse*, or *asfixiarse*, but not with verbs like *heder*, *trabajar*, *arrastrarse*, or *reflejarse*, which are atelic. This is summarized in Table 1.

INTRANSITIVE	*trabajar*	*heder*	*regresar*	*desaparecer*
	'work'	'stink'	'return'	'disappear'
PRONOMINAL	*arrastrarse*	*reflejarse*	*arrojarse*	*asfixiarse*
	'crawl'	'reflect'	'throw oneself'	'suffocate'
ATELIC	+	+	−	−
VOLITIONAL	+	−	+	−
			postverbal bare plural subject OK	

TABLE 1   Distribution of postverbal bare plural subjects.

Telicity also seems to play a role in determining the distribution of predicates in the GCC. Telic predicates like *regresar*, *desaparecer*, *arrojarse*, or *asfixiarse* are excluded from this construction. Not all atelic predicates, however, can appear in the GCC. While predicates like *arrastrarse* and *trabajar* do, other atelic predicates, like *heder* and *reflejarse*, are excluded. The critical factor here is volitionality. The events denoted by *arrastrarse* and *trabajar* are under the volitional control of the subject, but this is not the case with the events denoted by *heder* and *reflejarse*. What makes a predicate into a viable candidate for the GCC is the combined strength of being atelic and being under the volitional control of the subject. Volitional predicates are excluded from this construction if they are telic, as is the case with *arrojarse* and *regresar*. This is summarized in Table 2.[9]

---

[9]Marín and McNally (2011) discuss a class of Spanish pronominal verbs that refer to psychological events (i.e. *aburrirse* 'get bored', *enfadarse* 'get upset'). They notice that, like other pronominal verbs, they are inchoative, but differ from change-of-state predicates like *romperse* 'break' by being atelic. An anonymous reviewer judges psychological pronominal verbs like these to be OK in the GCC, which is consistent with my claim that telic predicates are excluded from it. However, it is not clear if these predicates are volitional. It may be that sentience is a more predictive feature of these predicates. I leave this issue for further research. The same reviewer, however, claims that atelic predicates like *pelearse* 'fight' and *confesarse* 'confess'.are excluded from the GCC, in spite of being volitional. But these predicates are ambiguous between an atelic and a telic interpretation. *Pelearse* can

INTRANSITIVE	*trabajar* 'work'	*heder* 'stink'	*regresar* 'return'	*desaparecer* 'disappear'
PRONOMINAL	*arrastrarse* 'crawl'	*reflejarse* 'reflect'	*arrojarse* 'throw oneself'	*asfixiarse* 'suffocate'
ATELIC	+	+	−	−
VOLITIONAL	+	−	+	−
			Excluded from generic causee construction	

TABLE 2 Distribution of predicates in the generic causee construction.

It is now easy to see where the mismatches in the test results occur. It is with verbs that are at once atelic and non-volitional. This generalization has consequences for a theory of split intransitivity.

4.5 Split intransitivity and proto-roles

Unaccusative mismatches have been found in languages that mark split intransitivity overtly. In Dutch, for instance, there are two tests for unaccusativity: auxiliary selection and formation of impersonal passives. In general, unaccusatives take *zijn* 'be' as the perfect auxiliary, and cannot form impersonal passives. But Perlmutter (1978) and Zaenen (1993) notice some remarkable exceptions. *Aankomen* 'arrive' takes *zijn* and appears in impersonal passives, whereas *stinken* 'stink' takes *hebben* 'have' (the auxiliary preferred by unergatives) but cannot form impersonal passives. Zaenen's explanation for the mismatches is a semantic one: Telic verbs combine with *zijn*, but verbs that appear in impersonal passives must be under the volitional control of the subject. The two tests, she concludes, are orthogonal to each other, and are not related to deep unaccusativity, as claimed in the syntactic analysis. Since the tests are sensitive to semantic differences, then split intransitivity should also be characterized semantically.

Zaenen's approach cannot be extended to Spanish directly, however, since one of the Spanish tests seems to be sensitive to a cocktail of semantic properties. Dowty (1991) proposes a semantic theory of argument selection that may be used to arrive at the desired analysis. He argues that unergative subjects are more like prototypical Agents, whereas unaccusative subjects are more like prototypical Patients. For

---

also mean 'fall out, become estranged', while *confesarse*, understood as 'going to confession', is not an activity but an accomplishment (confession ends when the subject tells all of his/her sins to the priest).

Dowty, thematic roles are sets of entailments, determined by the lexical semantics of the predicate. The two prototypical thematic roles, or proto-roles, are characterized by the following entailments:

Proto-agent Properties	Proto-patient Properties
VOLITIONAL	CHANGES STATE
SENTIENT	INCREMENTAL THEME
CAUSALLY ACTIVE	CAUSALLY AFFECTED
MOVING	STATIONARY
EXISTS INDEPENDENT FROM EVENT	EXISTS DEPENDENT ON EVENT

In a sentence with two arguments (i.e. a transitive verb), the subject will display a heavier proportion of proto-agent properties than the object. This principle allows for different combinations of semantic properties, defining degrees of prototypicality for agents and patients. This approach can be extended to account for patterns of split intransitivity. Subjects of unergative verbs, Dowty says, normally have more proto-agent properties than subjects of unaccusatives. The subject of a verb like *run*, often classified as unergative, must be volitionally involved in the event, and has the property of moving. A verb like *die*, on the other hand, which is typically unaccusative, is associated with the entailment that its subject undergoes a change of state, and is not volitionally involved in the event.

Dowty also notices that certain entailments about a predicate's arguments are determined by that predicate's aktionsart. In particular, subjects of telic intransitives are associated with proto-patient properties. First, telic predicates often have an argument that 'measures out' the event (as suggested in Krifka 1989 and Tenny 1992). In a sentence like *Max ironed the shirt* the condition of the shirt determines whether the ironing has been accomplished or not. Dowty introduces the notion of incremental theme to refer to these arguments, a property that he places among those characterizing a prototypical Patient.[10] Second, a telic verb of motion like *drop*, for instance, entails movement on the part of its object. Because the predicate is telic, movement is to a

---

[10]There are conflicting opinions as to whether arguments that measure out the event are always internal arguments. Tenny (1992) claims that subjects of transitive verbs are never incremental themes, but Dowty (1991) and Jackendoff (1996) disagree with that. In the majority of cases, however, incremental themes are realized as objects, and only when the incremental theme is associated with additional proto-agent entailments can it appear as a subject (in line with Dowty's Argument Selection Principle). For this reason, the classification of incremental themehood as a proto-patient property seems well grounded. Ackerman and Moore (1999, this volume) discuss additional issues regarding a proto-property theory of argument mapping.

definite location. This change of location counts as a change of state, and therefore as a proto-patient property. Atelic motion verbs like *rub*, *scratch*, *stomp*, or *pounce* also entail movement on the part of their subject. But when the manner of motion is more important than the specific change of location, movement does not count as a change of state and must be considered a proto-agent property. Telicity, then, is not directly involved in the classification of a predicate as unaccusative or unergative. Only the proto-patient properties associated with the argument of intransitive telic predicates are. This explains the observation that unaccusatives tend to be telic without invoking aktionsart as a direct factor in the classification of a predicate.

4.6 Proto-roles and unaccusative mismatches in Spanish

Dowty's theory of proto-roles, then, and its consequences for an analysis of split intransitivity, can be used to account for the distribution of embedded verbs in the GCC in Spanish. Volitional atelic verbs of the class of *arrastrarse* 'crawl' and *trabajar* 'work' can appear in the GCC because their subject is volitional (a key proto-agent property). Moreover, this argument is not associated with such prominent proto-patient properties as being causally affected by the event, undergoing a change of state, or measuring out the event. Of all the verbs in Table 2, then, *arrastrarse* and *trabajar* have the highest number of proto-agent entailments about their subject. At the other end of the spectrum there are verbs like *asfixiarse* 'choke' and *desaparecer* 'disappear', the subjects of which have no proto-agent properties. Neither one has a subject that controls the event volitionally. Moreover, the subject of *asfixiarse* undergoes a change of state, and so does the subject of *desaparecer*, with the additional proto-patient property of ceasing to exist as a consequence of the event. Verbs with these characteristics are excluded from the GCC, as most other typically unaccusative verbs would be. In between these two classes are verbs with a mixed set of entailments about their subjects. *Arrojarse* and *regresar*, which express motion verbs with a definite location, have a subject that undergoes a change of state (a proto-patient property) but are volitional (a proto-agent property). The subjects of *reflejarse* and *heder*, on the other hand, have none of the proto-patient properties associated with telicity, but they lack the proto-agent property of having a subject that controls the event volitionally.

The GCC, then, rejects anything but "top-shelf" unergatives, i.e. verbs associated with the highest number of proto-agent entailments.

The PVBS test, on the other hand, is less selective. Telicity (or the associated proto-role properties) is sufficient to determine whether a verb will pass or fail the PVBS test.[11] The syntactic analysis of split intransitivity could be saved by stating that unergatives like *heder* or *reflejarse* are arbitrarily excluded from the GCC, but this misses an important generalization having to do with the semantics of the predicates in question. The semantic analysis I have defended here, on the other hand, predicts that if any of the predicates which cannot have postverbal bare plural subjects are going to be excluded from the GCC, they will be like *heder*, and not like *trabajar*, i.e. the class of intransitives that are not associated with the heaviest proportion of proto-agent entailments about their subjects. The mismatch between the two tests for split intransitivity in Spanish, then, shows the semantic analysis of split intransitivity to be more explanatory than the syntactic analysis.

4.7 Argument realization with pronominal verbs

Returning now to the issue of whether all pronominal verbs are unaccusatives, it can be seen from the data discussed here that, in Spanish, some pronominal verbs pair up with unergatives. These are verbs like *arrastrarse, menearse,* and also *reflejarse*. These verbs are associated with proto-agent entailments about their subject. In a theory in which the tests for split intransitivity pick up semantic differences among different classes of intransitive verbs, this result is to be expected. There is no empirical evidence in Spanish to support the claim that the reflexive clitic is always a mark of unaccusativity, as claimed in Rosen (1988), Grimshaw (1990), and Levin and Rappaport (1995) for Romance at large. To be more precise, I claim that in Spanish there is no clear evidence of syntactic unaccusativity at all. In my search for unaccusativity tests in Spanish, I have found that even the evidence for deep unaccusativity in Spanish can be accounted for in semantic terms (Aranovich 2000, 2003b). When a language lacks strong evidence for deep unaccusativity, the motivation to represent some subjects as underlying objects disappears.

Clear evidence for deep unaccusativity in Romance is found in French and Italian, whose reflexive verbs take the 'be' auxiliary in the perfect tense.[12] However, as I have shown in this study, the Spanish pronominal

---

[11] A hierarchy of split intransitivity is also proposed in Sorace (2000) to account for variation in auxiliary selection in Italian.

[12] Old Spanish used to have a split auxiliary system as well, but it was also split across verbs with reflexive clitics. The diachrony of such split auxiliary systems gives additional support to the semantic approach to split intransitivity, as I argue in Aranovich (2003a, 2009).

verbs seem to display the same degree of variation in their lexical semantic properties as plain intransitives (Legendre and Smolensky 2009
reach a similar conclusion for French inchoatives). These considerations must be taken seriously in a semantic account of unaccusativity
in Romance, because if all reflexive verbs take the same auxiliary as
unaccusative verbs regardless of their semantics, the syntactic analysis
of split intransitivity can reclaim territory. Some of these issues have
been discussed in Centineo (1986), (1996), and Van Valin (1990), but
more work needs to be done. I hope my study of split intransitivity
in Spanish shows the kind of data that needs to be considered when
researching split intransitivity in Romance.

References

Ackerman, Farrell and John Moore. 1999. Syntagmatic and paradigmatic
dimensions of causee encoding. *Linguistics and Philosophy* 22:1–44.

Ackerman, Farrell and John Moore. 2012. Proto-properties in a comprehensive theory of argument realization. This volume.

Alsina, Alex. 1996. *The Role of Argument Structure in Grammar: Evidence
from Romance*. CSLI Publications.

Aranovich, Raúl. 2000. Split intransitivity and reflexives in Spanish. *Probus*
12:1–21.

Aranovich, Raúl. 2003a. The semantics of auxiliary selection in Old Spanish.
Studies in Language 27:1–37.

Aranovich, Raúl. 2003b. Two types of postverbal subjects in Spanish: Evidence from binding. In C. Beyssade, O. Bonami, P. C. Hofherr, and
F. Corblin, eds., *Empirical Issues in Formal Syntax and Semantics 4*, pages
227–242. Presses Universitaires de Paris-Sorbonne.

Aranovich, Raúl. 2009. From ESSE to *ser*: Diachronic mismatches in the
selection of perfect auxiliaries. In S. R. Rîpeanu, ed., *Studia Lingvistica in
Honorem Mariæ Manoliu. Bucureşti*, pages 21–35. Editura Universităţii
din Bucureşt.

Burzio, Luigi. 1986. *Italian Syntax: A Government-Binding Approach*. Reidel.

Centineo, Giulia. 1986. A lexical theory of auxiliary selection in Italian. In
Davis Working Papers in Linguistics, vol. 1, pages 1–35.

Centineo, Giulia. 1996. A lexical theory of auxiliary selection in Italian.
Probus 8:223–271.

Dowty, David. 1991. Thematic proto-roles and argument selection. *Language*
67:547–619.

Grimshaw, Jane. 1982. On the lexical representation of romance reflexive
clitics. In J. Bresnan, ed., *The Mental Representation of Grammatical
Relations*, pages 87–148. MIT Press.

Grimshaw, Jane. 1990. *Argument Structure*. MIT Press.

Jackendoff, Ray. 1996. The proper treatment of measuring out, telicity, and perhaps even quantification in English. *Natural Language and Linguistic Theory* pages 305–354.

Kayne, Richard. 1975. *French Syntax*. MIT Press.

Koontz-Garboden, Andrew. 2009. Anticausativiztion. *Natural Language and Linguistic Theory* 27:77–138.

Krifka, Manfred. 1989. Nominal reference, temporal constitution and quantification in event semantics. In R. Bartsch, J. van Benthem, and P. van Emde Boas, eds., *Semantics and Contextual Expression*, pages 75–115. Foris.

Legendre, Géraldine. 1989. Unaccusativity in French. *Lingua* 79:95–164.

Legendre, Géraldine and Paul Smolensky. 2009. French inchoatives and the uncusativity hypothesis. In D. Gerdts, J. Moore, and M. Polinsky, eds., *Hypothesis A/Hypothesis B: Linguistic Explorations in Honor of David M. Perlmutter*, pages 229–246. MIT Press.

Levin, Beth and Malka Rappaport. 1995. *Unaccusativity: At the Syntax-Lexical Semantics Interface*. MIT Press.

Marín, Rafael and Louise McNally. 2011. Inchoativity, change of state, and telicity: Evidence from Spanish reflexive psychological verbs. *Natural Language and Linguistic Theory* 29:467–502.

Mendikoetxea, Amaya. 2012. Passives and *se* constructions. In J. I. Hualde, A. Olarrea, and E. O'Rourke, eds., *The Handbook of Hispanic Linguistics*, pages 477–502. Blackwell.

Moore, John. 1996. *Reduced Constructions in Spanish*. Garland.

Perlmutter, David. 1978. Impersonal passives and the unaccusative hypothesis. In *Proceedings of the Fourth Annual Meeting of the Berkeley Linguistic Society*, pages 157–189.

Perlmutter, David. 1989. Multiattachment and the unaccusative hypothesis: The perfect auxiliary in Italian. *Probus* 1:63–119.

Rosen, Carol. 1988. *The Relational Structure of Reflexive Clauses: Evidence from Italian*. Garland.

Sorace, Antonella. 2000. Gradients in auxiliary selection with intransitive verbs. *Language* 76:859–890.

Tenny, Carol. 1992. The aspectual interface hypothesis. In I. Sag and A. Szabolcsi, eds., *Lexical Matters*, pages 1–27. CSLI Publications.

Torrego, Esther. 1989. Unergative-unaccusative alternations in Spanish. In *MIT Working Papers in Linguistics 10*, pages 253–272.

Valin, Robert Van. 1990. Semantic parameters of split intransitivity. *Language* 66:221–260.

Zaenen, Annie. 1993. Unaccusativity in Dutch: Integrating syntax and lexical semantics. In J. Pustejovsky, ed., *Semantics and the Lexicon*, pages 129–161. Kluwer.

Zubizarreta, María Luisa. 1985. The relation between morphophonology and morphosyntax: The case of Romance causatives. *Linguistic Inquiry* 16.

5

Lexical Mapping Theory Revisited

ONE-SOON HER

5.1 Introduction

The version of Lexical Mapping Theory (LMT) outlined in Bresnan and Zaenen (1990) (hereafter BZ), which replaced the earlier stipulated function-changing rules in Lexical Functional Grammar (LFG) and allowed principled accounts of the linking problems between argument roles and grammatical functions, remains the most widely adopted version of LMT among the many contenders, e.g., Zaenen (1988), Bresnan and Kanerva (1989), Bresnan (1989), Huang (1993), Butt et al. (1997), Ackerman and Moore (2001a,b), Kibort (2007, 2008), among many others. It is also the version of LMT adopted by Bresnan (2001), by now a standard reference of LFG's theoretical underpinnings, and Falk (2001), by far the most accessible textbook on LFG.[1]

In this paper I aim to propose an alternative version of LMT which, while maintaining not only the spirit of BZ but also its explanatory power, is more consistent in its principles and also simpler in organization. Section 2 first summarizes and reviews BZ's version of LMT, section 3 then presents the revisions proposed, and section 4 applies this revised LMT to the same transitive, unaccusative, unergative, and passive examples from BZ to demonstrate that this simpler version works equally well. I also review Zaenen (1988) and apply this revised LMT to the dative alternation and passive in English. Section 5 concludes

---

[1] I thank the anonymous external and internal reviewers for their very constructive comments, which led to improvement of the paper. I also thank Tracy Holloway King, co-editor of the current volume, for her kind assistance. All remaining errors are my own responsibility.

From Quirky Case to Representing Space: Papers in Honor of Annie Zaenen.
Tracy Holloway King and Valeria de Paiva.
Copyright © 2013, CSLI Publications.

the paper.

5.2 LMT in Bresnan and Zaenen (1990)

At the heart of LMT is the a(rgument)-structure, which consists of a predicator with its thematic roles, each of which is marked with a classification feature for its grammatical function. Two examples are given in (1) and (2), where $[-r]$ means unrestricted and $[-o]$, unobjective.

(1) pound <   ag   pt   >
             $[-o]$ $[-r]$

(2) freeze <   th   >
              $[-r]$

The argument roles in an a-structure are listed left-to-right in descending order according to their relative prominence in a universal hierarchy, as in (3) (e.g., Bresnan and Kanerva (1989)). The most prominent role in an a-structure, e.g., agent in (1) and theme in (2), is referred to as $\hat{\theta}$, or theta hat.

(3) Thematic Hierarchy:
     agent > beneficiary > experiencer/goal > instrument > patient/theme > locative

The syntactic features assigned to each role are $[\pm r]$, (un)restricted (whether a function is restricted as to its semantic role), and $[\pm o]$, (un)objective (whether a function is objective), which serve to classify grammatical functions into natural classes, as in (4). Negative features being unmarked, a hierarchy obtains, as in (5), where SUBJ is the least marked and thus the most prominent, and OBJ$_\theta$, the most marked and the least prominent. Note that in (5) OBJ and OBL$_\theta$ are indistinguishable for markedness.

(4) Feature Decomposition of Grammatical Functions:

	$-r$	$+r$
$-o$	SUBJ	OBL$_\theta$
$+o$	OBJ	OBJ$_\theta$

(5) Markedness Hierarchy of Grammatical Functions:
     SUBJ$_{([-r-o])}$ > OBJ$_{([-r+o])}$/OBL$_\theta{}_{([+r-o])}$ > OBJ$_\theta{}_{([+r+o])}$

Every role in an a-structure is associated with exactly one feature for its syntactic function by a set of universal unmarked choices, as in (6).

(6) Intrinsic Classification (IC) of A-Structure Roles:
   a. Patientlike roles: $\theta \longrightarrow [-r]$
   b. Secondary patientlike roles: $\theta \longrightarrow [+o]^2$
   c. Other roles: $\theta \longrightarrow [-o]$

The three unmarked choices in (6) ensure that all roles in an a-structure are underspecified with exactly one feature [r] or [o], never unspecified nor fully specified, for syntactic realization.

Following Bresnan and Kanerva (1989), morphological operations can alter the lexical stock of an a-structure by adding, suppressing, or binding thematic roles, e.g., passive, which suppresses the syntactic realization of $\hat{\theta}$, as shown in (7).

(7) Passive: $\hat{\theta} \longrightarrow \emptyset$

There are also universal mapping principles that determine the ultimate mapping of each of the expressed underspecified roles.

(8) Mapping Principles:
   a. Subject roles:
       (i) $\hat{\theta}[-o]$ is mapped onto SUBJ; otherwise:
       (ii) $\theta[-r]$ is mapped onto SUBJ.
   b. Other roles are mapped onto the lowest compatible function in the markedness hierarchy in (5).

As pointed out by Falk (2001, 104) and Her (2003, 6), there is an inconsistency between (8a) and (8b). Essentially, (8a) supplies only negative features to the role designated to be SUBJ, while (8b) does exactly the opposite and assigns only positive features. Thus, (8) can be restated as (9) in terms of feature supplements.

(9) Mapping Principles:
   a. Subject roles:
       (i)   Add negative features to $\hat{\theta}[-o]$; otherwise:
       (ii) Add negative features to $\theta[-r]$.
   b. Add positive features elsewhere.

Aside from the inconsistency in the mapping of subject roles and non-subject roles, the choice of the ultimate subject role is stipulated. Ideally, the mapping between a role and SUBJ, and indeed any other grammatical function, should be the consequence of a unified mapping principle for subject roles as well as non-subject roles. Furthermore, BZ's model, like most of the other contenders, also needs additional

---

[2] I shall ignore the distinction between symmetric versus asymmetric languages, where only the former allow the secondary patientlike roles to be [−r] as well (Bresnan and Moshi 1990).

output constraints, i.e., Function-Argument Biuniqueness (i.e., each a-structure role must be associated with a unique function, and conversely) and the Subject Condition (i.e., every predicator must have a subject) to ensure grammaticality. Again, ideally, such output constraints, instead of being ad hoc stipulations, should be consequences of a unified mapping principle (e.g., Her (1998, 1999, 2003, 2010), Kibort (2007, 2008)).

5.3 Revisions Proposed

The first change I propose relates to the markedness hierarchy of grammatical functions in (5), which assumes that a negative feature is less marked than its positive counterpart, as shown in (10a) below, but does not distinguish between the two negative features, $[-r]$ and $[-o]$. OBJ and OBL$_\theta$ are thus not distinguishable for markedness. That is why Bresnan (2001, 309) must call (5) a 'partial' ordering of functions. In the spirit of Zaenen (1993, 151), Ackerman and Moore (2001b, 44), and Kibort (2007), I propose that $[-r]$ should be seen as less marked than $[-o]$; intuitively, this is because $[-r]$ uniquely identifies argument roles that are 'empty', or athematic, as well as grammatical functions not restricted to a specific role (e.g., Bresnan (2001, 366)). The addition of (10b) enables a comprehensive ordering of argument functions, as in (11).

(10) Markedness Hierarchy of Grammatical Features (revised):
    a. $[-f] > [+f]$
    b. $[-r] > [-o]$

(11) Markedness Hierarchy of Grammatical Functions (revised):
    SUBJ$_{([-r-o])}$ > OBJ$_{([-r+o])}$ > OBL$_{\theta([+r-o])}$ > OBJ$_{\theta([+r+o])}$

The second change is regarding (6), the intrinsic classification of a-structure roles. Following Her (2003), I propose to simplify the classification and only assign patient or theme an intrinsic feature $[-r]$, repeated in (12). Other roles do not receive any intrinsic classification.

(12) Intrinsic Classification (IC) of A-Structure Roles (revised):
    patient/theme: $\theta \longrightarrow [-r]$[3]

In addition, I propose to follow Zaenen (1988), Bresnan and Kanerva (1989), Ackerman (1992), Markantonatou (1995), Kibort (2007,

---

[3] The IC is open to typological variation and thus parameterization, e.g., Her and Deng (2012) propose that there is no IC in Formosan languages, in order to allow a morphosyntactic operation to map any focused role to SUBJ. Thus, neither BZ's LMT nor the one proposed in this paper can account for ergative languages in general. See Manning (1996) for discussion.

2008), Her (2003, 2010), among others, and allow morphosyntactic operations, in addition to morpholexical operations such as passive. Ackerman (1992, 56) characterizes the difference between morphosyntactic and morpholexical operations as follows:

> Morpholexical operations affect the lexical semantics of predicates by altering the semantic properties associated with predicates.
>
> Morphosyntactic operations assign features supplemental to those supplied by IC assignment: these operations can affect the final GF assignments to arguments but cannot affect the lexical semantics.

Though all morphological operations are by definition language-specific, the default morphosyntactic operation in (13), that Her (2003) proposes for English and Chinese, has the potential to be universal.

(13) Language-specific Default Classification (DC):
  If $\theta \neq \hat{\theta}$, then $\theta \longrightarrow [+r]$

My strategy is to keep the IC maximally general, invariable, and thus elegant by leaving anything non-universal, thus parametric or language-specific, to the morphological component. This allows a more expressive a-structure, where roles can be unspecified (no [±r] nor [±o]), under-specified (only [±r] or [±o]), or fully specified (both [±r] and [±o]), while in BZ's model roles are uniformly underspecified (only [±r] or [±o]). Finally, the most significant revision proposed is to the internally-inconsistent mapping principles in (8). Adopting the spirit of a unified mapping principle in Her (1998, 1999, 2003, 2010) and Kibort (2007, 2008), I propose this precise formulation in (14).

(14) Unified Mapping Principle (UMP):
  Map each a-structure role that is available† onto the highest function in (13) that is compatible‡ and available†.
  † A role θ is *available* for mapping if all roles to the left of θ are mapped; a function F is *available* for mapping to θ if F is not fully specified for by another role and also not linked to a role to the left of θ.
  ‡ A function is *compatible* if it contains no conflicting feature.

The immediate advantage, aside from the obvious simplicity and consistency of this single principle, is that the two stipulated output constraints, Function-Argument Biuniqueness and the Subject Condition, are no longer needed, as both are already implicitly incorporated in (14) and thus can be seen as natural consequences of the mapping principle.

5.4 Illustrative Examples

The focus of grammatical data in BZ is on the phenomena of deep unaccusativity; so we shall start with the same illustrative examples in BZ to illustrate the revised LMT. Note that agent in our revised LMT is entirely unspecified in a-structure and yet does receive the desired mapping in (15) and (18).

(15) **Transitive** (e.g., *John pounded the metal*):

a-structure: pound < ag pt >
[−r]

$$\frac{\text{s/o/o}_\theta/\text{OBL}_\theta \quad\quad \text{s/o}}{}$$

UMP: SUBJ OBJ

(16) **Passive** (e.g., *the metal was pounded*):

a-structure: pound < ag pt >
[−r]
Passive: ∅

$$\frac{\text{s/o}}{}$$

UMP: SUBJ

(17) **Unaccusative** (e.g., *the river froze*):

a-structure: freeze < th >
[−r]

$$\frac{\text{s/o}}{}$$

UMP: SUBJ

(18) **Unergative** (e.g., *the dog barked*):

a-structure: bark < ag >

$$\frac{\text{s/o/o}_\theta/\text{OBL}_\theta}{}$$

UMP: SUBJ

Next, we illustrate how the dative alternation (e.g., *Lee gave her a book/Lee gave a book to her*) can be accounted for in this revised LMT. Zaenen (1988, 16) proposes the default classification in (19), in addition to the intrinsic classification of ag[−o] and pt/th[−r], to account for the dative construction in (20).

(19) Default Classification (DC) (Zaenen, 1988, 16):

    a.   the highest role $\longrightarrow$ $[-r]$

    b.   the next role $\longrightarrow$ $[+o]$

    c.   the third role $\longrightarrow$ $[+r]$

(20) **Dative** (e.g., *Lee gave her a book*):

a-structure:	give <	ag	go	th	>
IC		$[-o]$		$[-r]$	
DC		$[-r]$	$[+o]$		

		SUBJ	O/O_θ	S/O
Well-formedness Cond.		SUBJ	OBJ_{go}	OBJ

However, as pointed out by Her (2010, 112), this account does not allow the prepositional dative, where the goal links to OBL$_\theta$ marked by *to*. Thus, it can only derive the passivized theme SUBJ and goal OBJ in (21a), but fails to derive the goal OBL$_\theta$ (21b) and the passivized goal SUBJ in (21c).

(21) a. %A book was given her (by Lee). ($\checkmark$)

     b. A book was given to her (by Lee). (X)

     c. She was given a book (by Lee). (X)

     d. **Passivized dative:**

a-structure:	give <	ag	go	th	>
IC		$[-o]$		$[-r]$	
Passive		$\emptyset$			
DC			$[+o]$		

		O/O_θ	S/O
Well-formedness Cond.		OBJ/OBJ_{go}	SUBJ

Adopting the morphosyntactic operation of the dative alternation put forth in (22) by Her (1999) and thus assuming the prepositional dative, also known as the indirect-object construction (e.g., Haspelmath (2011)) and indirective (e.g., Dryer (1986), Siewierska (2003)), is the unmarked form and the double-object dative is marked, I now demonstrate how the dative alternation is accounted for in the model proposed here. See (23) and (24).

(22) Dative (English):

    If <ag go th>, then go $\longrightarrow$ $[+o]$

(23) **Prepositional dative** (e.g., *Lee gave a book to her*):

a-structure:	give <	ag	go	th	>
IC				$[-r]$	
DC			$[+r]$		

	$s/o/o_\theta/obl_\theta$	obl_θ/o_θ	s/o
UMP	SUBJ	OBL_{go}	OBJ

(24) **Double-object dative** (e.g., *Lee gave her a book*):

a-structure:	give <	ag	go	th	>
IC				$[-r]$	
Dative			$[+o]$		
DC			$[+r]$		

	$s/o/o_\theta/obl_\theta$	o_θ	s/o
UMP	SUBJ	OBJ_{go}	OBJ

The reason for posing the Dative as a language-specific operation instead of parameterized IC choices on the triadic argument structures is because the dative alternation is not universal. In the 378 languages examined by Haspelmath (2011), exactly 50%, or 189, have the indirect-object construction only; merely 83, or 22%, have the double-object form only. It is thus justifiable to derive the marked case of double-object morphologically.[4] Yet, the unmarked indirect-object form is not universal, as the operation in (22) is language-specific and is absent in the 189 direct-object languages, but it applies obligatorily in the 83 double-object languages and optionally in some 40 mixed languages like English, which have both constructions.[5]

Assuming that the morpholexical operation of passive, in addition to the suppression of $\hat{\theta}$, also includes a parameterized option to passivize goal, as in (25) (Her, 1999, 102-103), we can now see the interesting interaction between dative and passive in English. Again, the LMT model proposed here correctly accounts for the data observed.

(25) Passive (English)
    If $< \theta \ldots (go) \ldots >$, then $\theta \longrightarrow \emptyset$ (& go $\longrightarrow [-r]$)[6]

---

[4]This line of argument is well-accepted in typological accounts of word order variation in derivational approaches. Cinque (2005), for example, derives Greenberg's Universal 20, which concerns the word orders of D, Num, A, and N, and the attested exceptions, by base-generating the unmarked, most common, order of D > Num > A > N and obtaining all the other attested orders via movement of N.

[5]However, due to space limitations, this is still a partial account as it leaves primary object constructions (Dryer 1986), also known as the secundative (Siewierska 2003), unaccounted for.

(26) a. **Prepositional dative & passive w/o go[−r] option**
(e.g., *a book was given to her (by Lee)*):

a-structure:	give <	ag	go	th	>
IC				[−r]	
Passive		∅			
DC			[+r]		

		OBL$_\theta$/OBJ$_\theta$	s/o
UMP		OBL$_{go}$	SUBJ

b. **Prepositional dative & passive with go[−r] option**
(e.g., *she was given a book (by Lee)*):

a-structure:	give <	ag	go	th	>
IC				[−r]	
Passive		∅	[−r]		

		s/o	s/o
UMP		SUBJ	OBJ

Assuming that structures derived via a morphological operation are marked in relation to their counterparts derived without this operation, (26b) is more marked than (26a). In turn, structures in (26) are less marked, with only passive, than the ones in (27) below, with both dative and passive.[7]

(27) a. **Double-object dative & passive w/o go[−r] option**
(e.g., *%a book was given her (by Lee)*):

a-structure:	give <	ag	go	th	>
IC				[−r]	
Passive		∅			
Dative			[+o]		
DC			[+r]		

		OBJ$_\theta$	s/o
UMP		OBJ$_{go}$	SUBJ

---

[6]As demonstrated in Her (1999, 2010), while languages like English allow this option, languages like Chinese do not. The LMT model proposed here can account for this distinction; due to space limitations, I will not go into this interesting typological issue.

[7]This analysis does not bring in the co-variation in word order associated with this construction. See Siewierska and Hollmann (2007) for a corpus-based study.

b. **Double-object dative & passive with go[−r] option**
(e.g., *%a book was given her (by Lee)*:

a-structure:	give <	ag	go	th	>
IC			[−r]		
Passive		∅	[−r]		
Dative			[+o]		

	OBJ	S/O
	OBJ	S/O
UMP	OBJ	SUBJ

The fact that goal in (27) may map onto either OBJ and OBJ$_{go}$ further adds to the obscurity of the output of the interaction of dative and passive and thus further increases its markedness; this high degree of markedness may explain why this construction is only grammatical in British dialects or in certain literary styles (e.g., Jaeggli 1986, 596; Anderson 1988, 300; Dryer 1986, 833). To summarize, the several dative constructions in English are related by Dative, a morphosyntactic rule, and Passive, a morpholexical rule, as shown schematically in (28). The Dative rule marks (28a) and (28e), and the Passive rule marks (28c), (28d), and (28e). (28e) is the only construction marked by both. The degree of markedness is thus directly related to the application of these morphological rules.

(28) a. Lee gave a book to her. (unmarked)
  b. Lee gave her a book. (Derived from (a) via Dative, marked)
  c. A book was given to her. (Derived from (a) via Passive, marked)
  d. She was given a book. (Derived from (a) via Passive, marked)
  e. %A book was given her. (Derived from (a) via Dative and Passive, even more marked)

5.5 Conclusion

The version of Lexical Mapping Theory put forth in Bresnan and Zaenen (1990) (BZ) is the most widely accepted version in the literature of LFG. For example, it is adopted by Bresnan (2001), the most authoritative reference of LFG's theoretical underpinnings, and by Falk (2001), the most accessible textbook on LFG. The goal of this paper is to propose some revisions to BZ's model to further strengthen its internal consistency, formal rigor, and empirical coverage. Assuming the same two features [±r] and [±o] for the decomposition of grammatical functions and the unmarkedness of negative features, I further propose that [−r] is less marked than [−o]. This allows a comprehensive ordering of markedness, i.e., SUBJ > OBJ > OBL$_\theta$ > OBL$_\theta$. I also propose a single intrinsic [−r] classification of patient/theme and put in a default [+r] classification for all non-$\hat{\theta}$ roles. The latter morphosyntactic operations increase the expressivity of the theory but not at the expense of formal rigor. The most significant revision is replacing the stipulated mapping principles for SUBJ roles and non-SUBJ roles and the two output well-formedness conditions with a single unified mapping principle, which consistently favors the unmarked parallel matching between argument roles and grammatical functions. Finally, transitive, unaccusative, unergative, passive, and dative constructions in English are used as illustrations for the model of LMT proposed. Further applications should confirm that the simplicity and internal consistency of the proposed model broadens the LMT's empirical coverage.

References

Ackerman, Farrell. 1992. Complex predicates and morpholexical relatedness: Locative alternation in Hungarian. In I. Sag and A. Szabolcsi, eds., *Lexical Matters*. CSLI Publications.

Ackerman, Farrell and John Moore. 2001a. Dowtyian proto-properties and Lexical Mapping Theory. Paper presented at LFG 2001, Hong Kong University. Available online at: http://idiom.ucsd.edu/ moore/papers/hk-hout.pdf.

Ackerman, Farrell and John Moore. 2001b. *Proto-Properties and Grammatical Encoding. A Correspondence Theory of Argument Selection*. CSLI Publications.

Anderson, John M. 1988. Objects (direct and not-so-direct) in English and elsewhere. In C. Duncan-Rose and T. Vennemann, eds., *On Language*, pages 287–314. Routledge.

Bresnan, Joan. 1989. The syntactic projection problem and the comparative syntax of locative inversion. *Journal of Information Science and Engineering* 5.4:287–303.

Bresnan, Joan. 2001. *Lexical-Functional Syntax*. Blackwell Publishers.

Bresnan, Joan and Jonni Kanerva. 1989. Locative inversion in Chicheŵa: A case study of factorization in grammar. *Linguistic Inquiry* 20:1–50.

Bresnan, Joan and Lioba Moshi. 1990. Object asymmetries in comparative Bantu syntax. *Linguistic Inquiry* 21:147–185.

Bresnan, Joan and Annie Zaenen. 1990. Deep unaccusativity in LFG. In K. Dziwirek, P. Farrell, and E. Mejías-Bikandi, eds., *Grammatical Relations: A Cross-Theoretical Perspective*, pages 45–57. CSLI Publications.

Butt, Miriam, Mary Dalrymple, and Anette Frank. 1997. An architecture for linking theory in LFG. In M. Butt and T. H. King, eds., *Proceedings of the LFG97 Conference. CSLI On-line Publications*.

Cinque, Guglielmo. 2005. Deriving Greenberg's universal 20 and its exceptions. *Linguistic Inquiry* 36.3:315–332.

Dryer, Mathew S. 1986. Primary objects, secondary objects, and antidative. *Language* pages 808–845.

Falk, Yehuda N. 2001. *Lexical-Functional Grammar: An Introduction to Constraint-Based Syntax*. CSLI Publications.

Haspelmath, Martin. 2011. Ditransitive constructions: The verb *give*. In M. Dryer and M. Haspelmath, eds., *The World Atlas of Language Structures Online*, chap. 105. Max Planck Digital Library. Available online at http://wals.info/chapter/105 Accessed on 2012-04-01.

Her, One-Soon. 1998. Lexical mapping in Chinese inversion constructions. In M. Butt and T. H. King, eds., *Proceedings of the LFG98 Conference*. CSLI On-line Publications.

Her, One-Soon. 1999. Interaction of thematic structure and syntactic structures: On Mandarin dative alternations. In Y. Yin, I. Yang, and H. Chan, eds., *Chinese Languages and Linguistics V: Interaction of Form and Function*, pages 373–412. Academia Sinica.

Her, One-Soon. 2003. Chinese inversion constructions within a simplified LMT. *Journal of Chinese Linguistics, Lexical-Functional Grammar Analysis of Chinese* pages 1–31.

Her, One-Soon. 2010. *Interaction and Variation in the Chinese VO Construction*. Crane Publishing. Revised edition.

Her, One-Soon and Dun-Hong Deng. 2012. Lexical mapping in Yami verbs. Paper to be presented at LFG12, Bali; to appear in the proceedings.

Huang, Chu-Ren. 1993. Mandarin Chinese and the Lexical Mapping Theory: A study of the interaction of morphology and argument changing. *Bulletin of the Institute of History and Philology* 62.2:337–388.

Jaeggli, Osvald. 1986. Passive. *Linguistic Inquiry* 17:587–622.

Kibort, Anna. 2007. Extending the applicability of Lexical Mapping Theory. In M. Butt and T. H. King, eds., *Proceedings of the LFG07 Conference*. CSLI Publications.

Kibort, Anna. 2008. Impersonals in Polish: An LFG perspective. In A. Siewierska, ed., *Impersonal Constructions: Special Issue of the Transactions of the Philological Society*, vol. 106.2, pages 246–289.

Manning, Christopher D. 1996. *Ergativity: Argument structure and grammatical relations*. CSLI Publications.

Markantonatou, Stella. 1995. Modern Greek deverbal nominals: An LMT approach. *Journal of Linguistics* 31:267–299.

Siewierska, Anna. 2003. Reduced pronominals and argument prominence. In M. Butt and T. H. King, eds., *Nominals: Inside and Out*. CSLI Publications.

Siewierska, Anna and Willem Hollmann. 2007. Ditransitive clauses in English with special reference to Lancashire dialect. In M. Hannay and G. J. Steen, eds., *Structural-Functional Studies in English Grammar: In Honor of Lachlan Mackenzie*, pages 83–102. John Benjamins.

Zaenen, Annie. 1988. Lexical information in LFG, an overview. Unpublished ms. Xerox-PARC and CSLI, Stanford University.

Zaenen, Annie. 1993. Unaccusativity in Dutch: Integrating syntax and lexical semantics. In J. Pustejovsky, ed., *Semantics and the Lexicon*, pages 129–161. Kluwer Academic Publishers.

6

Argument Structure of Quirky Algonquian Verbs

AMY DAHLSTROM

6.1 Introduction

A hallmark of Annie Zaenen's work is the careful examination of mismatches between morphology and syntax, as in Icelandic quirky case, and of the role played by argument structure in unaccusativity and other syntactic phenomena (e.g. Zaenen, Maling, and Thrainsson 1985, Bresnan and Zaenen 1990).[1] In the present paper I investigate the argument structure associated with a 'quirky' pattern in Algonquian languages: not an instance of quirky *case*, but rather a mismatch between inflectional morphology and syntactic valence. This paper is a continuation of Dahlstrom (2009), which argued that a set of two-place verbs in the Algonquian language Meskwaki is associated with the valence of <SUBJ OBJ$_\theta$>, rather than the unmarked <SUBJ OBJ> pattern for transitive verbs. An example is given in (1):[2]

---

[1] An earlier version of this paper was presented at the 2011 LSA/SSILA meetings. Thanks to Matthew Dryer, Richard Rhodes, Lucy Thomason, and Aaron Broadwell for comments.

[2] Abbreviations: 3' obviative (in verb agreement), ANIM animate, AOR aorist (prefix or verb paradigm), EP epenthetic consonant, INAN inanimate, IND independent indicative, OBV obviative (nominal suffix), PL plural, SG singular. '>' separates subject and object features; an en dash indicates the boundary between preverb and verb stem. Obviative is a subtype of third person, used for third persons more peripheral to the discourse.

From Quirky Case to Representing Space: Papers in Honor of Annie Zaenen.
Tracy Holloway King and Valeria de Paiva.
Copyright © 2013, CSLI Publications.

(1) ahpe·nemo-wa   o-si·me·h-ani
depend.on-3/IND his-younger.sibling-ANIM.OBV.SG
'He relies on his younger brother.'

The stem *ahpe·nemo-* 'depend on, rely on' requires two arguments, but it is inflected only for the subject. In contrast, ordinary transitive verbs are inflected to agree with both subject and object:

(2) wa·pam-e·wa   o-si·me·h-ani
look.at-3>3'/IND his-younger.sibling-ANIM.OBV.SG
'He looks at his younger brother.'

The analysis in Dahlstrom (2009) presents a number of syntactic arguments demonstrating that the nonsubject argument of verbs like *ahpe·nemo-* in (1) is in fact OBJ$_\theta$, the thematically restricted object, and not OBJ or OBL. Little was said in Dahlstrom (2009) about the argument structure of such verbs. But in order to support the claim that the second argument of the verbs in question is a thematically restricted object, it is necessary to discover what the thematic restrictions on this set of objects might be. In the present paper I investigate the lexical semantics of this set of verbs, drawing examples not only from Meskwaki but also from the related languages of Kickapoo, Cree, Ojibwe, and Menominee.[3] (Unmarked examples below are Meskwaki.) It will be seen that the quirky pattern is widespread in the family, and should be reconstructed for the proto-language. Moreover, the quirky pattern is associated primarily with verbs which do not greatly affect the second argument, such as verbs of possession, or verbs expressing location.

Algonquianists call this quirky valence pattern "AI+O", an opaque label which requires explanation. "AI" stands for Animate Intransitive, one of the four stem classes in the language. (3) lists the four stem classes, which are sensitive to valence and the gender – animate or inanimate – of one of the verb's arguments. For transitive and ditransitive verbs subcategorized for OBJ, the gender of OBJ determines the stem class (e.g. *wa·pam-* 'look at' in (2) is Transitive Animate). Otherwise, the gender of the subject determines the stem class of the verb.[4]

---

[3]Sources: Kickapoo: Voorhis (1988); Cree: Wolfart and Ahenakew (1998); Menominee: Bloomfield (1975); Ojibwe: list provided by R. Rhodes in Valentine (2001:242). The various sources use different conventions for indicating long vowels: double vowels in Kickapoo and Ojibwe, a circumflex in Cree, and a raised dot in Meskwaki and Menominee. In the glosses of the various verb forms I have introduced the LFG symbol of OBJ$_\theta$ for the sake of uniformity.

[4]For the two intransitive stem classes, 'Animate' or 'Inanimate' precedes 'Intransitive' as a mnemonic that the gender of the subject is relevant; the gender specification follows 'Transitive' as a reminder that in transitive stems, it is the

(3) Animate Intransitive (AI)   Inanimate Intransitive (II)
     Transitive Animate (TA)   Transitive Inanimate (TI)
     cf. *meškosi-* (AI)   *meškwa·-* (II) 'be red'
     amw- (TA)   *mi·či-* (TI) 'eat'

For example, 'raspberry' is grammatically animate: to say that a raspberry is red the AI stem *meškosi-* would be selected; to say that someone ate a raspberry the TA stem *amw-* would be selected. 'Strawberry', on the other hand, is grammatically inanimate, so *meškwa·-* would be used to report its color and *mi·či-* to report eating a strawberry.

The valence pattern of interest here thus presents a mismatch between syntax and morphology: the verb requires two arguments but is inflected in the pattern appropriate for intransitive verbs. The Algonquianist label 'AI+O' means that it is inflected as an AI (Animate Intransitive) verb, but it takes an object (O) as well. This mismatch was noted by Bloomfield (1962:46; underlining in original):

> Many AI verbs behave, as to syntax and meaning, like transitive verbs: they are accompanied by substantive expressions, indifferent as to gender and number, which in syntactic behavior and meaning resemble objects. We shall say that these verbs take an implied object.

Below I recapitulate the findings of Dahlstrom (2009), and then turn to the lexical semantics of the verbs that appear in this marked valence pattern.

6.2   Syntax of the construction

Dahlstrom (2009) demonstrates that the non-subject argument of Meskwaki AI+O verbs is not an unrestricted OBJ but rather OBJ$_\theta$, the same grammatical function associated with the second object of ditransitive verbs.[5] This result was obtained by, first, establishing tests for the two object types using ditransitive verbs (e.g. *mi·n-* 'give'); second, showing that when the first object of a ditransitive is suppressed by lexical processes such as reflexive, reciprocal, or antipassive, the derived valence is <SUBJ OBJ$_\theta$> (e.g. *mi·šiwe·-* 'give OBJ$_\theta$ away'; antipassive). The final step is to show that the same valence is found with basic AI+O verbs, such as *ahpe·nemo-* 'depend on', which are not derived from underlying ditransitives.

I will here briefly recount the differences between the two objects

---

object's gender that determines the shape of the stem.

[5]Rhodes (1990) makes an analogous claim for Ojibwe, that the non-subject argument of the AI+O verbs is a 3 in Relational grammar terms. The details of the properties distinguishing the two objects of ditransitives varies from one language to another; see Rhodes (1990) for details of Ojibwe verb inflection.

found with ditransitives.[6] First, as implied in the quote from Bloomfield above, verbs inflect for OBJ; furthermore, the shape of the verb
stem (TA vs. TI) specifies the gender of OBJ. OBJ$_\theta$ neither triggers
agreement nor affects the stem shape. Second, OBJ in Meskwaki may
be suppressed by a number of valence-decreasing processes, including
antipassive, verbal reflexive, and reciprocal formation. The OBJ$_\theta$ argument, on the other hand, can never be so suppressed, either in ditransitive clauses or in the AI+O construction. Third, while Meskwaki
exhibits athematic ("dummy") SUBJ and OBJ, there are no athematic
OBJ$_\theta$s. Fourth, pronominal OBJs are expressed by inflectional affixes. In
contrast, pronominal OBJ$_\theta$s are expressed by zero anaphora or by independent pronouns built on possessed forms of the noun stem -$i\cdot yaw$-
'body' (see Dahlstrom 2009 for details).

Another property distinguishing OBJ from OBJ$_\theta$ in Meskwaki involves
noun incorporation. With verbs containing an incorporated body part
noun, an OBJ is construed as the body part's possessor. An OBJ$_\theta$ cannot
be so construed.

(4) mešketone·n-   'open OBJ's mouth by hand'
     mešk-etone·-en
     open-mouth-by.hand

(5) ahpanasite·ka·pa·-   'stand with one's feet on OBJ$_\theta$'
     ahp-anasite·-ika·pa·-   [not "stand on OBJ$_\theta$'s feet"]
     on-foot-stand

(4) is an example of the very productive Algonquian pattern of transitive verbs containing instrumental "finals".[7] The final -en means that
the subject acts upon an object by some action involving the subject's
hand(s), resulting in the state expressed in the stem-initial morpheme.
The medial position is optionally filled; if it is filled it is often filled
with a body-part noun. The body part medial in a transitive verb like
(4) is understood to belong to the object of the transitive verb. (5), on
the other hand, is an AI+O verb. The verb contains a body part noun
in the stem-medial position, but here the OBJ$_\theta$ is not construed as the
possessor. Rather it is the subject of the verb which is understood to
possess the incorporated body part noun.

---

[6]I here review arguments that the second argument of the AI+O construction is
not OBJ. For arguments that it is also not OBL, see Dahlstrom (2009).

[7]Many Algonquian verb stems are bipartite, combining an initial morpheme with
a final morpheme; another common schema is tripartite, with initial, medial, and
final stem components.

6.3 Classification of <SUBJ OBJθ > verb types

Having established that there is a syntactic difference between OBJ and OBJθ and that it is possible for Algonquian verbs to subcategorize for subject and OBJθ with no OBJ, we may now ask what types of verbs exhibit this marked valence pattern. This section describes several general semantic classes associated with the <SUBJ OBJθ> valence, plus some instances which are harder to account for.

We may first of all observe that the most prototypical transitive verbs, such as *nes-* 'kill' and *pakam-* 'hit' — that is, verbs with strongly affected patients — do not display the AI+O pattern. Nor do the numerous Algonquian verbs with instrumental finals, such as (4) above, where the final is *-en* 'by hand'. The schema exemplified in (4) — an initial specifying the resulting state, an optional medial, such as an incorporated body part noun, plus an instrumental final expressing the type of action — is uniformly associated with the unmarked transitive valence of <SUBJ OBJ>, never the AI+O pattern of <SUBJ OBJθ>.

The AI+O pattern, on the other hand, is most frequently found with less affected entities: e.g. certain subclasses of themes (things possessed, entities undergoing a transfer of possession), or locatives. We will examine instances of all these semantic roles below, beginning with possession.

6.3.1 Possession

Verbs derived from possessed nouns

The most productive set of verbs with the <SUBJ OBJθ> valence are the verbs derived from possessed nouns.[8] These include verbs expressing kinship relations, as well as possession of items such as drums and blankets, as seen in (6).

(6) a. ona·pe·mi- 'have OBJθ as a husband'
    b. oki- 'have OBJθ as a mother'
    c. otahkohkwi- 'have OBJθ as a drum'
    d. otakohpi- (Cree) 'use OBJθ as a blanket'

Such verbs may be used either as two place verbs, subcategorized for <SUBJ OBJθ>, or as one place verbs, subcategorized for only <SUBJ>. In other words, the verb stem in (6a) could be used to say of a woman that she is married (one place verb) or that she is married to him (two place verb). The same ambiguity of valence is found throughout this

---

[8]Note that the initial *o(t)-* of the stem is identical to the 3rd person possessive prefix on nouns. However, in verbs such as those in (6) the *o(t)-* does not function as agreement with, or pronominal reference to, a third person: it has simply been reanalyzed as part of the verb stem.

set of verbs.

Verbs with initial kek- 'having'

Another set of AI+O verbs expressing possession all have the stem-initial morpheme *kek-* (Cree *kik-*) 'having':

(7)	a.	kekišin-	'be buried with OBJ$_\theta$'
			(lit. 'lie having OBJ$_\theta$')
	b.	keko·mye·paho-	'run with OBJ$_\theta$ on back'
	c.	keki-kotawi·-	'go underwater with OBJ$_\theta$'
	d.	keke·ka·powew (Men)	'he stands having, holding OBJ$_\theta$'
	e.	kikâpôhkê- (Cree)	'add OBJ$_\theta$ to soup, enhance one's soup with OBJ$_\theta$'

In (7c) *keki* appears as a preverb (a phonologically independent word) compounded with the Animate Intransitive verb stem *kotawi·-* 'go underwater'. See Dahlstrom (2000) for discussion of preverb-verb compounds.

Other verbs of possession

Besides the verbs with initial *kek-* and the verbs derived from possessed nouns, we find other AI+O verbs expressing possessive relations; a few are listed in (8):

(8)	a.	dnid (Oj)	'possess OBJ$_\theta$'
	b.	gwid (Oj)	'wear OBJ$_\theta$'
	c.	naapeenemo- (Kick)	'adopt OBJ$_\theta$'
	d.	nwapod (Oj)	'take OBJ$_\theta$ along to eat'

(8c) from Kickapoo, *naapeenemo-* 'adopt OBJ$_\theta$', fits semantically with the kinship terms of (6).[9]

6.3.2 Loss

The opposite of possession is loss, and verbs expressing loss also often display the AI+O valence pattern:

(9)	a.	caakiθaa- (Kick)	'use OBJ$_\theta$ up'
	b.	jaagsed (Oj)	'run out of OBJ$_\theta$'
	c.	kehekwi-	'lose one's captive/prey (OBJ$_\theta$ gives s the slip)'
	d.	pakicî- (Cree)	'release, let go of OBJ$_\theta$'
	e.	wani·hke·-	'forget OBJ$_\theta$'
	f.	wanikiskisi- (Cree)	'forget OBJ$_\theta$; be forgetful'

---

[9] Cultural note: following a death in the family, the Meskwaki and Kickapoo ritually adopt someone else from the community to take the place of the deceased person, establishing a new kinship tie.

Verbs of forgetting, such as (9e) and (9f), fall into this pattern: to forget is to lose something mentally.

In some of the languages, the verbs for 'remember' are also AI+O; if forgetting is a mental loss, then the forms in (10) should perhaps be added to the verbs of possession in the previous section:

(10) a. kiskisi- (Cree)   'remember; remember OBJ_θ'
      b. kehkinooθoo- (Kick) 'remember OBJ_θ'

In Meskwaki, however, *mehkwe·nem-* (TA), *mehkwe·net-* (TI) 'remember' is a regular transitive verb, not AI+O.[10]

6.3.3 Verbs of exchanging

Semantically related to the verbs of possession are the verbs of exchange, such as 'buy', 'sell', and 'trade'. Here the possession of an object is transferred from one owner to another. This semantic domain is frequently associated with the <SUBJ OBJ_θ> valence in Algonquian languages:

(11) a. ata·we·-   'sell, trade OBJ_θ'
      b. daawed (Oj)   'trade/sell OBJ_θ'
      c. tepa·ha·kϵ·w (Men) 'he sells OBJ_θ'
      d. atâwê- (Cree)   'buy OBJ_θ'
      e. atâwâkê- (Cree)   'sell OBJ_θ, sell things'
      f. daawnged (Oj)   'borrow OBJ_θ'

To the class of verbs of exchange we may add the verb meaning 'steal', in which possession is also transferred, albeit against the wishes of the previous owner. This verb displays the AI+O pattern in all the languages under consideration:

(12) a. kemot-   'steal OBJ_θ'
      b. gmoodid (Oj)   'steal OBJ_θ'
      c. kemo·tew (Men) 'he steals OBJ_θ'
      d. kimoti- (Cree) 'steal OBJ_θ; be a thief'

The second gloss of (12d) 'be a thief' reflects the tendency of AI+O verbs to allow either two-place or one-place readings, discussed further below.

6.3.4 Activities, optionally taking an argument

Another set of verbs associated with the <SUBJ OBJ_θ> valence pattern may either be used as a one-place verb denoting an activity, such as cooking, or as a two-place verb in which the item cooked is identified.

---

[10]Ojibwe and Menominee also have regular transitive forms for 'remember'.

In the latter case the second argument is syntactically an OBJ$_\theta$. See also the Cree verbs for 'sell' in (11e) and for 'steal' in (12d) above.

(13) a. wača·ho-   'cook; cook OBJ$_\theta$'
      b. kaskikwâso- (Cree)   'sew, do one's sewing; sew OBJ$_\theta$'
      c. nawacî- (Cree)   'roast OBJ$_\theta$; roast one's food'
      d. bwed (Oj)   'roast; roast OBJ$_\theta$'

Note that this construction permits patients (affected by the action of the verb) as OBJ$_\theta$ as opposed to the theme OBJ$_\theta$s exemplified in previous sections.

6.3.5 Comitatives

Another set of <SUBJ OBJ$_\theta$> verbs associated with a specific morpheme is the set formed with *takw-* 'together with'. The thematic role of the OBJ$_\theta$ in such verbs is probably theme:

(14) a. takwi·-   'join OBJ$_\theta$'
      b. takwisen-   'lie together with OBJ$_\theta$'
                              (inanimate subject)[11]
      c. takwi-natom-   'summon OBJ together with OBJ$_\theta$'

(14c) is another example of a preverb-verb compound, comparable to (7c) above. The preverb *takwi-* 'together with' has been added to the Transitive Animate verb stem *natom-* 'summon'.

6.3.6 Lexicalized reciprocals, antipassives

A number of verb stems in Meskwaki and other Algonquian languages exhibit frozen forms of valence-decreasing morphemes such as Meskwaki *-eti·-* (reciprocal). For example, in (15a) *kakano·neti·-* now means simply 'converse', not necessarily 'converse with each other'; it can, for example, be used with a singular subject. Like the activity verbs in section 6.3.4 it may optionally take a second argument, expressing the person conversed with. If a second argument is used, its grammatical function is OBJ$_\theta$.

(15) a. kakano·neti·-   'converse; converse with OBJ$_\theta$'
      b. mi·ka·ti·-   'fight; fight against OBJ$_\theta$'
      c. ahčike·-   'plant OBJ$_\theta$'

(15b) likewise contains a frozen reciprocal suffix, while (15c) is a lexicalized antipassive form of *aht-* 'put', containing the antipassive suffix *-ike·-*.[12]

---

[11]Note that (14b) is an Inanimate Intransitive stem, requiring a subject in the inanimate gender, so this verb should in fact be labeled "II+O" rather than AI+O.

[12]When verbs such as (15a-b) are used with a singular subject and a lexically expressed OBJ$_\theta$ it is clear that they constitute an AI+O construction rather than a

6.3.7 'Drink', 'throw', and other verbs taking theme/patients

Finally, let us look at a few remaining verbs taking patient or theme arguments which do not seem to fit any of the categories mentioned so far.

One verb stem which is associated with the <SUBJ OBJ$_\theta$> valence pattern in all of the Algonquian languages under consideration here is 'drink'. It is hard to understand why 'drink' should have this unusual valence pattern when the verbs for 'eat' exhibit the regular transitive valence (cf. Meskwaki *amw-* (TA), *mi·či-* (TI) 'eat'). Both the entity drunk and the entity eaten are clearly affected by the action of the verb: based on what we have seen so far, one would predict that 'drink' would also exhibit the normal transitive pattern. Yet the uniformity of the <SUBJ OBJ$_\theta$> valence across the language family suggests that this is an old and stable pattern for 'drink'. Perhaps the 'drink' verbs are viewed like the activity verbs of section 6.3.4, where the focus is primarily on the one-place activity of drinking, and secondarily on the liquid being consumed.

(16)   a.   meno-   'drink OBJ$_\theta$; drink'
         b.   meno- (Kick)   'drink OBJ$_\theta$; drink'
         c.   menuah (Men)   'he drinks something, he drinks OBJ$_\theta$'
         d.   minihkwê- (Cree)   'drink OBJ$_\theta$'
         e.   mnikwed (Oj)   'drink OBJ$_\theta$ '

Another instance of the AI+O pattern is found with verbs of throwing in Meskwaki and Kickapoo, but not in Cree, Ojibwe, and Menominee. More precisely, the final *-a·hke·-* (Kickapoo *-aahkee-*) 'throw' is AI+O, and it combines very productively with numerous initials, often expressing direction. A sample of the throwing verbs is given in (17):

(17)   a.   we·pa·hke·-   'throw OBJ$_\theta$'
         b.   ina·hke·-   'fling OBJ$_\theta$ thither'
         c.   ni·sa·hke·-   'fling OBJ$_\theta$ down'
         d.   nowa·hke·-   'fling OBJ$_\theta$ out'
         e.   capookaahkee- (Kick)   'throw OBJ$_\theta$ in the water'

Finally, the two <SUBJ OBJ$_\theta$> verbs in (18) both exhibit theme OBJ$_\theta$s, but do not seem to fit any of the categories of theme arguments described above:

(18)   a.   nokaazod (Oj)   'use OBJ$_\theta$'
         b.   nitopahtwâ- (Cree)   'search for OBJ$_\theta$'

---

regular, symmetric reciprocal.

6.3.8 Location

In contrast to the examples of OBJ$_\theta$ given above, all instances of the thematic role of theme, the OBJ$_\theta$ in an AI+O verb may also express location:

(19) a. ahpeka·-   'dance on OBJ$_\theta$'
      b. ahpe·nemo-   'depend on OBJ$_\theta$'
      c. ahpapi-   'sit on OBJ$_\theta$'
      d. pabid (Oj)   'sit on OBJ$_\theta$'

The verbs in (19) all contain the same initial (Meskwaki *ahp*-, Ojibwe *p*- 'on'). Note that in (19b) *ahpe·nemo*- 'depend on OBJ$_\theta$' we see the same metaphorical extension of locative 'on' as is found in English *depend on* and *rely on*.

Other AI+O verbs without the initial *ahp*- also have locative OBJ$_\theta$s:

(20) a. aakzid (Oj)   'have a pain in OBJ$_\theta$
                                  [a part of the body]'
      b. θeeθikaapaa- (Kick)   'stand perched on OBJ$_\theta$'
      c. se·sapi-   'sit on top of OBJ$_\theta$'

The initial *θeeθ*- in Kickapoo is cognate with Meskwaki *se·s*-; both mean 'on top of'.

6.4   Conclusion

The above survey of Algonquian verbs exhibiting the quirky valence pattern reveals that OBJ$_\theta$ in two-place verbs is likely to be associated with nonaffected entities, such as possessums and other subtypes of the theme semantic role; also certain types of locatives. Although the most prototypical transitive verbs associated with patients, such as 'hit' and 'kill', do not occur with the quirky valence pattern, we cannot assert that patients are never associated with OBJ$_\theta$ in two-place verbs. The patient of 'drink' is realized as OBJ$_\theta$ in all the languages under consideration, and the activity verbs in 6.3.4 allow patient OBJ$_\theta$s as well.

Although the descriptive survey in this paper allows us to better understand the range of uses of the quirky valence pattern, it does not seem possible to predict absolutely whether a given argument will be realized as OBJ$_\theta$. Rather, the patient of 'drink' must be lexically specified as an OBJ$_\theta$, as opposed to the patient of 'eat', which can undergo the default realization as an OBJ. In terms of Lexical Mapping Theory, the Algonquian data present some interesting challenges. The theme and patient arguments of AI+O verbs could be intrinsically associated with the [+r] feature, to ensure their realization as OBJ$_\theta$; however, associating [+r] with the locative OBJ$_\theta$s seen in section 6.3.8 would not rule out the locatives being expressed as OBL, not the desired outcome. See Dahlstrom (2009) for further discussion comparing the Algonquian quirky pattern to other LFG analyses of differential object marking.

The recurrence of the quirky AI+O valence pattern in the daughter languages points to its antiquity and stability over time: it is not only an interesting theoretical and typological challenge, but it is also of central concern for descriptive and historical Algonquian work.

References

Bloomfield, Leonard. 1962. *The Menomini Language*. Yale University Press.

Bloomfield, Leonard. 1975. *Menominee Lexicon*. Milwaukee Public Museum.

Bresnan, Joan and Annie Zaenen. 1990. Deep unaccusativity in LFG. In K. Dziwirek, P. Farrell, and E. Mejías-Bikandi, eds., *Grammatical Relations. A Cross-Theoretical Perspective*, pages 45–57. CSLI Publications.

Dahlstrom, Amy. 2000. Morphosyntactic mismatches in Algonquian: Affixal predicates and discontinuous verbs. In A. Okrent and J. Boyle, eds., *Proceedings from the Panels of the Chicago Linguistic Society's Thirty-sixth Meeting*, pages 63–87. Chicago Linguistic Society.

Dahlstrom, Amy. 2009. OBJθ without OBJ: A typology of Meskwaki objects. In M. Butt and T. H. King, eds., *On-line Proceedings of the LFG09 Conference*, pages 222–239. CSLI Publications.

Rhodes, Richard. 1990. Secondary objects in Ojibwe. In K. Dziwirek, P. Farrell, and E. Mejías-Bikandi, eds., *Grammatical Relations: A Cross-theoretical Perspective*, pages 401–414. CSLI Publications.

Valentine, J. Randolph. 2001. *Nishnaabemwin Reference Grammar*. Toronto University Press.

Voorhis, Paul H. 1988. *Kickapoo Vocabulary*. Algonquian and Iroquoian Linguistics.

Wolfart, H. Christoph and Freda Ahenakew. 1998. *The Student's Dictionary of Literary Plains Cree*. Algonquian and Iroquoian Linguistics.

Zaenen, Annie, Joan Maling, and Höskuldur Thráinsson. 1985. Case and grammatical functions: The Icelandic passive. *Natural Language and Linguistic Theory* 3:441–483.

Part II

Views on Syntax

7

A Tour of Grammar Formalisms

ANETTE FRANK

Having worked with a number of grammatical frameworks over many years at varying depth, I have gained an understanding of their similarities and differences, their respective attractiveness and strengths, but also their biases, which relate to the specific architectural choices they make. In this contribution I will highlight some insights I have gained over years of theoretical and applied research on computational grammar in a multilingual context that might be of interest to researchers in this field – if only to see whether their insights line up with mine.

Our choice of LFG as a guiding theoretical framework is what brought Annie and me together. My first encounter with her, dating back to the time when I finished my studies, was related to discussing linking theory in LFG – a research theme Annie has greatly influenced and that still bears many open questions. I have fond memories of a number of years working with Annie at XRCE Grenoble, investigating LFG from many perspectives. In later work I could compare the insights I gained to my experiences with other frameworks, like HPSG and LTAG.

My personal lesson from the synopsis I give below[1] is that none of the frameworks I discuss is the ultimate answer to how to describe natural languages uniformly within a linguistically sound and expressive computational grammar formalism. Still, I hope that these thoughts can contribute to a better understanding of how these frameworks are similar despite their differences, and different despite their similarities.

---

[1] The ideas I summarize here were presented in a survey talk at the ACL 2007 Workshop *Deep Linguistic Processing*, where I first reflected on the nature of various grammar formalisms, and dimensions of similarities and differences between them.

From Quirky Case to Representing Space: Papers in Honor of Annie Zaenen.
Tracy Holloway King and Valeria de Paiva.
Copyright © 2013, CSLI Publications.

7.1 Characterizing Grammatical Frameworks

The design of a mathematically defined grammar formalism makes strong predictions as to the grammaticality of linguistic constructs. If the grammatical theory that is built on top of is expected to reflect important characteristics of language crosslinguistically, we also expect it to be able to accommodate typologically distinct languages.[2] In this contribution I will investigate the formal and theoretical-linguistic underpinnings of major computational grammar frameworks from different perspectives.[3] A guiding question will be to what extent architectural choices and linguistic assumptions effect linguistic modeling of particular phenomena, within and across languages.

I will concentrate on a selection of grammatical frameworks that have been subject to intensive research in theoretical and computational linguistics: Lexical-Functional Grammar, LFG (Bresnan, 2001), Head-driven Phrase Structure Grammar, HPSG (Pollard and Sag, 1994), (Lexicalized) Tree Adjoining Grammar, (L)TAG (Joshi, 1988, Joshi and Schabes, 1997), and Combinatory Categorial Grammar CCG (Steedman, 2000). They represent major exponents of lexicalized, constraint- and unification-based grammar (especially LFG and HPSG), different types of tree adjunction grammars (TAGs), and CCG as a special type of categorial grammar (CG).[4]

These frameworks have evolved from different linguistic traditions. (C)CG has its roots in Montague Semantics (Dowty et al., 1981). HPSG, LFG and TAGs are grounded in the tradition of Generative Grammar, even though they arose in opposition to this framework, in a 'lexicalist' turn that questioned the transformation-centered views of Chomskyan syntax. Dependency Grammar, DG (Tesnière, 1959), finally, stands in a long tradition of grammar dating from antiquity. It encodes core grammatical concepts, but has not been extensively studied in modern theoretical syntax.

The particular design choices of these frameworks show interesting differences in how they account for general linguistic properties, such as constituency, word order, and valency. This will be illustrated in a concise overview in Section 7.2. Section 7.3 will further analyze differences and similarities of these frameworks by looking at various aspects of comparison, including (i) architectural choices, focusing on representation levels and linguistic concepts, (ii) adoption of special constructs,

---

[2]I deliberately avoid any discussion of 'language universals'.

[3]Given space restrictions, I will assume familiarity with the respective frameworks. For a concise introduction to these frameworks see Müller (2010).

[4]Dependency Grammar (DG) will only briefly be discussed in the conclusion.

and (iii) generalization across languages. In Section 7.4, I will show that we can reach even deeper insights into the strengths or biases of specific formalization choices by examining how they fare with notoriously difficult phenomena that 'strain' core assumptions of syntax and their implementation in a given framework. To this end, we will look at two notoriously difficult phenomena: complex predicates and coordination.[5]

7.2 Grammar Architecture and Formal Constructs

Obvious design choices that characterize a grammatical theory are its general architecture and the formal constructs used to describe linguistic structures.

Head-driven Phrase Structure Grammar, HPSG

In HPSG *all* levels of linguistic descriptions are uniformly encoded in *typed feature structures*, with *unification* and *type inheritance* as the main formal devices. This uniform perspective on the encoding of grammar is complemented with a rich inventory of hierarchically structured linguistic objects and interacting principles. A grammar is defined as a set of *principles* that define linguistic structures, some 'universal', some language-specific, and language-specific *lexicons*. The principles define constraints across different levels of linguistic description. Subcategorization requirements are defined through lexically defined valence lists and principles coordinating their realization and saturation in diverse structural configurations. This includes the treatment of long-distance constructions, which are covered by the interplay of subcategorization, non-local-feature projection and constituency principles, through stepwise projection of *nonlocal* elements from gap to filler position.

The most striking characteristics of HPSG are (i) uniform encoding of linguistic structure in typed feature structures, ranging from phonology to semantics, (ii) free interaction of modular principles across typed structures, which jointly determine grammaticality, and (iii) tight integration of syntax and semantics. The latter is seen most clearly in the collapsed **synsem** type that specifies the nature of subcategorized arguments. (iv) In contrast to LFG or DG, HPSG does not treat grammatical functions as primitive concepts in its grammar archictecture.

Lexical-Functional Grammar, LFG

LFG's architecture encodes a system of *functional projections* that distinguish constituent, functional and semantic structure as independent

---

[5]Müller (2010) offers a by-far more rigorous description and comparison of grammatical frameworks than what is possible within the scope of this article. Our main novel contribution is related to the discussion in Section 7.4.

levels of grammatical description. Each level is encoded using an individually motivated formalism: tree structures for constituency, and attribute-value (feature) structures for the encoding of functional and morphosyntactic properties and subcategorization. Principles governing grammatical wellformedness are stated on individual levels (most prominently, f-structure), but also across levels, constraining structure-to-function correspondences, or argument linking. This co-description architecture accommodates non-isomorphism between structures, especially word order variation and discontinuity in surface structure. For *non-local* dissociations of constituency and functional embedding, as in long-distance dependencies, LFG adopts *functional uncertainty* as a formal device that bridges the (potentially unlimited) dissociation of argument realization in the mapping between c- and f-structure.

The most striking characteristics of LFG are (i) its distributed projection architecture, which makes it possible to (ii) study and process syntax independently from semantics, (iii) its strong focus on grammatical functions as a primitive concept for (crosslingual) grammatical description, and (iv) the dissociation of context-free surface constituency encoding vs. functional representation in feature structures.

Lexicalized Tree Adjoining Grammar, LTAG

LTAG shares with LFG the encoding of surface syntactic properties in constituent tree structures and a modular interface to semantic representation so that syntax can be defined and processed independently from semantics. Its grammar architecture is based on *tree adjunction* as the central mechanism for structure composition. The grammar is built from lexicalized *elementary trees (etrees)* that are composed by *substitution* and *adjunction operations*. The latter is not restricted to syntactic modification, but serves as a general device for *factoring recursion* – one of the most prominent characteristics of language and a guiding principle for finite grammatical description. *etrees* fulfill two functions: they encode *argument structure* and they pre-define surface properties that account for order variation, diatheses such as the passive, or *wh-* and relative clause constructions. A wide variation of such etree variants is organized in automatically generated *tree families*.

The most striking characteristics of LTAG are (i) its formalization of recursion in terms of adjunction applied to tree fragments, i.e. *tree adjunction*. By this move, it does not require additional devices for capturing long-distance dependencies. (ii) LTAG offers *derived* and *derivation trees* as parallel syntactic structures. The derivation tree records the history of tree compositions and traditionally serves as the basis for semantic projection. (iii) LTAG does not adopt grammatical functions as a central notion of grammar. (iv) The theory puts less emphasis on constraints that govern the internal structure of etrees, and thus on the shape of the resulting derived tree. This would be possible by adopting core X'-principles, similar to LFG.

Combinatory Categorial Grammar, CCG

CCG differs from the previous frameworks in that it is strongly influenced by semantics, notably Montague Grammar. It employs a small number of *syntactic composition operations*: i.a., forward and backward application, composition and type raising. Syntactic composition is guided by semantic composition that operates in parallel with syntax. *Syntactic categories* are either atomic or complex categories that encapsulate the way the category can be embedded in its constructional context by syntactic/semantic composition rules. In this way, syntax is modeled as a composition process driven by complex categories that externalize their constructional context, rather than by traditional construction-specific rules. *Type raising* in conjunction with composition accounts for *non-local dependencies* and other nonstandard constructions such as raising and coordination. In contrast to LTAG, which derives dependency-like structures from the history of derivations, CCG records and outputs predicate-argument dependencies as defined in lexical types. Saturation of argument structure is achieved by deriving the target category.

The most striking characteristics of CCG are (i) that syntax and semantics are highly intertwined, with syntax merely considered a sideprocess running in parallel with semantic composition. (ii) Syntactic categories can be type-raised to complex categories that encapsulate their constructional context. (iii) The categories are defined to reflect core syntactic properties, but the derived constituents can diverge considerably from traditional assumptions.

7.3 Architectural Choices and Linguistic Modeling

Looking at these characteristics, we can map out similarities and differences between the frameworks along various dimensions (cf. Fig.1).

Architecture and Main Focus

LFG and LTAG assume a clear *separation between syntax and semantics*, while for HPSG and CCG it is more difficult to dissociate semantics from syntax. We characterize this as *modular vs. integrated architectures*. At the same time, HPSG and CCG are fundamentally different in that HPSG models syntax in a highly articulated structure representing core syntactic properties and wellformedness constraints, while CCG mainly defines valid surface structures in a generative process driven by syntactic/semantic compositions. That is, CCG's focus is on *semantics and the syntactic encoding of argument structure*, including a proper treatment of core syntactic constructions, such as binding, reflexivization, control or raising and the like. HPSG takes a somewhat broader look at grammar. Its core theory encompasses an articulated representation of linguistic objects that is constrained by general interacting *syntactic and semantic principles of composition*. Syntax and semantics are strongly intertwined and can only be described jointly.[6]

LFG and LTAG syntax is more clearly dissociated from semantics. Here, syntax is conceived of as an independent grammatical system. Both have been coupled with various semantic representation layers and diverse semantics construction architectures.[7]

Formal Devices, Representation and Generalization

Looking at formal devices, HPSG employs a rich formalization using *typed feature structures*, with sophisticated encoding of linguistic objects and structures that are constrained by interacting principles. The rich representation of structural layers and interacting principles readily accounts for the treatment of long-distance dependencies in a feature propagation analysis that is reminicent of dislocation analyses in Generative Grammar. While 'classical' HSPG analyses control surface order by way of phrase structure schemata, *linearization-based accounts* allow for dissociation of surface realization and phrasal constituent structure by way of independent linearization constraints.

LFG, with its system of parallel projections and especially its *dissociation of constituency and functional structure*, allows for a very flexible encoding of surface realization within and across languages. Non-local realization of arguments is mediated by *functional uncertainty* – an equivalent to the unbounded feature passing devices of HPSG-like formalisms that operates on the level of f-structure.[8] [9]

HPSG and LFG share a constraint-based view of grammatical structure with articulated representations and principles of wellformedness

---

[6]See for instance the semantic construction algebra of Copestake et al. (2001).

[7]For LFG see the co-description vs. description-by-analysis architectures (Halvorsen and Kaplan, 1988) and the resource-logic account (Dalrymple, 2001, Crouch et al., 2001). For LTAG see Kallmeyer and Joshi (1999) or Gardent and Kallmeyer (2003) and synchronous TAG (Shieber and Schabes, 1990).

[8]Advantages of functional vs. constituent-based constraints on extraction and binding have been discussed in Kaplan and Zaenen (1995) and Dalrymple (1993).

[9]Discontinuous phrases marked by morphological case as discussed in Nordlinger (1998) can be resolved in HPSG using a feature-passing device similar to long-distance dependencies (Bender, 2008). This is largely equivalent to the LFG analysis using functional uncertainty.

operating on them. LTAG and CCG take a more generative perspective on syntax, with sparser representational devices. Linguistic and constructional properties of words and phrases are captured in a theory of complex lexical categories, or complex encoding of families of etrees, which are carefully designed to generate valid surface structures for a given language or as a basis for semantic construction from predicate-argument structures.

LTAG encapsulates argument structure in *etrees* and applies *tree adjunction* as its main syntactic composition operation. Since etrees must express a wide variety of structures, an important line of research pursues a 'meta grammar' approach as a general framework for describing and factoring TAG grammars that offers an abstract level of grammatical description for defining the set of admissible etrees for a given language.[10] In LTAG, due to tree adjunction as a general compositional device, no additional devices are required to account for non-local dependencies.[11] Yet this specific take on recursion comes at the price of an asymmetry between adjunction as a recursion building process as opposed to adjunction as a structural indicator of linguistic modification, as traditionally assumed in X′ syntax.[12]

In CCG, type raising and composition account for a wide spectrum of constructions, including long-distance dependencies. Type-raised categories may also be used to encode notions of case, in terms of externalized structural configurations. Argument structure is defined by complex lexical categories, in terms of the arguments they specify. From these lexical definitions full-fledged dependency representations can be derived in parsing (Clark et al., 2002). Thus, the syntactic formalism proves homogeneous and representationally sparse and offers great variety in structural exponence of syntactic properties and semantic content. While syntacticians do not find traditional notions of constituency and projectivity in the syntactic derivation structure, core syntactic properties and constructions are modeled in a lexicon theory of complex categories.[13]

---

[10] See i.a. Candito (1996), Doran et al. (2000), Crabbé et al. (2012).

[11] Though this requires careful definition of lexical or tree families, see above.

[12] Since LTAG's preferred structure for semantic construction is the derivation tree, this lack of discrimination between modification and complementation has implications for the projection of semantics from syntax. Alternatively, semantic construction can be based on the derived tree. See Frank and van Genabith (2001), Gardent and Kallmeyer (2003) and Cimiano et al. (2007) for more detail.

[13] See Steedman and Baldridge (2011) on the encoding of binding, extraction, raising and control, and gapping.

Cross-linguistic Language Modeling

As seen above, the different formalisms have differing foci in expressing and representing linguistic structure and generalizations. This may have an impact on insights gained by cross-linguistic language modeling.

The *principle-driven formalism of HPSG* offers strong formal support for cross-linguistic syntactic description, which is documented by the *Grammar Matrix* and its extension to grammar fragments for a great variety of languages (Bender et al., 2002). Generalizations can be defined using type inheritance, as well as language-specific parameterizations of general principles (for constituent order, case, etc.).

LFG's focus is on *f-structure as an independent level of grammatical description*. Consequently, the theory draws important cross-linguistic generalizations linked to the concept of grammatical functions. This includes argument realization in linking theory and constraints observed in extraction and binding constructions.[14] Less prominent have been its generalizations regarding constituency and mapping principles to f-structure (Bresnan, 2001).[15] Multilingual grammar development in the ParGram project has proven that f-structure can offer a pivot for aligning grammars cross-linguistically, requiring little variation across typologically diverse languages (King et al., 2005).

In both frameworks, the encoding of interactions between word order, constituency and morphological marking has led to important insights into the grammar of nonconfigurational languages and morphological marking strategies across languages.

Research in LTAG and CCG is restricted to a smaller community. Accordingly the range of multilingual studies is less diverse.[16] However, it has been shown, by wide-coverage treebank-based grammar induction and parsing of corpora in different languages, that these formalisms are able to analyze a wide range of linguistic constructions.[17]

7.4 Straining Theories

The grammatical frameworks under discussion show considerable differences in how they encode grammatical concepts, most importantly argument structure and its interplay with surface realization. Yet the consequences of these formalization choices are limited, as long as we

---

[14]See Bresnan and Zaenen (1990), Dalrymple (1993), Kaplan and Zaenen (1995) and Butt et al. (1997).

[15]But see the formalization of mapping principles in treebank-based LFG grammar induction (Frank et al., 2001).

[16]See e.g. Kroch and Joshi (1985), Becker et al. (1991), Kinyon et al. (2006) for LTAG and the overview in Steedman and Baldridge (2011).

[17]See references above and the overview in van Genabith et al. (2006).

concentrate on core constructions and ignore questions of personal taste or adherence to traditional notions of grammatical description.

In fact, it is by looking at linguistic phenomena that 'strain' general assumptions about grammar encoding that we can gain more insight into possible biases of particular formalization choices. I will thus take a closer look at two phenomena related to argument structure realization that present true challenges to any grammatical framework, and reflect on their way of handling these. For exposition I will concentrate on their analyses in LFG and HPSG. But our observations will bring out further aspects of formalization choices that clearly differentiate LFG from HPSG, and also LTAG from CCG.

Complex Predicates (such as causatives or coherently constructed infinitive embedding verbs) are subject to intensive research in HPSG and LFG. Linguistic evidence calls for an analysis in terms of *clause union* or *argument composition* that conflates the arguments of two predicates into a monoclausal structure to account for the argument relation changes and surface realizations characterized as *long scrambling*.

Complex predicates present a particular challenge for LFG: in order to account for their monoclausal properties, two lexical predicates need to be turned into a single predicator with redefined argument characteristics. Butt (1995) and Alsina (1996) employ a *restriction operator* that constructs a joint predicate 'on the fly' in syntax. This causes a disruption in the functional projection and leads to problems in defining relation changing processes (e.g., reflexivization, passivization) that need to apply in the lexicon. Frank (1996), and more recently Bouma and Kuhn (2009), therefore proposes an alternative analysis with lexical rules that (re)define the involved predicates as co-predicators in the lexicon, where relation changing processes can apply in the usual way.

These contrastive approaches reveal a bias in LFG's grammar architecture: syntactic arguments that may be realized in dissociated phrasal structures are integrated into complete, fully specified f-structure nuclei by means of functional head projection rules. This mechanism allows for an elegant analysis of local and nonlocal surface realization phenomena by means of f-structure equations defined over functional paths. At the same time, this characteristic of LFG makes it difficult to accommodate dynamic changes of argument structures in complex predicate formation.

In HPSG we do not find a layer comparable to f-structure that represents the complete syntactic argument structure of a clause. Argument structure is essentially defined in the lexicon's SUBCAT list, where it is directly linked to the semantic representation. In syntactic composition, the SUBCAT list is *redefined* in each phrasal projection to record saturation and the realization of arguments. In this architecture complex predicate formation can be defined through *argument composition in syntax*, yet *(pre)defined in the lexicon*, as proposed by Hinrichs and Nakazawa (1994): the SUBCAT list of the main predicate attracts the arguments of a co-predicate into its own argument list. This produces a joint argument structure as soon as the co-predicate is encountered in syntax. At the same time, lexical syntactic processes can apply to the incorporated or the composed SUBCAT list in the lexicon.[18]

(Asymmetric) Coordination presents another challenge related to argument realization, as it typically involves factorization of one or more arguments that are shared between coordinated predicates.

Coordination is handled in similar ways in LFG and HPSG, yet here, the differences we highlighted above favor LFG's way of coding syntax by means of a monostratal and fully connected f-structure representation. This can be observed by looking at a special type of *asymmetric* coordination that is frequently observed in German, and illustrated in (1).[19] The puzzle this construction presents is that the joint subject of the coordinated sentential phrases is deeply embedded within the first conjunct (German is V2), but seems to be accessible for binding the subject gap in the second conjunct. This construction presents a true challenge for any theory that is based on notions of constituency.

(1) Im Park   sitzen Leute und erzählen Geschichten.
    in the park sit   people and recount stories
    People are sitting in the park and are recounting stories.

LFG and HPSG both account for shared arguments in coordination by joint reference to a single argument (cf. Fig. 2). In HPSG (upper left), this is encoded in the lexical entry of the coordinating conjunction: the non-consumed arguments of all coordinated phrases are coindexed with the arguments on the phrase's SUBCAT list. This allows for standard coordination structures with a shared subject realized outside the coordinated VP. In LFG, a SUBJECT that is realized outside of the

---

[18]This difference between LFG's and HPSG's representation architecture becomes apparent in Andrews and Manning (1999)'s reformulation of LFG in a *spreading information* account that dissociates the contribution of different feature types into separate layers. Here, LFG's uniform $\uparrow=\downarrow$ head projection rules are dissociated according to feature types f: $\uparrow_f=\downarrow_f$. This mimics an HPSG-like architecture, with the possibility of redefining individual features in phrasal composition, and thus allows for argument composition along the lines of Hinrichs and Nakazawa (1994).

[19]See Höhle (1983), Wunderlich (1988), Steedman (1990), Kathol (1999), and Frank(2002, 2006) for more detailed discussion of this construction.

coordinated VP is defined in the conjoined phrase's f-structure. From there it is *distributed* into the f-structures of the coordinated phrases and thus fills their respective subcategorization requirements (cf. Dalrymple (2001)). Neither of these standard analyses for coordination accounts for cases of asymmetric coordination as in (1).

Frank (2002, 2006) motivates an analysis of asymmetric coordination in analogy to modal subordination constructions. In this analysis the first sentential conjunct licenses an *extension of its discourse-functional domain* that includes the second conjunct. Operators that can perform such domain extensions are *grammaticalized discourse functions*, here the SUBJECT. Domain extension is defined by asymmetric projection of the SUBJECT from the first conjunct's clausal node to the coordinated phrase (Fig. 2, middle left). From there, the SUBJECT is distributed to the second conjunct by applying LFG's distribution mechanism.

Could a similar analysis be designed for HPSG? This is not possible without further ado, precisely because HPSG does *not*, in contrast to LFG, offer an integrated monostratal syntactic argument structure where all arguments 'float' up and down along syntactic head projection lines. In HPSG's coordinated phrase for (1), the subject of the first conjunct is not accessible from the SUBCAT list of the first conjunct to 'fill' the open subject slot of the second conjunct (cf. Fig. 2): The conjuncts are symmetric with regard to their constituent phrases, but asymmetric regarding saturation. One way of solving this problem is to resort to the ARG-ST list, usually employed for expressing binding constaints, that represents a copy of the complete SUBCAT list, as defined in the lexical entry (cf. Pollard and Sag (1994)).[20]

Lesson I. Levels of Representation. In sum, by looking at exceptional linguistic structures that strain basic assumptions of linguistic formalization, a principled difference in the representation architecture of LFG and HPSG shows up. LFG's encoding of a complete clausal nucleus in functional structure defines its interface to semantics (Dalrymple, 2001) and also offers great flexibility in accessing argument functions non-locally along head projections. The latter turns out as an advantage in the case of asymmetric coordination, yet as a problem

---

[20]Indeed, related problems have been faced in the description of Germanic V2 and generally, verb initial constructions. Borsley (1989) proposed a *double slash* feature DSL that makes the *complete* lexical SUBCAT list available along the head projection, mimicking local head movement. A similar mechanism had been proposed for CG by Jacobson (1987). Thus, one could adopt the ARG-ST or the DSL mechanism to make the SUBCAT list (and with it the subject) available along the head projection, to make it accessible from the second conjunct. Technically, this opens the way for an analysis along the lines of Frank (2002, 2006), yet it needs to be integrated with HPSG's core analysis of coordination.

when trying to integrate complex predicate constructions in a monoclausal syntactic representation. HPSG, by contrast, lacks an integrated syntactic representation layer. Syntactic arguments defined in the SUBCAT list are directly linked to semantics. The SUBCAT feature is discharged stepwise, as arguments are realized syntactically. This way of specifying and controlling clausal argument structure explains the greater flexibility of HPSG in accounting for complex predicates: composed argument structures can be built on the fly, without requiring full integration into a monoclausal syntactic structure. Yet, the lack of such a representational layer is what prevents non-local access to arguments along the head projection, and thus the binding of subject gaps in asymmetric coordination structures.

Lesson II: Argument Encoding and Surface Realization in LTAG & CCG. This observation brings us back to LTAG and CCG. These theories offer sparser formalizations than LFG and HPSG in terms of representational devices. Do they fare better with these exceptional construction types?

LTAG, with its free encoding of argument structure in etrees, could be expected to flexibly accommodate structural asymmetries in coordination. But for LTAG it is the *factorization* of arguments in coordination that challenges its strongest assumption: the encoding of *full argument structures* in etrees. The problem is illustrated in Fig. 2 (lower, right) for symmetric VP coordination: LTAG has to cope with multirooted derived structures in parsing, and needs to focus on derivation structure to derive valid argument and semantic structures.[21]

CCG bears a strong resemblance to the way arguments are processed in HPSG. Argument structure is defined in lexical types, i.e. families of complex categories that account for diverse structural realizations. The stepwise reduction of complex categories to infer a clausal category is similar to the reduction of the SUBCAT list, as is the composition of the encountered arguments into full argument structures in a concurrently processed semantic structure. CCG shows even stronger flexibility than HPSG, in that it does not encode a rich system of general principles of linguistic structure, especially, phrasal structure. The free application of composition operations may produce structures that do not correspond to traditional notions of phrase structure.[22] In fact, Steedman (1990) shows how a special *decomposition operation* detaches the em-

---

[21]Sarkar and Joshi (1996) propose a *conjoin* operator to merge identical nodes. This approach is further developed in recent work by Banik (2004), Seddah (2008) and Lichte and Kallmeyer (2010).

[22]Steedman and Baldridge (2011) motivate such exceptional phrase structures as a natural way of integrating information structure with semantics.

bedded subject in asymmetric coordination constructions and makes it accessible as a shared subject in the second conjunct (cf. Fig. 2, upper right).[23]

In sum, when it comes to coordination, CCG's discharging processes for argument structure realization prove to be highly flexible, whereas LTAG suffers from a more rigid encoding of full argument structures in etrees. In this respect, it bears similarities to LFG's representation of clausal nuclei in terms of subcategorized grammatical functions, yet at the level of phrase-structural encoding. Finally, for sake of completeness, let us note that nonlocal argument serialization in complex predication constructions has been studied extensively in (MC)TAG and CCG.[24] While it has been assumed that the LTAG and CCG formalisms are equivalent in terms of serialization capacities, recently Hockenmaier and Young (2008) established that there are configurations that can be generated with CCG that cannot be generated with TAG (see also Kuhlmann et al. (2010)).

7.5   Conclusions

Beyond the aspects of linguistic modeling proper, formal design choices have implications for grammar engineering and processing complexity, as well as techniques for grammar induction and automatic disambiguation.[25] All the frameworks under discussion have developed sophisticated grammar engineering platforms and efficient parsing techniques, including stochastic disambiguation. It is with techniques for automatic grammar induction from treebanks that we can again observe that different views on grammar constructs and detail of representation are clearly reflected in the proposed techniques: articulated frameworks like HPSG and LFG require considerable ingestion of linguistic knowledge to define finer-grained distinctions or linguistic principles not reflected in classic treebanks, whereas, at least theoretically, algorithms for LTAG and CCG grammar inducion can rely on leaner methods.

This survey tries to shed some light on similarities and differences among grammatical frameworks in how their particular take on the formalization of linguistic concepts is reflected in different foci of research as well as potential biases in the formalization of syntactic phenomena.

---

[23]Note that the *decomposition* operator is not in the scope of constructors generally considered in CCG formalizations.

[24]See e.g. Becker et al. (1991), Rambow (1994), Joshi et al. (2000), and Steedman and Baldridge (2011).

[25]These aspects could not be discussed in this contribution, but are integrated in Fig. 1 for completeness. For an overview regarding the generative capacity of the respective formalisms see e.g. Müller (2010).

These stand out most clearly in the treatment of special constructs that strain the borders of general syntactic principles.

From our observations we may conclude that HPSG's take on grammar is the most articulated one and is the most closely related to traditional structure-oriented, GB-style notions of syntax, through its traditional take on non-local dependencies and its principle-driven account of grammar formalization. CCG, LTAG and LFG each adopt specific assumptions and constructs, with LFG being closely related to HPSG in offering a representation- and constraint-based theory of syntax that stays close to traditional notions of syntactic description. LFG is special in choosing grammatical functions as its main descriptive device, and is thus close to Dependency Grammar, a framework that is seeing a strong revival, supported by efficient parsing algorithms. It has been shown in recent multilingual parsing challenges that dependency-based syntactic analysis is applicable to many languages without major adjustments. It offers a lean representational view on syntax that is close to LFG's f-structure representation with all its strengths and weaknesses, yet little emphasis on surface constituency. CCG maybe in fact turn out to be the most versatile and flexible grammar framework, one that is capable of bridging large discrepancies between surface form and semantic encoding, across a wide variety of languages and constructions. However, this enormous flexibility needs to be paired with the cautious statement of linguistic constraints that restrict the space of possible structures to those that are (cross-linguistically) grammatical and adhere to linguistic constraints on the association of form and meaning.

Acknowledgements. Thanks go to Claire Gardent and Julia Hockenmaier, as well as two anonymous reviewers for insightful comments on an earlier version of this paper. Any errors are my own responsibility.

References

Alsina, Alex. 1996. *The Role of Argument Structure in Grammar*. CSLI Publications.

Andrews, Avery D. and Christopher D. Manning. 1999. *Complex Predicates and Information Spreading in LFG*. CSLI Publications.

Banik, Eva. 2004. Semantics of VP coordination in LTAG. In *Proceedings of the Seventh International Workshop on Tree Adjoining Grammar and Related Formalisms, TAG+7*, pages 118–125.

Becker, Tilman, Aravind K. Joshi, and Owen Rambow. 1991. Long-distance scrambling and Tree Adjoining Grammars. In *Proceedings of the Fifth Conference of the European Chapter of the Association for Computational Linguistics*, pages 21–26.

	CCG	HPSG	LFG	LTAG
architecture	integrated	integrated	modular	modular
main focus	semantics	syntax & semantics	f-structure	derivation tree
main constructs	function composition	principles & unification	functional projection	tree composition
theory-specific devices	type raising	word order domains	functional uncertainty	tree adjunction
languages	E, G, NL, Tur, ...	many (Matrix)	many (Pargram)	E, Zh, F, I, G, ..
means of abstraction	lexical families	types & inheritance	templates & macros	tree families
processing efficiency	–	packing	packing	–
grammar induction	yes	yes	yes	–
statistical selection	supertagging	supertagging	–	supertagging
statistical disambiguation	yes	yes	yes	yes

FIGURE 1 Facets and Dimensions across Frameworks

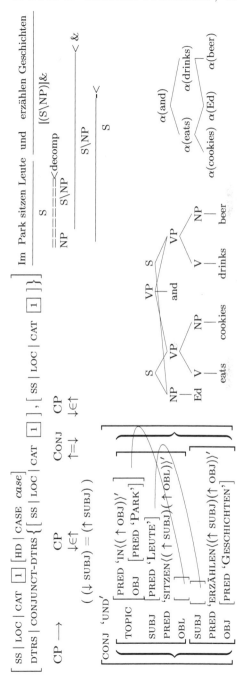

FIGURE 2 Cross-framework Analyses of Coordination: left: HPSG (upper), LFG (lower); right: CCG (upper), LTAG (lower)

Bender, Emily M. 2008. Radical non-configurationality without shuffle operators: An analysis of Wambaya. In S. Müller, ed., *The Proceedings of the 15th International Conference on Head-Driven Phrase Structure Grammar*, pages 6–24. CSLI Publications.

Bender, Emily M., Dan Flickinger, and Stephan Oepen. 2002. The Grammar Matrix: An open-source starter-kit for the rapid development of cross-linguistically consistent broad-coverage precision grammars. In *Proceedings of the Workshop on Grammar Engineering and Evaluation at the 19th International Conference on Computational Linguistics*, pages 8–14.

Borsley, Robert D. 1989. Phrase-structure grammar and the barriers conception of clause structure. *Linguistics* pages 843–863.

Bouma, Gerlof and Jonas Kuhn. 2009. On the split nature of the Dutch laten-causative. In M. Butt and T. H. King, eds., *Proceedings of the LFG'09 Conference*, pages 167–187. CSLI Publications.

Bresnan, Joan. 2001. *Lexical-Functional Syntax*. Blackwell Publishers.

Bresnan, Joan and Annie Zaenen. 1990. Deep unaccusativity in LFG. In K. Dziwirek, P. Farrell, and E. Mejias-Bikandi, eds., *Grammatical Relations. A Cross-Theoretical Perspective*, pages 45–57. CSLI Publications.

Butt, Miriam. 1995. *The Structure of Complex Predicates in Urdu*. CSLI Publications.

Butt, Miriam, Mary Dalrymple, and Anette Frank. 1997. An architecture for linking theory in LFG. In M. Butt and T. H. King, eds., *Proceedings of the LFG-97 Conference*, CSLI Online Publications.

Candito, Marie-Helene. 1996. A principle-based hierarchical representation of LTAGs. In *Proceedings of the 16th International Conference on Computational Linguistics (COLING)*, pages 194–199.

Cimiano, Philipp, Anette Frank, and Uwe Reyle. 2007. UDRT-based semantics construction for LTAG — and what it tells us about the role of adjunction in LTAG. In *Proceedings of the 7th International Workshop on Computational Semantics, IWCS-7*.

Clark, Stephen, Julia Hockenmaier, and Mark Steedman. 2002. Building deep dependency structures using a wide-coverage CCG parser. In *Proceedings of 40th Annual Meeting of the Association for Computational Linguistics*, pages 327–334. Philadelphia, Pennsylvania, USA: Association for Computational Linguistics.

Copestake, Ann, Alex Lascarides, and Dan Flickinger. 2001. An algebra for semantic construction in constraint-based grammars. In *Proceedings of the 39th ACL*.

Crabbé, Benoit, Denis Duchier, Claire Gardent, Joseph Leroux, and Yannik Parmentier. 2012. XMG: eXtensible MetaGrammar. *Computational Linguistics* to appear.

Crouch, Richard, Anette Frank, and Josef van Genabith. 2001. Glue, underspecification and translation. In H. C. Bunt, ed., *Computing Meaning Volume 2*. Kluwer Academic Publishers.

Dalrymple, Mary. 1993. *The Syntax of Anaphoric Binding*. CSLI Lecture Notes. CSLI Publications.

Dalrymple, Mary. 2001. *Lexical-Functional Grammar*, vol. 34 of *Syntax and Semantics*. Academic Press.

Dalrymple, Mary, Ronald M. Kaplan, John T. Maxwell III, and Annie Zaenen, eds. 1995. *Formal Issues in Lexical-Functional Grammar*. CSLI Lecture Notes, No. 47. CSLI Publications.

Doran, Christy, Beth Ann Hockey, Anoop Sarkar, B. Srinivas, and Fei Xia. 2000. Evolution of the XTAG system. In A. Abeillé and O. Rambow, eds., *Tree Adjoining Grammars: Formalisms, Linguistic Analysis and Processing*, pages 371–404. CSLI Publications.

Dowty, David R., Robert E. Wall, and Stanley Peters. 1981. *Introduction to Montague Semantics*. Reidel, Dordrecht.

Frank, Anette. 1996. A note on complex predicate formation: Evidence from auxiliary selection, reflexivization, passivization and past participle agreement in French and Italian. In M. Butt and T. H. King, eds., *Proceedings of the 1st LFG Conference*. CSLI Online Publications.

Frank, Anette. 2002. A (discourse) functional analysis of asymmetric coordination. In *Proceedings of LFG 2002*, pages 174–196.

Frank, Anette. 2006. A (discourse-) functional analysis of asymmetric coordination. In M. Butt, M. Dalrymple, and T. H. King, eds., *Intelligent Linguistic Architectures: Variations on themes by Ronald M. Kaplan*, pages 259–285. CSLI Publications.

Frank, Anette, Louisa Sadler, Josef van Genabith, and Andy Way. 2001. From treebank resources to LFG f-structures. Automatic f-structure annotation of treebank trees and CFGs extracted from treebanks. In A. Abeille, ed., *Building and Using Syntactically Annotated Corpora*. Kluwer Academic Publishers.

Frank, Anette and Josef van Genabith. 2001. LL-based semantics for LTAG — and what it teaches us about LFG and LTAG. In *Proceedings of LFG 2001*, pages 104–126.

Gardent, Claire and Laura Kallmeyer. 2003. Semantic construction in F-TAG. In *Proceedings of the 10th Conference of the European Chapter for the Association of Computational Linguistics, EACL 2003*, pages 123–130.

Halvorsen, Per-Kristian and Ronald M. Kaplan. 1988. Projections and semantic description in Lexical-Functional Grammar. In *Proceedings of the International Conference on Fifth Generation Computer Systems*, pages 11–16. Reprinted in: Mary Dalrymple et al. 1995. eds.: *Formal Issues in Lexical Functional Grammar*, CSLI Publications.

Hinrichs, Erhard and Tsuneko Nakazawa. 1994. Linearizing finite AUX in German complex VPs. In J. Nerbonne, K. Netter, and C. Pollard, eds., *German in Head-Driven Phrase Structure Grammar*, vol. 46 of *CSLI Lecture Notes*. CSLI Publications.

Hockenmaier, Julia and Peter Young. 2008. Non-local scrambling: The equivalence of TAG and CCG revisited. In *Proceedings of The Ninth International Workshop on Tree Adjoining Grammars and Related Formalisms (TAG+9)*.

Höhle, Tilman. 1983. Subjektlücken in Koordinationen. Unpublished manuscript, University of Cologne.

Jacobson, Pauline. 1987. Phrase structure, grammatical relations, and discontinuous constituents. In G. J. Huck and A. E. Ojeda, eds., *Discontinuous Constituency*, vol. 20 of *Syntax and Semantics*, pages 27–69. Academic Press.

Joshi, Aravind K. 1988. Tree Adjoining Grammars. In D. Dowty, L. Karttunen, and A. Zwicky, eds., *Natural Language Parsing*. Cambridge University Press.

Joshi, Aravind K., Tilman Becker, and Owen Rambow. 2000. Complexity of scrambling: A new twist to the competence-performance distinction. In A. Abeillé and O. Rambow, eds., *Tree Adjoining Grammars: Formalisms, Linguistic Analysis and Processing*, pages 167–181. CSLI Publications.

Joshi, Aravind K. and Yves Schabes. 1997. Tree Adjoining Grammars. In A. Salomma and G. Rosenberg, eds., *Handbook of Formal Languages and Automata*. Springer Verlag.

Kallmeyer, Laura and Aravind K. Joshi. 1999. Factoring predicate argument and scope semantics: Underspecified semantics with LTAG. In P. Dekker, ed., *Proceedings of the 12th Amsterdam Colloquium*, pages 169–174.

Kaplan, Ronald M. and Annie Zaenen. 1995. Long-distance dependencies, constituent structure, and functional uncertainty. In M. Dalrymple, R. Kaplan, J. M. III, and A. Zaenen, eds., *Formal Issues in Lexical Functional Grammar*, CSLI Lecture Notes, pages 137–165. CSLI Publications.

Kathol, Andreas. 1999. Linearization vs. phrase structure in German coordination constructions. *Cognitive Linguistics* 10(4):303–342.

King, Tracy Holloway, Martin Forst, Jonas Kuhn, and Miriam Butt. 2005. The feature space in parallel grammar writing. *Research on Language and Computation* 3(2-3):139–163.

Kinyon, Alexandra, Owen Rambow, Tatjana Scheffler, SinWon Yoon, and Aravind K. Joshi. 2006. The metagrammar goes multilingual: A crosslinguistic look at the V2-phenomenon. In *Proceedings of The Eighth International Workshop on Tree Adjoining Grammar and Related Formalisms, TAG+8*, pages 17–24.

Kroch, Anthony S. and Aravind K. Joshi. 1985. The linguistic relevance of Tree Adjoining Grammar. Tech. rep., University of Pennsylvania.

Kuhlmann, Marco, Alexander Koller, and Giorgio Satta. 2010. The importance of rule restrictions in CCG. In *Proceedings of the 48th Annual Meeting of the Association for Computational Linguistics (ACL)*, pages 534–543.

Lichte, Timm and Laura Kallmeyer. 2010. Gapping through tag derivation trees. In *Proceedings of the 10th International Workshop on Tree-Adjoining Grammar and related Formalisms (TAG+10)*.

Müller, Stefan. 2010. *Grammatiktheorie*. No. 20 in Stauffenburg Einführungen. Tübingen: Stauffenburg Verlag.

Nordlinger, Rachel. 1998. *Constructive Case: Evidence from Australian Languages*. CSLI Publications.

Pollard, Carl and Ivan Sag. 1994. *Head-Driven Phrase Structure Grammar*. The University of Chicago Press.

Rambow, Owen. 1994. *Formal and Computational Aspects of Natural Language Syntax*. Ph.D. thesis, University of Pennsylvania.

Sarkar, Anoop and Aravind K. Joshi. 1996. Coordination in Tree Adjoining Grammars: Formalization and implementation. In *Proceedings of the 16th International Conference on Computational Linguistics (COLING)*, pages 610–615.

Seddah, Djamé. 2008. The use of MCTAG to process elliptic coordination. In *Proceedings of The Ninth International Workshop on Tree Adjoining Grammars and Related Formalisms (TAG+9)*.

Shieber, Stuart M. and Yves Schabes. 1990. Synchronous Tree-Adjoining Grammars. In *Proceedings of the 13th International Conference on Computational Linguistics (COLING)*, pages 253–258.

Steedman, Mark. 1990. Gapping as constituent coordination. *Linguistics and Philosophy* 13:207–264.

Steedman, Mark. 1996. *Surface Structure and Interpretation*. No. 30 in Linguistic Inquiry Monograph. MIT Press.

Steedman, Mark. 2000. *The Syntactic Process*. MIT Press.

Steedman, Mark and Jason Baldridge. 2011. Combinatory Categorial Grammar. In R. Borsley and K. Borjars, eds., *Non-Transformational Syntax: Formal and Explicit Models of Grammar*. Wiley-Blackwell.

Tesnière, Lucien. 1959. *Éléments de syntaxe structurale*. Éditions Klincksieck.

van Genabith, Josef, Julia Hockenmaier, and Yusuke Miyao. 2006. Treebank-based acquisition of LFG, HPSG and CCG resources. ESSLI 2006 Advanced Course.

Wunderlich, Dieter. 1988. Some problems of coordination in German. In U. Reyle and C. Rohrer, eds., *Natural Language Parsing and Linguistic Theories*, pages 289–316. Reidel.

8

"They whispered me the answer" in Australia and the US: A Comparative Experimental Study

Marilyn Ford and Joan Bresnan

8.1 Introduction

Mismatches between grammaticality judgments of linguists and actual usage are surprisingly common, particularly where linguists invoke subtle contrasts such as between different types of dative transfer verbs or between different types of dative communication verbs.[1] For example, as Levin's (1993) compendium of verb classes in the linguistic literature shows, linguists have judged verbs of manner of communication like *mutter* or *whisper* as ungrammatical in the double object form in contrast to the prepositional alternative (**whisper John the answer* vs. *whisper the answer to John*), while they have judged verbs of communication by instrument like *phone* or *text* grammatical in each of the alternative structures (*phone John the answer, phone the answer to John*). Similarly, linguists have judged verbs of continuous transfer like *lower* or *carry* as ungrammatical in the double object form (**lower John the rope* vs. *lower the rope to John*) in contrast to verbs of instantaneous transfer like *throw, toss* (*throw John the rope* vs. *throw the rope to John*). The verbs that are judged ungrammatical in one of the alter-

---

[1] We dedicate this work to Annie Zaenen, for her critical perspective on lexical semantics and her long-standing interest in experimental and corpus data for linguistic studies. This material is based upon work supported by the National Science Foundation under Grant No. BCS-1025602.

From Quirky Case to Representing Space: Papers in Honor of Annie Zaenen.
Tracy Holloway King and Valeria de Paiva.

native structures are termed "non-alternating". Yet the non-alternating verbs can be found in the reportedly ungrammatical kinds of structures in actual usage, in contexts where they appear grammatical (Fellbaum 2005, Bresnan, Cueni, Nikitina, and Baayen 2007, Bresnan and Nikitina 2009).

Why do these mismatches between judgments and usage occur? Although we lack specific probability estimates for all of the relevant verbs, we know that differing classes of dative verbs have different frequencies of usage in the double object form in internet samples (Lapata 1999). It is also known that different argument types are more likely to occur in double object structures. That is, the sequence V [... Pronoun ...] NP is far more frequent than V [... Noun ...] NP in a corpus of telephone conversations (Bresnan 2007).

Bresnan 2007 hypothesized that ratings of the naturalness of non-alternating verbs in reportedly ungrammatical structures would be higher when these verbs appeared in more probable syntactic contexts; specifically, in the context V [... Pronoun ...] NP compared to V [... Noun ...] NP. She used datives with six alternating verbs (verbs of communication by instrument, *phone*, *text*, and *IM*, and verbs of instantaneous transfer, *flip*, *throw*, and *toss*). She also used datives with eight reportedly non-alternating verbs (verbs of manner of communication, *whisper*, *mutter*, *mumble*, *yell*, and verbs of continuous transfer, *carry*, *push*, *drag*, and *lower*). Thirty items were constructed by searching for examples from the internet and then creating their alternative double object form. Half of the items used alternating verbs and half used reportedly non-alternating verbs. Each item consisted of the context for the original dative followed by the two alternative dative forms, as exemplified by (1).

(1) My mother and I went out of our way to go to Scottsdale. When we got there, she drove to the Luau, a good hotel, one they'd listed in Town and Country. I sat in a chair on one side of the lobby while she went up to the desk. She came back
(i) and whispered the price to me.
(ii) and whispered me the price.

Participants were asked to read each passage and rate the relative naturalness of the numbered alternatives using 100 points divided between the two alternatives. The results showed that for all verb classes, datives with the pronominal recipient were rated higher than datives with the lexical NP recipient and for supposedly non-alternating datives with a pronominal recipient the ratings were as high as those for alternating datives with lexical NP recipients. These results are consistent with findings from other studies indicating that language users have implicit knowledge of syntactic frequencies and probabilities (Ford, Bresnan, and Kaplan 1982; Gahl and Garnsey 2004; Bresnan, Cueni, Nikitina, and Baayen 2007; Diessel 2007; Bresnan and Hay 2008; Szmrecsányi and Hinrichs 2008; Tily, Gahl, Arnon, Snider, Kothari, and Bresnan 2009; Bresnan and Ford 2010; Jaeger 2010).

If knowledge of syntax is probabilistic, then one might expect to find different responses to the same verb classes across varieties of the same language. Bresnan and Ford 2010, using dative items, have found differences between Americans and Australians in ratings and in processing dative structures while reading, and Ford and Bresnan *submitted* have found differences in mini databases of datives and genitives obtained from Americans and Australians in a completion task where participants complete richly contextualized sentence fragments. The converging evidence obtained from different types of studies gives added weight to the suggestion that there is more to grammaticality than a simple categorical division.

The previous work comparing Americans and Australians in dative ratings and processing did not consider possible differences in dative verb classes across the varieties. In the present study, we investigate the responses of the two varieties in rating and processing datives with different verb classes, including reportedly non-alternating verb classes.

8.2 The Ratings Study

Twenty Australian participants from Griffith University who had grown up in Australia speaking only English were given the same 30 items used by Bresnan 2007, although with the contexts localized to Australian English. Thus, for example, (1) was modified slightly for the Australians as shown in (2), with changes shown in bold.

(2) My mother and I went out of our way to go to **Canberra**. When we got there, she drove to the **Plaza**, a good hotel, one they'd listed in **Travel Australia**. I sat in a chair on one side of the lobby while she went up to **reception**. She came back
   (i) and whispered the price to me.
   (ii) and whispered me the price.

The participants performed the same split-100 ratings task as the American participants.

The ratings of the Americans and Australians for the double object alternatives were analyzed using mixed effects regression models (Baayen 2008, Baayen, Davidson, and Bates 2008, Jaeger 2008, Johnson 2008, Quené and van den Bergh 2008) as implemented in the lme4 package in R (Bates, Maechler, and Dai 2009). In one model, the data from the communication verbs were analyzed and in another the transfer verbs were analyzed. For both models, the effects of interest were variety, verb type within the broad verb class (either communication by instrument and manner of communication or instantaneous transfer and continuous transfer), recipient pronominality, and the possible interaction of these factors. Given that the order in which participants receive the items could influence ratings, item order was also included in the models. There were three random effects incorporated into the initial models. These were the participant, the verb, and item order interacting with participant. For both models it was found by likelihood ratio tests (Bates et al. 2009) that the random effect of item order interacting with participant was not needed and so it was eliminated. In this and other analyses presented here, we tested whether fixed effect variables and their interactions could be removed by seeing if the magnitudes of the estimates were less than the standard error, but it was found that none could be eliminated. Here, as elsewhere, we use * for significant at $p < 0.05$, ** for significant at $p < 0.01$, and *** for significant at $p < 0.001$. The resulting models for the communication verbs and the transfer verbs are shown in Tables 1 and 2, respectively.

Positive coefficients indicate higher ratings, while negative coefficients indicate lower ratings. The results in Table 1 show that for the communication verbs, ratings for the double objects increased with item order and that there is an interaction between variety and pronominality, such that the Americans, but not the Australians, showed a pronominality effect. Examination of the mean ratings showed that for the Americans the pronominal recipient increased rating of the communication by instrument datives by 12.86 and increased rating of the manner of communication datives by 9.87, while for the Australians, the corresponding increases were only 4.38 and 5.22, respectively.

Turning now to the transfer verbs, the results in Table 2 show, again, that ratings of the double object datives increased with item order. There was also a significant main effect of pronominality, such that the datives with a pronominal recipient were rated higher than those with a lexical NP recipient for both varieties. Examination of the mean ratings for the two transfer verbs showed that both varieties have a large, consistent, pronominality effect; for Americans the pronominal recipient increased rating by 24.49 for the instantaneous transfer datives and 18.33 for the continuous transfer datives, and for the Australians the corresponding increases in rating were 20.06 and 22, respectively.

We see, then, that both varieties show a pronominality effect for transfer verbs, but only the Americans show a pronominality effect

Fixed Effects				
		95% Confidence Limits		
	Estimate	Lower	Upper	p
(Intercept)	30.323	20.748	40.006	0.0000 ***
variety = US	-6.553	-14.226	1.361	0.1168
verb type = manner	-8.377	-19.050	2.545	0.0555
recipient = pronoun	-3.563	-11.041	4.066	0.3553
item order	0.664	0.374	0.932	0.0000 ***
verb type (manner): recipient (pronoun)	9.784	-0.167	19.740	0.0548
variety (US): verb type (manner)	-0.947	-10.175	8.017	0.8358
variety (US): recipient (pronoun)	14.291	4.199	23.873	0.0048 **
variety (US): verb type (manner): recipient (pronoun)	-9.641	23.522	3.287	0.1561
Random Effects				
participant standard deviation		8.275		
verb standard deviation		3.808		

TABLE 1 Model parameters for the American and Australian ratings for communication verb double object datives

	Fixed Effects			
		95% Confidence Limits		
	Estimate	Lower	Upper	p
(Intercept)	25.363	12.877	37.866	0.0000 ***
variety = US	-6.083	-15.547	3.297	0.2248
verb type = instantan.	4.283	-14.041	22.635	0.5812
recipient = pronoun	22.417	15.391	29.716	0.0000 ***
item order	0.295	0.014	0.584	0.0368 *
verb type (instantan.): recipient (pronoun)	-2.350	-14.075	9.414	0.6901
variety (US): verb type (instantan.)	1.458	-10.487	14.096	0.8150
variety (US): recipient (pronoun)	-3.667	-12.870	6.448	0.4477
variety (US): verb type (instantan.): recipient (pronoun)	8.292	-7.353	23.180	0.278
	Random Effects			
participant standard deviation			9.7666	
verb standard deviation			8.1920	

TABLE 2 Model parameters for the American and Australian ratings for transfer verb double object datives

for communication verbs. Hence for transfer verbs, both varieties show that more frequent contexts improve the ratings of reportedly non-alternating verbs as would be expected given Bresnan 2007, while for communication verbs, only the American variety shows the effect. As suggested previously, such differences between varieties are to be expected for speakers of different variants of a language. Given the pervasive variability of usage probabilities for different structures in a language (Hinrichs and Szmrecsányi 2007; Schneider 2007; Bresnan and Hay 2008; Rohdenburg and Schlüter 2009; Wolk, Bresnan, Rosenbach, and Szmrecsányi to appear), it would be purely coincidental for probabilistic knowledge of language to be the same across varieties. Of course much more research needs to be done to determine the exact differences in probabilistic knowledge.

8.3 The Word-by-Word Processing Task

While the contextualized ratings task is sensitive to probabilistic differences in sentence types (Bresnan and Ford 2010, Ford and Bresnan to appear), it does not capture time-bounded effects on sentence processing tasks such as reading. For this reason we undertook a second study using a word-by-word reaction time task during reading as a measure of sentence processing complexity. Our expectation was that more probable sentence types would require fewer resources during reading, so that processing complexity during reading would decrease in predicted high-probability sentences.

Thus, given the ratings results, we expected that Americans would process both communication and transfer verb double object datives faster when there is a pronominal recipient, whereas the Australians would only show this pronominality effect for transfer verb datives.

In the self-paced reading task, participants are presented with a sentence one word at a time on a computer screen and must press a button as quickly as possible each time they read a word. For our purposes, a context is presented before the word-by-word presentation of the part of the sentence we are interested in. The task is similar to that used by Bresnan and Ford 2010, though without any lexical decision being made for each word. Twenty experimental items were used, half had communication by instrument verbs, and half had continuous transfer verbs. There were two basic versions of the items. In both versions, half of the communication verb items and half of the transfer verb items used a pronominal recipient and half used a lexical NP recipient. Any item with a pronominal recipient in one version used a lexical NP in the other version. This was balanced over variety and gender. Each context was given as a block and the word-by-word decision making began with the dative verb. The points of interest were the determiner and noun after the recipient.

The participants were 36 US speakers (18 males and 18 females) and 36 Australian speakers (18 males and 18 females). The US speakers received the US versions of the items, while the Australians received the items contextualized for Australians. The US participants were paid volunteers from the Stanford University community and had grown up in the US speaking only English. The Australians were paid volunteers from the Griffith University community and had grown up in Australia speaking only English. The participants had not taken part in the ratings study.

The data were analyzed using mixed effects regression models. Examination of the data showed that the Americans had faster reaction times (RTs) than the Australians, with a mean reaction time of 322.19 milliseconds compared with 396.27. Further, while the Americans showed no significant effects at the determiner except item order, for the Australians it was at the noun position that there was no effect except item order. Significant effects appeared at the determiner for the Australians, and at the following noun for the Americans. In other words, for the Americans the expected linguistic effects lagged the Australians, occurring later in the sentence — perhaps because the Americans were processing the sentences more quickly. Here we will present the results for the Australians at the determiner and the Americans at the noun. For both models, the effects we were interested in were verb class, recipient pronominality, and their possible interactions. We also collected gender information and so included that in the possible interaction. Item order was also included in the model. The random effects were participant, verb, and item order interacting with participant. For neither model could any of these be eliminated. All RTs were logged to reduce the effect of extreme values (Baayen 2008).

The model parameters for the Australians at the determiner are presented in Table 3, though due to space limitations possible 3- and 4-way interactions, which could not be eliminated but which were all non-significant, are not presented. Positive coefficients indicate higher RTs, while negative coefficients indicate lower times.

It can be seen that RTs significantly decreased with item order. There is also a significant interaction between verb class and pronominality of the recipient. As predicted, the Australians have faster RTs after a pronominal recipient for transfer verbs, but not communication verbs. Examination of the raw data for the Australians shows that RTs for the transfer verb datives with a pronominal recipient were on average 45.21 milliseconds less than for transfer verb datives with a lexical recipient. The difference for communication verb datives due to recipient pronominality was only 24.55.

The model parameters for the Americans at the noun are presented in Table 4, though due to space limitations possible 3- and 4-way interactions are not presented.[2] Once again RTs decreased with item order. As predicted, the Americans have a significant main effect of pronominality but no interaction between verb class and pronominality. Examination of mean RTs showed that the decrease in RTs due to a pronoun recipient was 46.54 milliseconds. There were significant interactions found in the data, as shown in Table 4, though none concerned

---

[2] The 3- and 4-way interactions could not be eliminated, and all bar one of these interactions (item order*gender*pronominality) were non-significant. The effects shown remain significant when a further control for previous word RT is added.

Fixed Effects				
		95% Confidence Limits		
	Estimate	Lower	Upper	p
(Intercept)	6.159	5.985	6.323	0.0000 ***
verb type = transfer	0.102	-0.100	0.326	0.3337
recipient = pronoun	-0.044	-0.205	0.118	0.5786
gender = male	-0.046	-0.247	0.161	0.7079
item order	-0.023	-0.036	-0.011	0.0002 **
verb type (transfer): recipient (pronoun)	-0.233	-0.487	-0.007	0.0468 *
gender (male): verb type = transfer	-0.229	-0.475	-0.004	0.0505
gender (male): recipient (pronoun)	0.068	-0.156	0.307	0.5487
item order: verb type = transfer	-0.006	-0.025	0.011	0.4830
item order: recipient (pronoun)	-0.002	-0.015	0.010	0.7053
item order: gender = male	0.003	-0.013	0.017	0.7379
Random Effects				
participant standard deviation			0.2830	
verb standard deviation			0.0704	
participant / item order standard deviation			0.0118	

TABLE 3 Model parameters for all main effects and 2-way interactions for Australian RTs at the determiner after the recipient in double object datives

any verb class pronominality interaction.

With the word-by-word processing task as our measure of sentence processing complexity we expected that more probable / more highly rated sentence types would require fewer resources during reading, so that RTs measured in the task would decrease in high-probability / highly rated sentences. Specifically, Americans would process both communication and transfer verb double object datives faster when there is a pronominal recipient, whereas the Australians would only show this pronominality effect for transfer verb datives. With the proviso that the effect for the American participants lagged by one word, this is what we found.

	Fixed Effects			
		95% Confidence Limits		
	Estimate	Lower	Upper	p
(Intercept)	6.183	5.993	6.363	0.0000 ***
verb type = transfer	-0.189	-0.420	0.059	0.1184
recipient = pronoun	-0.318	-0.509	-0.128	0.0008 **
gender = male	-0.238	-0.451	-0.007	0.0568
item order	-0.037	-0.051	-0.023	0.0000 ***
verb type (transfer): recipient (pronoun)	0.152	-0.115	0.427	0.2731
gender (male): verb type = transfer	0.159	-0.116	0.435	0.2504
gender (male): recipient (pronoun)	0.347	0.090	0.631	0.0096 **
item order: verb type = transfer	0.015	-0.004	0.037	0.1332
item order: recipient (pronoun)	0.019	0.004	0.033	0.0117 *
item order: gender = male	0.011	-0.005	0.029	0.1854
	Random Effects			
participant standard deviation		0.2431		
verb standard deviation		0.0752		
participant / item order standard deviation		0.0130		

TABLE 4 Model parameters for all main effects and 2-way interactions for American RTs at the noun after the recipient in double object datives

8.4 Concluding Remarks

Our data in two very different experimental tasks have pointed to the same finding: overall, there seems to be more variation between speakers of the two varieties in judging and reading pronominal recipient objects with communication verbs than with transfer verbs. Why should this be?

In the transfer events with our dative verbs, the theme is expressed as an NP, never as a clause or PP. The semantics of these dative verbs, whether instantaneous (*flip, throw, toss*) or continuous (*push, drag, lower*) constrain the relations among the participants in the described action quite specifically in comparison to the communication verbs. With the communication verbs, there is much more choice about how to convey the theme. The topic of communication could be a clause, a quotation, or a PP. Consider:

(3) she texted me with all the details

(4) he texted me on the weekend saying he has a surprise for me

Using Google with the searches "verb you" and "verb her" in a sample of both Australian and American web pages and for all verbs used, we were able to confirm the intuition that, in usage, transfer verbs are quite constrained in the manner in which a theme and recipient are expressed, with 30/64 results for communication verbs being other than *NP NP* or *NP to NP* and only 1/37 results for transfer verbs being other than *NP NP* or *NP to NP*. A Fisher's Exact test shows that this is a highly significant difference, p = .000. So, with the transfer verbs, there are fewer ways the Australian and US populations can differ in their usage. But with communication verbs, there are many more possible differences in usage preferences. These considerations suggest that the true explanation for the covariation may lie in the varying usage probabilities of specific verb-argument combinations in Australia and the US. More research in the future will clarify ways in which usage varies for the two varieties.

References

Baayen, R. Harald. 2008. *Analyzing Linguistic Data. A Practical Introduction to Statistics Using R*. Cambridge University Press.

Baayen, R. Harald, Doug Davidson, and Douglas M. Bates. 2008. Mixed effects modeling with crossed random effects for subjects and items. *Journal of Memory and Language* 59:390–412.

Bates, Douglas, Martin Maechler, and Bin Dai. 2009. lme4: Linear mixed effects models using s4 classes. R package version 0.999375–31.

Bresnan, Joan. 2007. Is knowledge of syntax probabilistic? Experiements with the English dative alternation. In S. Featherston and W. Sternefeld, eds., *Roots: Linguistics in Search of its Evidential Base, Series: Studies in Generative Grammar*, pages 75–96. Mouton de Gruyter.

Bresnan, Joan, Anna Cueni, Tatiana Nikitina, and R. Harald Baayen. 2007. Predicting the dative alternation. In G. Bourne, I. Kraemer, and J. Zwarts, eds., *Cognitive Foundations of Interpretation*, pages 69–94. Royal Netherlands Academy of Science.

Bresnan, Joan and Marilyn Ford. 2010. Predicting syntax: Processing dative constructions in American and Australian varieties of English. *Language* 86:168–213.

Bresnan, Joan and Jennifer Hay. 2008. Gradient grammar: An effect of animacy on the syntax of *give* in New Zealand and American English. *Lingua* 118:245–259.

Bresnan, Joan and Tatiania Nikitina. 2009. The gradience of the dative alternation. In L. Uyechi and L. H. Wee, eds., *Reality Exploration and Discovery: Pattern Interaction in Language and Life*, pages 161–184. CSLI Publications.

Diessel, Holger. 2007. Frequency effects in language acquisition, language use, and diachronic change. *New Ideas in Psychology* 25:108–127.

Fellbaum, Christiane. 2005. Examining the constraints on the benefactive alternation by using the World Wide Web as a corpus. In M. Reis and S. Kepser, eds., *Evidence in Linguistics: Empirical, Theoretical, and Computational Perspectives*, pages 207–236. Mouton de Gruyter.

Ford, Marilyn. 1983. A method for obtaining measures of local parsing complexity throughout sentences. *Journal of Memory and Language* 58:161–187.

Ford, Marilyn and Joan Bresnan. submitted. Generating data as a proxy for unavailable corpus data: The contextualized completion task. Unpublished manuscript, Griffith University and Stanford University.

Ford, Marilyn, Joan Bresnan, and Ronald M. Kaplan. 1982. A competence-based theory of syntactic closure. In J. Bresnan, ed., *The Mental Representation of Grammatical Relations*, pages 727–796. MIT Press.

Gahl, Susanne and S. M. Garnsey. 2004. Knowledge of grammar, knowledge of usage: Syntactic probabilities affect pronunciation variation. *Language* 80:748–775.

Hinrichs, Lars and Benedikt Szmrecsányi. 2007. Recent changes in the function and frequency of standard English genitive constructions: A multivariate analysis of tagged corpora. *English Language and Linguistics* 11:437–74.

Jaeger, T. Florian. 2008. Categorical data analysis: Away from ANOVAs (transformation or not) and towards logit mixed models. *Journal of Memory and Language* 59:434–446.

Jaeger, T. Florian. 2010. Redundancy and reduction: Speakers manage syntactic information density. *Cognitive Psychology* 61:23–62.

Johnson, Keith. 2008. *Quantitative Methods in Linguistics*. Blackwell.

Lapata, Mirella. 1999. Acquiring lexical generalizations from corpora: A case study for diathesis alternations. In *Proceedings of the 37th Meeting of the North American Chapter of the Association for Computational Linguistics*, pages 397–404.

Levin, Beth. 1993. *English Verb Classes and Alternations: A Preliminary Investigation*. University of Chicago Press.

Quené, Hugo and Huub van den Bergh. 2008. Examples of mixed-effects modeling with crossed random effects and with binomial data. *Journal of Memory and Language* 59:413–425.

Rohdenburg, Gü and Julia Schlüter, eds. 2009. *One Language, Two Grammars? Differences between British and American English*. Cambridge University Press.

Schneider, Edgar W. 2007. *Postcolonial English: Varieties around the World*. Cambridge University Press.

Szmrecsányi, Benedikt and Lars Hinrichs. 2008. Probabilistic determinants of genitive variation in spoken and written English: A multivariate comparison across time, space, and genres. In T. Nevalamen, I. Taavitsainen, P. Pahta, and M. Korhonon, eds., *The Dynamics of Linguistic Variation: Corpus Evidence on English Past and Present*, pages 291–309. Benjamins.

Tily, Harry, Susanne Gahl, Inbal Arnon, Neal Snider, Anubha Kothari, and Joan Bresnan. 2009. Syntactic probabilities affect pronunciation variation in spontaneous speech. *Language and Cognition* 1:147–165.

Wolk, Christopher, Joan Bresnan, Anette Rosenbach, and Benedikt Szmrecsányi. to appear. Dative and genitive variability in late modern English: Exploring cross-constructional variation and change. To appear in *Diachronica*.

9

Nothing Personal? A System-internal Syntactic Change in Icelandic

JOAN MALING AND SIGRÍÐUR SIGURJÓNSDÓTTIR

9.1 Introduction

In their 1985 paper entitled "Case and Grammatical Functions: The Icelandic Passive," Zaenen, Maling and Thráinsson demonstrated that morphological case does not map 1-1 onto grammatical functions in Icelandic, a language famous for having both oblique subjects and nominative objects. This typologically unusual property has inspired a great deal of research. The heart of that paper consisted of detailed syntactic characteristics for subjecthood. Some of the diagnostic properties were cross-linguistic, while others were language-specific. In the spirit of that classic paper, we provide an update from the field, reporting on a major syntactic change now underway in Icelandic, which has inspired lively debate. This ongoing change is another intriguing phenomenon, the apparent reanalysis of passive morphology; at the heart of our work on understanding this change is the identification of syntactic properties which distinguish active from passive clauses.

Any description of Icelandic syntax distinguishes two kinds of passive clauses: (i) canonical passives of transitive and ditransitive verbs and (ii) impersonal passives of intransitive verbs, e.g. *Það var dansað* 'it was danced' (example (13)). The Icelandic canonical passive has the same basic syntactic properties as its counterpart in English or German, but adds much richer agreement and a greater variety of morphological case-marking. If the matrix verb takes accusative (structural) case on its object, that argument will correspond to a nominative subject in the

From Quirky Case to Representing Space: Papers in Honor of Annie Zaenen.
Tracy Holloway King and Valeria de Paiva.
Copyright © 2013, CSLI Publications.

passive voice (usually the subject, but the direct object in certain cases; see Zaenen, Maling and Thráinsson 1985), which triggers agreement with both the finite verb and the participle. If the verb governs lexical case on its object, either dative or genitive, that case is preserved in the passive, but NP-movement to subject position is still obligatory, giving rise to one class of the "quirky subjects" for which Icelandic is famous. Since there is no nominative argument, there is no agreement with the finite verb and participle, which occur in the default 3rd person neuter singular. See Thráinsson (2007) for a thorough description.

A new transitive impersonal passive construction has arisen in recent decades, and is gaining ground. The innovative construction is illustrated in (1a,b).[1]

(1) a. Það var beðið **mig** að vaska upp
it$_{expl}$ was asked-N.SG. me-ACC to wash up
Literally: it was asked me to do the dishes
Intended: 'I was asked to do the dishes' or 'they asked me to do the dishes'

b. Loks var fundið **stelpuna** eftir mikla leit.
finally was found-N.SG. girl.the-ACC after great search
Literally: finally was found the girl after a long search
Intended: 'the girl was finally found after a long search' or 'they finally found the girl after a long search'

We provide two different translations of the examples in (1), one passive (e.g. "I was asked to do the dishes"), the other active with an indefinite nonspecific human subject like "they" (e.g. "they asked me to do the dishes"). Because of the participial morphology, some linguists have labeled this construction "the New Passive" following Kjartansson (1991); in this paper, however, we refer to it as the "new impersonal" (NI).

Data on the NI has been collected in two nationwide studies. The first was conducted in 1999-2000 and reported in Sigurjónsdóttir and Maling (2001) and Maling and Sigurjónsdóttir (2002) (henceforth referred to collectively as M&S). Our study focused on the syntactic characteristics of the innovative construction. We developed a questionnaire which was distributed to 1,731 tenth graders (age 15-16) in 65 schools throughout Iceland (10th grade is the last year of compulsory education in Iceland). This number represents 45 percent of the children born in Iceland in 1984. The questionnaire was also given to 205 adult controls in various parts of the country. The questionnaire

---

[1]Note that the expletive *það* is not a grammatical subject; in finite clauses, both main and subordinate, it is a place-holder confined to initial position, and thus does not occur in questions, or if a non-subject constituent has been fronted, as in (1b).

was a grammaticality judgment task. For each of the 68 test sentences, subjects were asked to check one of two options: "Yes, this is something one can say" or "No, this is something one cannot say." A large study on syntactic variation in modern Icelandic was conducted in 2005-2007, and reported in Thráinsson et al. (in press). 2,241 subjects throughout Iceland were tested on various syntactic construction, including the NI (n=772). Subjects in four different age groups were asked to judge whether the test sentences were natural, questionable or impossible.

Both studies show that sentences like those in (1) are sharply ungrammatical in the standard language. The example of the New Impersonal shown in (1a) was one of the test sentences in the M&S survey. As shown in Table 1, 93 percent of adults (n=200) judged this sentence ungrammatical, while over 73 percent of the teenagers (n =1695) judged it to be acceptable.

TABLE 1 Acceptability Judgments for New Impersonal in (1a)

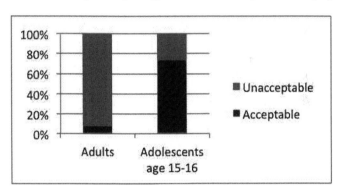

The sentence in (1a) was also included in the second nationwide survey, which confirmed the age-related variation found in the first study; in fact, the variation is even more striking because there are three different groups of adult subjects, as shown in Table 2. Nearly 60 percent of adolescents in this survey accepted the sentence in (1a) as natural, as compared to only 22 percent of subjects in their early twenties, and almost no one in the two oldest age groups.

This is clearly a major syntactic change, one which seems to have sprung up spontaneously in various parts of the country. The proper analysis of this construction has been much debated in recent years, but there is no disagreement about the fact that a major syntactic innovation is taking place and that the construction is rapidly gain-

TABLE 2 Age-related Variation in Acceptability Judgments for the NI
Example in (1a)

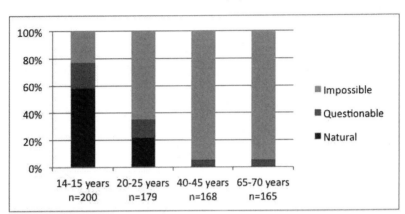

ing ground. Because this is an on-going change, it provides historical linguists with a rare opportunity to observe and document a syntactic change at a relatively early stage; the evidence available in written records can be complemented with native speaker judgments of acceptability. On-going research supports the hypothesis that the NI is acquired by young children and not adopted by adults. Forty of the subjects tested by M&S in 1999-2000 were retested in 2010; children who acquire the NI do not seem to outgrow it (Thráinsson, Sigurjónsdóttir and Eythórsson, 2010).

9.2 Syntactic analysis

What exactly is this innovative construction? The debate about how to analyze the NI has focused on whether it is syntactically passive or active. Barðdal and Molnár (2003) describe it as a subtype of the passive construction, albeit a construction with "an actional character" which is therefore "much closer to an ACTIVE reading than the promotional types" (p. 242). Eythórsson (2008) suggests that the New Construction is an impersonal "expletive passive" that has lost the definiteness constraint that exists in the standard language. In his analysis, the direct object is marked accusative because it is a "non-promotional" passive, a construction with an empty [e] subject but no NP-movement, as in (2a). M&S on the other hand have argued in various papers for an alternative analysis under which the construction is a syntactically active impersonal with a null pro_{arb} [+human] pronoun subject, as in (2b).

(2) a. $[_S$ ___ Aux $[_{VP}$ V$_{ppart}$ NP]] Passive Impersonal
    b. $[_S$ pro$_{arb}$ Aux $[_{VP}$ V$_{ppart}$ NP]] Active Impersonal

Halldór Á. Sigurðsson (2011) takes an intermediate position, coming to the conclusion that "the New Passive is an unusually 'active passive'" (p. 174) and that it "is not an alien but a member of the passive family, albeit a somewhat odd one" (p. 176). Einar Freyr Sigurðsson (2012) presents new evidence that the NI shares syntactic properties with active constructions, and differs in important ways from the canonical passive.

9.2.1 Cross-linguistic evidence

Why would anyone think that this innovative impersonal construction is syntactically active? The controversy indicates the importance of developing concrete syntactic diagnostics for an active vs. a passive analysis of a given construction. We know that this reanalysis has occurred in other languages. The Polish *–no/to* construction and the Irish autonomous form each developed from a past participle; both have been shown to be active impersonals. Based on her study of these constructions, Maling (1993) selected the four syntactic properties in (3) to use as diagnostics (see also Maling and Sigurjónsdóttir 2002:102, ex. 7):

(3) Syntactic properties of active construction with an impersonal subject:
    a. No agentive *by*-phrase is possible.
    b. Binding of anaphors (reflexive and reciprocal) is possible.
    c. Control of subject-oriented adjuncts is possible.
    d. Nonagentive ("unaccusative") verbs can occur.

The underlying assumption is that a syntactically present agent argument blocks an agentive *by*-phrase. However, a subject argument that is syntactically present licenses binding of lexical anaphors and control of subject-oriented adjuncts, and unaccusative verbs should be able to occur in the construction (provided that the verb selects for a human subject). A syntactically active impersonal construction with an overt grammatical subject, e.g. French *on* or German *man*, has all four of these properties; the canonical passive construction lacks all four.

The comparison of Polish and Ukrainian is particularly instructive. Maling and Sigurjónsdóttir (2002:100-107) compared and contrasted the syntactic properties of the accusative-assigning participial *–no/to-* construction in Polish and Ukrainian, exemplified in (4).

(4) a. Polish (=Maling and Sigurjónsdóttir 2002, ex. 8b)
    Świątynię   zbudowano w 1640 roku.
    church-F.ACC build-*no*   in 1640 year
    'The church was built in 1640'

   b. Ukrainian (=Sobin 1985:653, ex. (13a))
    Cerkvu   bulo zbudovano v 1640 roc'i.
    church-F. ACC was build-*no*   in 1640 year

We showed that despite their common historical origin and superficial similarity (i.e. the shared morphological properties of assigning accusative case and consequent lack of agreement), the Polish and Ukrainian constructions are polar opposites in terms of syntactic behavior (Table 3). Both Polish and Ukrainian have a canonical passive with the expected properties; what is important to observe is that the Ukrainian *–no/to*-construction behaves like a true passive, whereas its Polish counterpart does not (for Polish see Kibort 2004; Blevins 2003). Despite their common origin, they are polar opposites syntactically.

More detailed discussion can be found in Maling and Sigurjónsdóttir (2002) and Maling (2006).

TABLE 3 Syntactic properties of constructions in Polish and Ukrainian

syntactic property	Pol/Ukr Active	Pol/Urk Passive	Polish *–no/to*	Ukrainian *–no/to*
agentive *by*-phrase	*	ok	*	ok
bound anaphors in object position	ok	*	ok	*
control of subject-oriented adjuncts	ok	*	ok	*
nonagentive ("unaccusative") verbs	ok	*	ok	*

9.2.2 Syntactic behavior of the Icelandic New Impersonal

The obvious question, then, is this: which of the two polar opposites does the innovative Icelandic construction most resemble? Both possible answers have been offered.

(5) a. The NI is parallel to the *–no/to*-construction in Polish, an active impersonal with a thematic pro_{arb} subject (M&S 1997, 2001, 2002; Maling 2006)

b. The NI is directly "comparable to the *–no/to*-construction in Ukrainian, a passive preserving structural accusative case" (Eythórsson 2008:216)

Eythórsson (2008) and Jónsson (2009) argue that the Icelandic NI is a "true passive", and claim that as such, it behaves more like the accusative-assigning passive in Ukrainian than like the Polish counterpart, which has the syntactic properties of an active impersonal (Maling 2006). M&S hypothesized that this on-going syntactic change in Icelandic is parallel to the completed development of the *–no/to*-construction in Polish, as well as the Irish autonomous construction (Maling 1993). We predicted that although the actuation may take several centuries to complete, the New Impersonal construction in Icelandic will eventually pattern with the Polish *–no/to*-construction with regard to all four syntactic properties listed in (3) (see Table 3).

Because the change is still very much in progress, the dichotomy between the NI and the canonical passive in Icelandic is not as clear cut as it is in Polish. But nonetheless, the survey data show that the NI is different from the canonical passive, thus supporting the Active Impersonal analysis. As predicted by Maling and Sigurjónsdóttir (2002:127), the NI is even beginning to extend its usage to nonagentive verbs which do not form passives in the standard language. Sentence (6a), which is an instance of the NI, was tested in the Thráinsson et al. (in press) study. The results across the four age groups are shown in Table 4.

(6) a. Það var samt alltaf átt marga hesta.
it$_{expl}$ was still always had many horses-ACC
'People still owned many horses.' (New Impersonal)

b. *Hundurinn er áttur (af þeim)
dog.the-NOM is had (by them)
'The dog is owned (by them).' (Thráinsson 2007:152, ex.
4.15b) (Canonical Passive)

The data show that many speakers accept this sentence, and that the younger the speakers, the more likely they are to accept it. It is worth noting that in both Polish and Irish, where a similar syntactic reanalysis has already been completed, nonagentive "unaccusative" verbs do occur with the relevant "impersonal" morphology provided that the understood subject is [+human].

9.3 Possible models for the syntactic change

Why is this syntactic change happening? We assume that the NI has its origins in child language, as first suggested by Kjartansson (1991). The question then, is what features of the primary linguistic data avail-

TABLE 4   Acceptability judgments for NI of a verb that does not form the
canonical passive

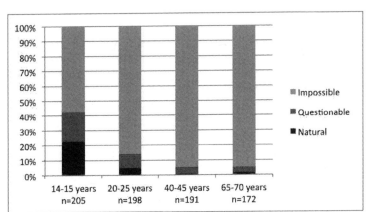

able to the child might be the source of this innovation. Researchers
have suggested different constructions as the model: impersonal passives with PP complements (Kjartansson 1991; Barðdal and Molnár
2003; Sigurðsson 2011); impersonal passives of reflexive verbs (Kjartansson 1991:20; M&S 2001, 2002; Maling 2006); transitive expletive
passives with an indefinite postverbal NP (Eythórsson 2008; Thráinsson 2007); an impersonal ditransitive reflexive construction (Eythórsson
2008). Given space limitations, we discuss only two possible models.

9.3.1   Transitive expletive passives

One hypothesis is that the "... the New Passive emerged from a reanalysis of the canonical existential passive (það-passive) with a postverbal
NP" (Eythórsson 2008:173). Eythórsson (2008) looks for parallels in
other Scandinavian languages and points to the expletive passive, or
"transitive existential passive," as a possible parallel for the Icelandic
innovation. He hypothesizes that the NI is an impersonal "expletive passive" that has lost the definiteness constraint that exists in the standard
language.

Many sentences in standard Icelandic can be analyzed as either
the canonical passive or the NI (Sigurjónsdóttir and Maling 2001:128;
Thráinsson 2007:276; Eythórsson 2008). This ambiguity arises because
neuter nouns have the same form for NOM/ACC in both singular and
plural. When the postverbal NP is unambiguously nominative, as for
the masculine noun strákur 'boy' in (7a), then the clause can only be
analyzed as a canonical passive; however, when the postverbal NP is

a neuter singular noun as in (7b), then the child cannot tell from the morphology that the postverbal NP is marked nominative.

(7) a. Það var barinn strákur.
   it$_{expl}$ was hit-M.SG. boy-NOM M.SG.
   'A boy was hit.'

   b. Það var skammað lítið barn.
   it$_{expl}$ was scolded-N.SG. little child-N.SG(NOM/ACC)
   'A little child was scolded.' (Eythórsson 2008, ex.73a)

As a result, the child may hypothesize that the postverbal NP in (7b) is an accusative object rather than a postposed nominative subject. If this happens, we have a case of 'misanalysis' or 'reanalysis'. Moreover, a sentence with an indefinite oblique NP as in (8) is always ambiguous between the NI and the canonical passive (Sigurjónsdóttir and Maling 2001).

(8) Það var hrint litlum strák.
   it$_{expl}$ was pushed-N.SG. little-DAT boy
   'A little boy was pushed.' (Eythórsson 2008, ex.73b)

However, sentences like those in (9a,b) are unambiguously instances of the NI because the postverbal NP is definite.

(9) a. Það var skammað litla barnið.
   it$_{expl}$ was scolded-N.SG little child.the
   'The little child was scolded.' (Eythórsson 2008, ex.74a)

   b. Það var hrint litla stráknum.
   it$_{expl}$ was pushed-N.SG little boy.the-DAT
   'The little boy was pushed.' (Eythórsson 2008, ex. 74b)

Intuitively, sentences like those in (9) are less "glaring" or salient to the speaker's ear in that the only nonstandard feature is the violation of the Definiteness Effect, whereas with accusative-assigning verbs there are the additional morphological signs of case-marking and the lack of verb agreement. Indeed, in the M&S study, examples of the NI with dative-assigning verbs had slightly higher acceptability rates than those with accusative-assigning verbs. The same was true in Polish; for centuries, the only examples of the innovative −no/to construction contained neuter NPs which could just as well have been canonical passives (Zbigniew Kański, p.c.). Anthony Naro's work on Brazilian Portuguese showed that the use of non-standard forms goes down as the surface salience of the deviation from the standard goes up (Naro 1981).[2]

---

[2]We are grateful to Anthony Kroch for the reference to Naro's work on Portuguese.

Thráinsson (2007) seems to agree with Eythórsson's suggestion that existential passives with indefinite postverbal NPs were the model for the innovation. He notes (p. 276) that "there is considerable overlap between the two dialects" with the result that "in the primary linguistic data (PLD) available to the child acquiring the language there is a lot of ambiguity even if the data all come from speakers of the standard dialect." We agree that the input available to the child underdetermines the grammar; indeed, as discussed in Section 3.2, we have argued that two different analyses of impersonal passives of intransitive verbs are available even to speakers of the standard language. However, the suggestion that existential passives with an indefinite postverbal NP were the model for the innovation is not compelling. First, there is the actuation problem: why is the NI developing only now, in the late 20th century, when existential passives have existed throughout the entire recorded history of Icelandic? There do not seem to be any unambiguous examples of the NI containing either full NPs in the accusative or pronouns until the mid-20th century (Maling and Sigurjónsdóttir 2002:129).[3] Eythórsson (2008:212) accepts this timeline.

Second, on this account, it is mysterious why the NI is developing only in Icelandic and not in, e.g. Norwegian. The "transitive expletive passive" construction also occurs in the other Scandinavian languages, as illustrated in (10) for Norwegian, where there is no evidence of a similar syntactic change.

(10) Det var lagt   eit document/*det framfor oss.
     it was placed a document/*it   before us
     'A document was placed before us.' (=Eythórsson 2008, ex. 66a)

Eythórsson claims that "the Norwegian *det*-passive is a close parallel to the New Passive in Icelandic in that the postverbal argument is an object rather than a subject ... the difference is that the direct object NP must generally be indefinite in Norwegian" (Eythórsson 2008:206). We find the claimed parallelism unconvincing; personal pronouns are

---

[3] A search of the entire IcePaHC corpus (Wallenberg et al. 2011) uncovered only one unambiguous example of an accusative NP object with a passive participle, from Jón Steingrímsson's diary/autobiography (1791):

i En þá   kvöl, ...,   verður ei af mér útmálað.
   but the-ACC torment-F.SG... becomes not by me out.painted-N.SG.

ii En þá kvöl, sem eg hafði að bera af kitlum, sem eg hafði í yljum og tám, verður ei af mér útmálað.
   "But the torment which I had to endure from the tickling that I had in the soles of my feet and toes will not be described by me."

This example is less clear than one would like because two relative clauses intervene between the fronted accusative object and the participle (Wallenberg et al. 2010).

excluded in Norwegian, whereas they are common in the Icelandic NI.

There are also theoretical problems with Eythórsson's analysis of the existential passive. He says that "the postverbal NP is standardly argued to be an object, assigned structural accusative case" (2008: 205), and continues, "In sum, the Norwegian *det*-passive is a close parallel to the New Passive in Icelandic in that the postverbal argument is an object rather than a subject ... the difference is that the direct object NP must generally be indefinite in Norwegian" (p. 206). Eythórsson seems to dismiss the significance of the Definiteness Effect (DE). A hallmark of the Icelandic NI is the lack of NP-movement, and because the DE only applies to postverbal subjects, it does not constrain the postverbal object in the NI. In the Norwegian existential passive, however, the postverbal NP is a postposed subject, and must be indefinite. Since personal pronouns are excluded, any argument that the postverbal NP receives accusative case in Norwegian (e.g. Hestvik 1986) is theory-internal. In Icelandic, on the other hand, personal pronouns are common in the NI, and there is overt morphological case marking on nouns as well. Eythórsson (2008:212-213) provides an analysis for the Icelandic NI under which accusative is the default structural case on objects. "Once the postverbal NP has been reanalyzed as an object that is assigned structural accusative case, the New Passive emerges" and "Since the NP is not a subject but an object, the DE no longer applies." By this same logic, however, we would expect (contrary to fact) that the DE should also not apply to Norwegian *det*-passives, since under his hypothesis, the postverbal NP in Norwegian is an object assigned structural accusative.

Eythórsson suggests that the predicted lack of the DE is found in Norwegian ditransitives, since the Indirect Object of a ditransitive verb can be definite. Observe, however, that only the Indirect Object can be definite; the direct object must be indefinite, as shown in (11).

(11) Det   vart overrekt vinnaren   ein pokal /*pokalen.
     it$_{expl}$ was given   the.winner a   cup   /*the.cup
     'The winner was given a cup/*the cup.' (= Eythórsson 2008, ex.
     66b)

The *det*-passive construction is an existential with a (personal) passive base. The construction targets the Direct Object, the theme, and the Definiteness Effect follows; the Indirect Object is inert. We conclude that it is misleading to describe the Icelandic NI as a "parallel development" to the Norwegian *det*-construction. We know of no evidence that Norwegian is extending it along the same lines to transitive verbs, apart from the reflexive passive allowed by some speakers (Åfarli

1992:128). Crucially, however, only the simple reflexive *seg* is allowed, and not the *selv* 'self' anaphor:

(12) Det ble låst   seg (*selv) inn   i fabrikken.
     it$_{expl}$ was locked REFL (self)   inside in the.factory
     'Someone/People locked themselves/himself in the factory' (cf.
     Maling 2006, ex. 26b)

This contrast supports the suggestion that for those Norwegian speakers who do accept the reflexive passive, the simple reflexive *seg* serves as an intransitivizing suffix (cf. Sells, Zaenen and Zec 1987; Maling and Sigurjónsdóttir 2010).

9.3.2 Impersonal passives of intransitive verbs

The two nationwide surveys included examples of both the NI construction and the Canonical Passive. But they also included examples of the traditional so-called "Impersonal Passive" exemplified in (13), a construction which all linguists (including us) considered to be passive.

(13) Það var dansað   alla nóttina.
     it$_{expl}$ was danced-N.SG all   night
     'there was dancing all night' or 'people danced all night'

Perhaps the most surprising result from the M&S survey was the data from the 200 adult controls. What we discovered is that for many of the adult subjects, the traditional Impersonal Passive displayed two of the properties that we had identified as being associated with being syntactically *active*, namely control of bound anaphors and subject-oriented adjuncts. The example of an impersonal passive with a reflexive object shown in (14) was included in both nationwide surveys. The results from the second survey, shown in Table 5, clearly show the striking age-related variation.

(14) Svo var bara drifið   sig   á ball.
     then was just hurried REFL to dance
     'Then everyone just hurried (themselves) off to the dance' (Maling
     and Sigurjónsdóttir 2002, ex. 30a)

For all age groups, the acceptance rate of reflexive impersonal passives is higher than the acceptance rate for the NI. In other words, the Impersonal Passive was showing the same *active* syntactic property as the New Impersonal, but at even higher levels of acceptance (compare Table 5 with Table 2).

It turns out that the reflexive impersonal passive is a 20th century innovation. Eythórsson (2008:189) observes: "I have not been able to find any cases of [impersonal passives] with reflexive verbs in Old Icelandic;

TABLE 5   Impersonal Passive of Reflexive Verb

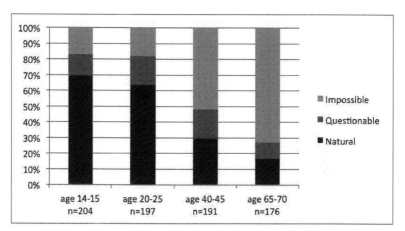

...Thus, the reflexive [impersonal passive] seems to be an innovation of Modern Icelandic which is increasingly gaining ground and is accepted by many speakers who do not accept the [New Impersonal] ..." The historical timeline has been studied in more detail by Árnadóttir, Eythórsson and Sigurðsson (2011).

The development of reflexive impersonal passives is a syntactic change which had not been noticed before linguists began to investigate the syntactic properties of the NI in detail. Our initial assumptions about the standard (adult) language were based on the grammaticality judgments of a few adult speakers (see also Sigurðsson 1989:355). Barðdal and Molnár (2003:246) disagreed with the judgments reported in M&S on the acceptability of adjuncts with impersonal passives, and suggested as an alternative explanation that participial adjuncts can be "controlled by the underlying agent in impersonal passive sentences." But they were unaware of the variation that exists among adult speakers.

To account for the variation we found among our adult controls, we suggested that impersonal passives of intransitive verbs are *in principle* syntactically ambiguous between active and passive (Maling and Sigurjónsdóttir 2002:126).[4] If this suggestion is correct, then there are two possible grammars, as sketched in (15a,b):

(15)   a.   [e] [$_{VP}$ var dansað]   Grammar 1: syntactically passive
       b.   [pro_{arb}] [$_{VP}$ var dansað] Grammar 2: syntactically active

---

[4]Haspelmath (1990) independently made the same claim in a different framework with different terminology.

The data generally available to the child learning Icelandic under-determine the analyses. We suggested that roughly half of the adult speakers responding to our survey analyzed the traditional Impersonal Passive as a **passive** construction. The other half analyzed it as **active**, i.e. having a syntactically accessible null subject. This makes bound anaphors and adjuncts possible. So if a speaker's grammatical representation of the Impersonal Passive is as sketched in (15a), then she will not accept control of adjuncts because there is nothing to control them. There is some anecdotal evidence which supports this claim. Consider the example of an impersonal passive with a subject-oriented participial adjunct in (16):

(16) Það var komið   skellihlæjandi í   tímann
     it$_{expl}$ was come-N.SG laughing   into class
     'People came into class laughing.'

When asked to judge this example, one speaker in her 70s commented: *Það vantar einhvern* 'Someone is missing.' She reacted the way an English speaker might react to a sentence like "There was running into class"; the attempt to add an adjunct like "laughing" or "drunk" creates the same feeling of a missing agent participant.

The hypothesis that there are two different grammars makes an interesting prediction: those speakers who accept the adjuncts in the Impersonal Passive should be more likely to accept the bound anaphors in the Impersonal Passive, because their syntactic representation of the construction provides for both. This prediction is borne out: for both adolescents and adults in our study, acceptance of subject-oriented participles was significantly correlated with acceptance of reflexives in impersonal passives. For adolescents, the correlation was very significant ($r = 0.433$, n=1693, $p = .000$, 2-tailed); for adults, the correlation was also very significant ($r = 0.532$, n=199, $p = 0.000$, 2-tailed) (Maling and Sigurjónsdóttir 2002:126, note 15). Our hypothesis is that speakers who *accept* subject-oriented participles and reflexives have an *active* representation of the "Impersonal Passive" as sketched in (15b), while speakers who reject subject-oriented participles and reflexives have a passive representation of the "Impersonal Passive" as sketched in (15a).

The age-related variation uncovered in the two nation-wide surveys, complemented with the historical evidence on the recent spread of reflexive impersonal passives over the last century, suggests the following stages in the development of the NI (Maling and Sigurjónsdóttir 2010).

(17) a. Stage 1. Impersonal passives occur only with intransitive verbs
        (e.g. *dansa* 'dance')

b. Stage 2. Impersonal passives start to occur with reflexive verbs in the 20th century, as some speakers reanalyze the impersonal passive as a syntactically active construction with a pro_{arb} subject.

c. Stage 3. For Grammar 2 speakers, impersonal "passives" occur with all transitive verbs, with ACC on the postverbal object.

Stage 1 represents Icelandic before c. 1900; all speakers have Grammar 1, that is, they have the passive analysis sketched in (15a). In Stage 2, there are two competing grammars of impersonal passives. In Stage 3, the active analysis of impersonal passives of intransitive verbs extends to transitive verbs, with accusative case occurring on any postverbal object not assigned lexical case by the verb. This is what we now recognize as the "New Impersonal."

9.4 Conclusion

Why is this change happening? One explanation that we can exclude is borrowing. Although a similar syntactic change took place independently in Polish and Irish several centuries ago, none of the languages commonly spoken by Icelanders have the construction, so the usual scapegoats for linguistic contamination, namely, Danish and English, cannot be blamed. Nor is this the result of any phonological change or morphological weakening. This is a system-internal change which challenges the claim in generative theories that syntax is inert, as pointed out to us by Anthony Kroch (p.c.). According to the Principle of inertia, proposed by Keenan (2001) and developed by Longobardi (2001), syntax does not change on its own; rather syntactic change must be triggered either by external forces (i.e., language contact), or some prior change in another domain, e.g. phonology or morphology. Neither of these triggers apply to the Icelandic situation. Rather, a highly marked option of Universal Grammar, namely a construction with an accusative object but no apparent nominative subject, in violation of Burzio's Generalization, arose spontaneously in the language without any prior relevant change in Icelandic morphology or phonology.

M&S suggested that we need to look beyond the historical identity of the morphemes involved in order to understand the nature of this ongoing change. The hypothesis that the NI still behaves like a grammatical passive does not account for the variation among the adult controls first revealed in the M&S study and now even better documented in the Thráinsson et al. (in press) study. Conflicting grammaticality judgments have sometimes been reported (cf. Barðdal and Molnár 2003 and Eythórsson 2008, who disagree with judgments reported in M&S). Now with large survey data, we can see the complex dimensions of the problem. It can be difficult to deal with the inherent messiness/murkiness of data found in surveys, large-scale corpora, and experimental studies, but we need to account for the variation in syntactic judgments that exists among adult speakers. We do not believe that all (adult) native speakers necessarily come to the same grammatical analysis of every construction; on the contrary, we believe that speakers may come to radically different analyses of the same data. The readily observable data underdetermines the analysis; it is only by pushing the speaker to judge more complex, or less common (even "vanishingly rare") sentences that we can see the empirical consequences of choosing one syntactic representation over another.

Acknowledgments

This research was supported by grants from Vísindasjóður Rannsóknarráðs Íslands (RANNÍS), Rannsóknarsjóður Háskóla Íslands, and Lýðveldisjóður; the original pilot study reported in Maling and Sigurjónsdóttir (1997) was supported in part by NSF grant BCS-9223725 to Brandeis University. Special thanks to Halldór Ármann Sigurðsson, Jim Wood, and an anonymous reviewer for helpful comments on an earlier draft. The material in this paper is based in part on work done while the first author was serving as Director of NSF's Linguistics Program. Any opinions, findings and conclusions expressed in this material are those of the authors, and do not necessarily reflect the views of the U.S. National Science Foundation.

References

Åfarli, Tor A. 1992. *The Syntax of Norwegian Passive Constructions*. John Benjamins.

Árnadóttir, Hlíf, Thórhallur Eythórsson, and Einar Freyr Sigurðsson. 2011. The passive of reflexive verbs in Icelandic. In T. E. Strahan, ed., *Nordlyd 37: Relating to Reflexives*, pages 39–97. CASTL. http://www.ub.uit.no/munin/nordlyd.

Barðdal, Jóhanna and Valéria Molnár. 2003. The passive in Icelandic compared to mainland Scandinavian. In J. Hetland and V. Molnár, eds., *Structures of Focus and Grammatical Relations [Linguistische Arbeiten 477]*, pages 231–60. Max Niemeyer Verlag.

Blevins, James P. 2003. Passives and impersonals. *Journal of Linguistics* 39:473–520.

Eythórsson, Thórhallur. 2008. The new passive in Icelandic really is a passive. In T. Eythórsson, ed., *Grammatical Change and Linguistic Theory: the Rosendal papers*, pages 173–219. John Benjamins.

Haspelmath, Martin. 1990. The grammaticization of passive morphology. *Studies in Language* 14:25–72.

Hestvik, Arild. 1986. Case theory and Norwegian impersonal constructions. *Nordic Journal of Linguistics* 9:181–197.

Jónsson, Jóhannes Gísli. 2009. The new impersonal as a true passive. In A. Alexiadou, J. Hankamer, T. McFadden, J. Nuger, and F. Schäfer, eds., *Advances in Comparative Germanic Syntax*, pages 281–306. John Benjamins.

Keenan, Edward. 2001. Explaining the creation of reflexive pronouns in English. In D. Minkova and R. Stockwell, eds., *Studies in the History of English: A Millennial Perspective*, pages 325–355. Mouton de Gruyter.

Kibort, Anna. 2004. *Passive and Passive-like Constructions in English and Polish: A Contrastive Study with Particular Reference to Impersonal Constructions*. Ph.D. thesis, University of Cambridge.

Kjartansson, Helgi Skúli. 1991. Nýstárleg þolmynd í barnamáli [A new passive in child language]. *Skíma* 14:18–22.

Longobardi, Giuseppe. 2001. Formal syntax, diachronic minimalism and etymology: The history of French 'chez'. *Linguistic Inquiry* 32:275–302.

Maling, Joan. 1993. Unpassives of unaccusatives. Unpublished ms. Brandeis University. Talks presented at the University of Massachusetts at Amherst, the University of California San Diego, the University of Helsinki, and the University of Iceland. Revised version published as Maling 2010.

Maling, Joan. 2006. From passive to active: Syntactic change in progress in Icelandic. In B. Lyngfelt and T. Solstad, eds., *Demoting the Agent. Passive and Other Voice-related Phenomena*, pages 197–223. John Benjamins.

Maling, Joan. 2010. Unpassives of unaccusatives. In D. B. Gerdts, J. Moore, and M. Polinsky, eds., *Hypothesis A/Hypothesis B: Linguistic Explorations in Honor of David M. Perlmutter*, pages 275–292. MIT Press.

Maling, Joan and Sigríður Sigurjónsdóttir. 1997. The "new passive" in Icelandic. In *Proceedings of the 21st Annual Boston University Conference on Language Development*, pages 378–389. Cascadilla Press.

Maling, Joan and Sigríður Sigurjónsdóttir. 2002. The new impersonal construction in Icelandic. *Journal of Comparative Germanic Linguistics* 5:97–142.

Maling, Joan and Sigríður Sigurjónsdóttir. 2010. From passive to active: Stages in the Icelandic "new impersonal". Paper presented at Diachronic Generative Syntax XII conference, University of Cambridge, July 14-16, 2010. To appear in *Syntax over Time: Lexical, Morphological and Information-Structural Interactions*. Studies in Diachronic and Historical Linguistics. T. Biberauer and G. Walkden (eds.), Oxford University Press.

Naro, Anthony J. 1981. The social and structural dimensions of a syntactic change. *Language* 57:63–98.

Sells, Peter, Annie Zaenen, and Draga Zec. 1987. Reflexivization variation: Relations between syntax, semantics and lexical structure. In M. Iida, S. Wechsler, and D. Zec, eds., *Working Papers in Grammatical Theory and Discourse Structure: Interactions of Morphology, Syntax, and Discourse*, pages 169–238. CSLI Publications.

Sigurjónsdóttir, Sigríður and Joan Maling. 2001. Það var hrint mér fyrir framan blokkina; þolmynd eða ekki þolmynd? *Íslenskt mál* 23:123–180.

Sigurðsson, Einar Freyr. 2012. Germynd en samt þolmynd: Um nýju þolmyndina í íslensku [Active but still passive: On the new passive in Icelandic.]. M.A.-thesis, University of Iceland, Reykjavík.

Sigurðsson, Halldór Ármann. 1989. *Verbal Syntax and Case in Icelandic*. Ph.D. thesis, University of Lund. Republished 1992, Institute of Linguistics, Reykjavík.

Sigurðsson, Halldór Ármann. 2011. On the new passive. *Syntax* 14:148–178.

Sigurðsson, Halldór Ármann and Verner Egerland. 2009. Impersonal null-subjects in Icelandic and elsewhere. *Studia Linguistica* 63:158–185.

Sobin, Nicholas. 1985. Case assignment in Ukrainian morphological passive constructions. *Linguistic Inquiry* 16:649–62.

Thráinsson, Höskuldur. 2007. *The Syntax of Icelandic*. Cambridge University Press.

Thráinsson, Höskuldur et al., ed. in press. *Tilbrigði í íslenskri setningagerð. [Variation in Icelandic Syntax.]*. Háskólaútgáfan.

Thráinsson, Höskuldur, Sigríður Sigurjónsdóttir, and Thórhallur Eythórsson. 2010. Linguistic change in real time in the phonology and syntax of Icelandic. Poster presentation, Conference on Nordic Language Variation: Grammatical, Sociolinguistic and Infrastructural Perspectives, University of Iceland, Reykjavík, October 8, 2010.

Wallenberg, Joel C., Anton Karl Ingason, Einar Freyr Sigurðsson, and Eiríkur Rögnvaldsson. 2010. Icelandic parsed historical corpus (IcePaHC): Stability? patterns that die and others that don't. Presented at the Nordic Language Variation Network / RILiVS Workshop, October 9, 2010, University of Iceland.

Wallenberg, Joel C., Anton Karl Ingason, Einar Freyr Sigurðsson, and Eiríkur Rögnvaldsson. 2011. Icelandic parsed historical corpus (IcePaHC). Version 0.5. http://www.linguist.is/icelandic_treebank.

Zaenen, Annie, Joan Maling, and Höskuldur Thráinsson. 1985. Case and grammatical functions: The Icelandic passive. *Natural Language and Linguistic Theory* 4:441–483.

10

Down *with* Obliques?

GYÖRGY RÁKOSI

10.1 Introduction

There is virtually no disagreement among linguists that idiosyncratically marked dependents of a verb are syntactic arguments and not
adjuncts. The PPs in (1) are idiosyncratically marked in the sense that
the choice of the preposition is fixed with respect to the relevant verbal meaning, and the preposition does not contribute compositionally
to the meaning of the verb phrase. Such PPs tend to be syntactically
obligatory, or at least their presence is required for the intended verbal
reading to hold.

(1) a. I rely on you/*in you.

    b. I believe in you/*on you.

In contradistinction, the syntactic status of *semantically marked PPs* is
less obvious. These, like the directional *to* and the source-marker *from*
in (2) below, appear to make a systematic contribution to the meaning
of the clause across relatively well-definable classes of verbs.

(2) a. John sent flowers to/for Mary.

    b. John drove from/past the house to/towards the school.

Furthermore, such PPs often are syntactically optional. It is not a priori
obvious whether they should be classified as syntactic arguments or
adjuncts.

    Therefore in any linguistic theory where the argument-adjunct dis-
tinction is treated as a valid dichotomy, a choice has to be made in
the syntactic analysis of semantically marked PPs. Lexical-Functional

From Quirky Case to Representing Space: Papers in Honor of Annie Zaenen.
Tracy Holloway King and Valeria de Paiva.
Copyright © 2013, CSLI Publications.

Grammar is one such framework, where the argument analysis has been the accepted practice ever since the birth of the theory. Bresnan (1982) takes many types of these prepositional phrases to be *possible grammatical arguments of the verb*, which are f-structure obliques (OBLS). More recently, Needham and Toivonen (2011) analyzed them as *derived arguments*. The underlying assumption in both works is that semantically marked oblique arguments can be added relatively freely under specific licensing conditions to the argument structure of what we can consider the basic lexical entry of the verb.

Zaenen and Crouch (2009), however, argue that there are advantages in treating *all* semantically marked obliques as syntactic adjuncts. Their concerns are mostly implementational: other things being equal, the oblique analysis of semantically marked optional PPs will generally create OBL/ADJ ambiguities in parsing. Given that, for example, *send* has both a dyadic and a triadic entry under this analysis, sentence (2a) can be analyzed either as construction involving the dyadic *send* with an adjunct PP, or as the realization of a triadic entry with an oblique. Such ambiguities multiply when several semantically marked obliques are present in the clause. So, they argue, it is better to treat all such PPs as adjuncts, whose range of interpretation is merely *constrained* by the verb they apply to. This increases the efficiency of the parser by reducing the number of ambiguities, and, furthermore, it obviates the *theoretical* burden of distinguishing arguments from adjuncts in a good number of cases.

In this paper, I want to contribute to this discussion by presenting some remarks on the behaviour of two types of *with*-phrases: *instrumentals* (3) and *comitatives* (4).

(3) a. John cut the meat with a knife.
    b. John wrote the letter with a pen.

(4) a. John corresponded with Kate.
    b. John sang with Kate.

It is common to both pairs that the preposition *with* appears to make essentially the same semantic contribution to the respective sentences: it denotes an instrument controlled by the agent argument in both (3a) and (3b), and it marks an individual who accompanies the agent subject argument in the activity it pursues in both (4a) and (4b). Thus each of the four *with*-phrases seems to be a semantically marked oblique. Yet, the (a)-examples have been treated as arguments in much of the literature, whereas the (b)-examples are traditionally considered adjuncts. For Zaenen and Crouch (2009), all four examples would presumably be adjuncts, whereas in the classical LFG approach, as well as in its revised version in Needham and Toivonen (2011), each would be a (derived or basic) argument.

What I argue for is that there is good motivation to treat both *with*-phrases in (3) as adjuncts, but an argument-adjunct distinction needs to be drawn to account for (4a) and (4b), respectively. This conclusion lends some further support to the general program of reducing the number of semantically marked obliques, as Zaenen and Crouch (2009) suggest — even if there may be pockets of the lexicon where semantically marked oblique arguments still abide.

10.2 Instrumentals

Instrumental *with*-phrases show a mixture of argument and adjunct properties with respect to well-known syntactic and semantic tests. Here I only quote apparently contradictory pieces of data from Schütze (1995), and refer the reader to his article for a detailed overview of this issue. The *do so* VP pro-form test shows that instrumentals (5a) pattern up with adjuncts (5b), and not with arguments (5c). On the other hand, instrumentals allow direct preposition stranding in complex constructions (6a), unlike true adjuncts (6b).

(5) a. John stirred the soup with a spoon, and Fred did so with a fork.

    b. John opened the bank on Tuesday, and Peter did so on Friday.

    c. *John put the book on the table, and Kate did so on the shelf.

(6) a. This flimsy key is extremely hard to convince yourself to be willing to open such a heavy door with.

    b. *This lousy day is extremely hard to convince yourself to be willing to go out on.

Schütze concludes that instrumentals *have several argument properties* (1995: 132). In the LFG literature, a similar claim is made by Donohue and Donohue (2004) in their survey of instrumentals in several Austronesian and Papuan languages. Needham and Toivonen (2011) argue that all instrumentals are *derived arguments*.

The more restrictive approach is to assume that only some instrumentals are arguments. Reinhart (2002), for example, argues that Levin's (1993) *verbs of cutting* and Levin and Rappaport's (1995) *manner verbs* are triadic verbs that have exactly such an instrument *argument*. *Peel* in (7) below represents this class, other members of which are *cut, screw, sow* or *drill*. These verbs take an agent (7a) or an instrument (7b) subject, but not a pure cause (7c), and they do not undergo the anticausative alternation (7d).

(7) a. John peeled the apple with a knife.

    b. This knife wouldn't peel the apple.

    c. *The heat peeled the apple.

    d. *The apple peeled.

Example (8) includes the not-necessarily agentive verb *break*. *Break* is a dyadic verb that can take either agent (8a), instrument (8b) or cause (8c) subjects, and it undergoes the anticausative alternation (8d).

(8) a. John broke the glass with this hammer.

    b. This hammer broke the glass.

    c. The storm broke the glass.

    d. The glass broke.

Thus it is clear that the two classes of verbs are not equivalent grammatically.

It is less evident though that this difference should include a difference between argument and adjunct instrumentals. Notice that the (a) and (b) examples superficially appear to be representatives of the same alternation. In the absence of the (c) and (d) examples, it is not so easy to argue why the (a) and (b) examples involve instrumentals of non-identical types. The two certainly do not differ much with respect to the tests that Schütze (1995) catalogues, except for one: the intuition that underlies the argument analysis of *cut*-instrumentals is that these verbal concepts necessarily include an instrument participant. In other words, the existence of the instrument is entailed by the verb in (7), but not in (8).

But this is a rather contentious issue. We have no similar linguistic intuitions in the case of *write*, for example, and it is not immediately obvious why. Most writing events that occur in the world do include some sort of an instrument (a pen, a board marker, or a keyboard). In fact, such events are probably an overwhelming majority. It is true that one *can* write words in the sand with his or her fingers, but one can also cut someone's face with his or her nails — no instrument external to the agent is used in either situation. Thus, given that lexical semantic intuitions are a somewhat unreliable guide anyway and that there does not seem to be a radical grammatical difference between the two instrumentals in (7a) and (8a), we can treat the two as representatives of the same grammatical type of semantically marked PPs.

To support this claim, I conducted a small-scale pilot corpus study of the *Corpus of Contemporary American English* (Davis 2008-2012). The survey includes four *cut*-type verbs (*cut, peel, chop,* and *carve*), and four others that can also take instruments (*write, open, break, close*). I searched for *verb lemma* plus *any pronominal* strings (e.g., *cut it*), and did a separate search on *verb lemma+pronoun+with* strings (e.g., *cut it with*). This search covered all the inflected forms of the respective verbs. Within the *with*-list, I manually separated true instrumental uses from other uses of the preposition. The non-instrumental uses include cases where the base verb has an irrelevant reading (9a), or where the *with*-PP has some other function, like the expression of manner (9b). For the purposes of this survey, body-part *with*-PPs (10a) and metaphoric extensions (10b) were treated as instrumental uses. The results are summarized in Table 1.

(9) a. That argument doesn't cut it with folks like Freddy Yoder.

b. I had to write it with a great deal of discretion.

(10) a. He peeled the orange with his fingers.

b. She was peeling me with her eyes.

I. verb	II. V + pronoun	III. V + pronoun + *with*	
		III.1. total	III.2. instrumentals
Cut	7,711	137	113
Peel	374	9	9
Chop	362	2	1
Carve	255	5	4
Write	8,425	62	8
Open	6,435	95	68
Break	3,975	31	19
Close	3,563	24	11

TABLE 1 Instrumentals in the Corpus of Contemporary American English

The figures in the cells are raw frequencies of occurrence. For example, the string 'lemma *cut*+pronoun' occurs 7,711 times in the corpus (Column II), and it is only in 137 cases that this string is immediately followed by the preposition *with* (Column III.1.). Of these 137 occurrences, I classified 113 as truly instrumental (Column III.2).

The figures are surprisingly low, especially in the first four rows (*cut, peel, chop, carve*). This is not what we would expect if *cut*-verbs indeed took instrumental arguments. There seems to be a difference between these verbs and the last four, inasmuch as the ratio of the true instrumental uses and the total number of *with*-PPs is somewhat lower in the latter group. Whether that difference is real and significant is a question that requires more data to settle.

The upshot of this discussion is that there is no massive corpus evidence for the presence of an instrumental argument in the *cut*-class. If these verbs have such an argument, why does it remain implicit in 98-99 percent of the cases and why is it realized as an oblique only in the rest? Furthermore, the frequency of instrumental *with*-phrases is so low across the board that we might indeed be better off as far as implementational issues are concerned if we treat all of these instrumentals as adjuncts. This is the suggestion that Zaenen and Crouch (2009) make, and I fully concur with them on the basis of the considerations I presented here.

10.3   Comitatives

Comitative phrases can be added to agentive predicates relatively freely, and they denote participants who actively accompany the referent of the subject argument in the event ((4) repeated as (11)). A subset of agentive predicates, Levin's (1993) *verbs of social interaction*, also take what looks like a comitative phrase ((4a) repeated as (11a)).

(11)   a. John corresponded with Kate.

     b. John sang with Kate.

The so-called *discontinuous construction* in (11a) has been taken to include a dyadic reciprocal verb by a number of authors, including, among others, Dowty (1991), Dimitriadis (2004, 2008), Rákosi (2003, 2008), Siloni (2001, 2008, 2011), as well as Hurst (2010) in the LFG literature. In this section, I briefly argue that the *with*-phrase is a semantically marked PP in both constructions, but it indeed is an argument in (11a) and a true adjunct in (11b). Thus, unlike in the case of instrumentals, here we have good empirical motivation not to collapse the grammar of the two *with*-PPs.

The claim that the discontinuous *with*-PP is a semantically marked oblique is supported by the fact that its presence is predictable across relatively well-definable classes of verbs. In English, most *verbs of social interaction* take *with*-phrases (12a), some optionally take a *with*-phrase or an object (12b), and some only take an object (12c).

(12)   a. John corresponded/flirted/negotiated with Kate.

     b. John consulted/fought/met (with) Kate.

     c. John embraced/kissed/married (*with) Kate.

It is a quirk of the English language that some of these verbs cannot or may only optionally combine with a *with*-PP. However, the majority of them do so (see Dowty 1991 and Levin 1993 for a more comprehensive list). Such variation is not characteristic of other languages. In Hungarian, for example, each of these verbs co-occurs with a comitative case-marked oblique (the same case marker is used on instruments):

(13) János levelezett/találkozott/csókolózott Kati-val.
 John corresponded/met/kissed   Kate-with
 'John corresponded with/met/reciprocally-kissed Kate.'

Thus it is plausible to conclude that comitative *with*-phrases are a productive feature of the grammar of English verbs of social interaction, even if their use is blocked by overriding lexical specifications in some cases.

Verbs of social interaction denote reciprocal relations that are distributed over the subject set and the comitative set in the discontinuous construction (hence the name; see Dimitriadis 2004). Comitative adjunct constructions (11b) do not involve such an underlying reciprocal relation. Nevertheless, the contribution of the *with*-phrase may be considered to be constant in the two cases: it introduces a participant who accompanies the agent in the action denoted by the verb. Any further differences can be deduced from the fact that the discontinuous construction in (11a) has reciprocal semantics, and the *with*-phrase fills in one of the two argument slots of this relation (cf. Siloni 2011 for related discussion).

The argument status of the comitative PP of reciprocal verbs is supported by a number of independent considerations. Superficially, one could assume that the following two pairs are representative of the same sort of alternation.

(14) a. John negotiated with Kate.
 b. John and Kate negotiated.

(15) a. John ran with Kate.
 b. John and Kate ran.

Indeed, whether expressed as an oblique or as part of the subject, in (14) Kate plays essentially the same role in the two sentences (but see Dowty (1991) and Rákosi (2003, 2008) for arguments that the discontinuous construction does license asymmetric interpretations). On the other hand, the comitative adjunct construction in (15a) cannot be reduced to the coordinate structure in (15b) without loss of meaning. (15a) may also be true if Kate does not run but she is carried by John. And (15b) has a distributive reading — on which there are two separate running events, one performed by Kate and one by John — but (15a) seems to allow for the collective reading only. Such facts point toward an analysis where (14) is treated as an argument alternation, but (15) is not.

The semantic argument status of the comitative of reciprocal social verbs is also evidenced by the intuition that (16a), unlike (16b), entails the existence of an extra participant not expressed directly in the sentence.

(16) a. John has always corresponded with pleasure.

b. John has always run with pleasure.

Here the intuitions are much clearer than in the case of instrumentals. In fact, comitative arguments cannot normally be dropped in episodic contexts in the presence of a singular subject, which is a clear indication of their argument status.

As discussed in the literature cited in the first paragraph of this section, the two types of comitatives show differences in their grammar across a variety of languages. Let me quote here two illustrative tests concerning Hungarian comitatives (and I refer the reader to Rákosi (2003) for a more detailed presentation).

In Hungarian, a reciprocal anaphor is only licensed as a comitative argument, but not as a comitative adjunct (see also Komlósy 1994). Compare (17a) with (17b).

(17) a. János és   Kati csókolóztak egymás-sal.
         John and Kate kissed   each.other-with
         'John and Kate reciprocally-kissed each other.'

b. *János és   Kati futottak egymás-sal.
         John and Kate ran   each.other-with
         'John and Kate ran with each other.'

And, given that the two fall into two distinct syntactic categories, comitative adjuncts and comitative arguments can co-occur in the same clause:

(18) Péter-rel   ritkán flörtölt-em Kati-val.
     Peter-with rarely flirted-1SG Kate-with
     'I rarely flirted with Kate (together) with Peter.'

To sum up, a number of semantic and syntactic considerations support an analysis in which the comitative phrase by reciprocal verbs of social interaction is treated as semantically marked oblique argument of the verb. Such comitative arguments exist beside true comitative adjuncts, which can freely be added to any agentive predicate.

Finally, I would like to add that the comitative analysis of this well-defined class of social verbs offers implementational advantages, too, as even a quick search in the Corpus of Contemporary American English testifies (Davis 2008-2012). I searched for four verbs in this class, once for the lemma only (including all inflected forms), and then for 'verb lemma plus *with*' sequences. The results are summarized in Table 2.

I. verb	II. V-lemma	III. V-lemma +*with*	III/II ratio
correspond	5,020	758	15.10%
flirt	2,714	1,539	56.71%
meet	140,775	14,272	10.14%
consult	8,394	1,937	23.08%

TABLE 2 Social verbs in the Corpus of Contemporary American English

Though the frequencies vary across the verbs, it is clear that comitative arguments are much more frequent in the corpus than any of the instrumentals discussed in the previous section (cf. Table 1). And, as one reviewer points out, the verbs in Table 2 also have other subcategorization frames which are either non-reciprocal (e.g., *correspond to*) or less reciprocal than the basic social interaction entry (e.g., transitive *meet* and *consult*). Thus the frequency of the comitative arguments *relative to* truly 'verb of social interaction' uses must be even higher than the raw frequencies in Table 2 suggest. This fact also supports an analysis in which these *with*-phrases are treated as arguments.

10.4   Conclusions

Having briefly overviewed the grammar of two types of *with*-phrases, I have concluded that instrumentals are best treated as adjuncts across the board as in (3), but a distinction has to be made between comitative arguments of reciprocal social verbs as in (4a) and comitative adjuncts that freely appear with agentive predicates as in (4b).

(3)   a. John cut the meat with a knife.

    b. John wrote the letter with a pen.

(4)   a. John corresponded with Kate.

    b. John sang with Kate.

On the whole, these results give support to the program that Zaenen and Crouch (2009) recommends: semantically marked PPs can generally be treated as syntactic adjuncts. The comitative scene only reminds us that there may be certain well-definable classes of verbs which do contain semantically marked obliques on their argument list. That conclusion is necessitated by observable grammatical differences between comitative adjuncts and arguments, and, as I have tried to show, this distinction may only add to parsing efficiency rather than decrease it.

These conclusions are at odds with the classical LFG approach by Bresnan (1982), or its revised version by Needham and Toivonen (2011).

(19) a. John corresponded with Kate. < Agent, Comitative >
　　 b. John sang. < Agent >
　　 c. John sang with Kate. < Agent, Comitative >

In this analysis, all semantically marked obliques are introduced at the level of argument structure. That makes it non-trivial to account for the observed differences between what I call here comitative arguments and comitative adjuncts, for the two argument structures in (19a) and (19c) are technically non-distinct. Needham and Toivonen (2011: 413) propose that arguments listed in the basic argument structure of a verb as in (19a-b) have a different status than what they call derived arguments of non-basic predicates (the comitative in (19c)). But it is not obvious how the difference between basic and derived arguments can be captured in LFG, unless one is ready to mark the latter category by some non-canonical feature specification.

The approach I suggest here in the footsteps of Zaenen and Crouch (2011) is to treat all but some specific classes of semantically marked PPs as adjuncts, rather than semantic arguments realized as syntactic obliques. This is not to deny that, as Needham and Toivonen (2011) carefully show, all semantically marked PPs tend to be characterized by a mixture of adjunct and argument properties, and their argument properties must also be accounted for. This target, however, can possibly be reached by assuming that such PP adjuncts receive thematic specification. I argue for such an analysis in Rákosi (2006), and similar claims have been made by Webb (2008) and Hurst (2010) in the LFG literature.

10.5 Acknowledgments

I thank the two anonymous reviewers for their comments. Any remaining errors are solely mine.

I acknowledge that the research reported here is supported, in part, by OTKA (Hungarian Scientific Research Fund), grant number K 72983; by the TÁMOP-4.2.1/B-09/1/KONV-2010-0007 project, which is co-financed by the European Union and the European Social Fund; and by the Research Group for Theoretical Linguistics of the Hungarian Academy of Sciences at the University of Debrecen.

References

Bresnan, Joan. 1982. Poliadicity. In J. Bresnan, ed., *The Mental Representation of Grammar*, pages 149–172. The MIT Press.

Davies, Mark. 2008–2012. The corpus of contemporary American English: 425 million words, 1990-present. Available online at http://corpus.byu.edu/coca/.

Dimitriadis, Alexis. 2004. Discontinuous reciprocals. Manuscript, Utrecht Institute of Linguistics, Utrecht, The Netherlands.

Dimitriadis, Alexis. 2008. Irreducible symmetry in reciprocal constructions. In E. König and V. Gast, eds., *Reciprocals and Reflexives: Cross-linguistic and Theoretical Explorations*, pages 375–410. Mouton de Gruyter.

Donohue, Catherine and Mark Donohue. 2004. On the special status of instrumentals. In M. Butt and T. H. King, eds., *Proceedings of the LFG04 Conference*, pages 209–225. CSLI Publications.

Dowty, David. 1991. Thematic proto-roles and argument selection. *Language* 67:547–619.

Hurst, Peter. 2010. The syntax of reciprocal constructions. In M. Butt and T. H. King, eds., *The Proceedings of The LFG10 Conference*, pages 290–310. CSLI.

Komlósy, András. 1994. Complements and adjuncts. In F. Kiefer and K. É. Kiss, eds., *The Syntactic Structure of Hungarian. Syntax and Semantics Volume 27*, pages 91–178. Academic Press.

Levin, Beth. 1993. *English Verb Classes and Alternations. A Preliminary Investigation*. The University of Chicago Press.

Levin, Beth and Malka Rappaport Hovav. 1995. *Unaccusativity at the Syntax - Lexical Semantics Interface*. The MIT Press.

Needham, Stéphanie and Ida Toivonen. 2011. Derived arguments. In M. Butt and T. H. King, eds., *Proceedings of the LFG11 Conference*, pages 401–421. CSLI Publications.

Rákosi, György. 2003. Comitative arguments in Hungarian. In W. Heeren, D. Papangeli, and E. Vlachou, eds., *Uil-OTS Yearbook 2003*, pages 47–57. Utrecht Institute of Linguistics OTS.

Rákosi, György. 2006. On the need for a more refined approach to the argument-adjunct distinction: The case of dative experiencers in Hungarian. In M. Butt and T. H. King, eds., *Proceedings of the LFG06 Conference*, pages 416–436. CSLI Publications.

Rákosi, György. 2008. The inherently reflexive and the inherently reciprocal predicate in Hungarian: Each to their own argument structure. In E. König and V. Gast, eds., *Reciprocal and Reflexives. Theoretical and Typological Explorations. Trends in Linguistics Studies and Monographs 192*, pages 411–450. Mouton de Gruyter.

Reinhart, Tanya. 2002. The theta system — An overview. *Theoretical Linguistics* 28:229–290.

Schütze, Carson. 1995. PP attachment and argumenthood. In C. T. Schütze, J. B. Ganger, and K. Broihier, eds., *Papers on Language Processing and Acquisition: MIT Working Papers in Linguistics Volume 26*, pages 95–151. MIT.

Siloni, Tal. 2001. Reciprocal verbs. In Y. N. Falk, ed., *Proceedings of the Israel Association of Theoretical Linguistics*. online publication at http://atar.mscc.huji.ac.il/ english/IATL/17/.

Siloni, Tal. 2008. The syntax of reciprocal verbs: An overview. In E. König and V. Gast, eds., *Reciprocals and Reflexives: Crosslinguistic and Theoretical Explorations*, pages 451–498. Mouton de Gruyter.

Siloni, Tal. 2011. Reciprocal verbs and symmetry. *Natural Language and Linguistic Theory* 30:261–320.

Webb, James. 2008. Instruments in LFG's argument structure. Master's thesis. University of Oxford.

Zaenen, Annie and Dick Crouch. 2009. OBLs hobble computations. In M. Butt and T. H. King, eds., *Proceedings of the LFG09 Conference*, pages 644–654. CSLI Publications.

11

Nested and Crossed Dependencies and the Existence of Traces

MARY DALRYMPLE AND TRACY HOLLOWAY KING

11.1 Introduction

Constraints on long-distance dependencies have long fascinated syntacticians. Recent work in constraint-based syntax has explored the issue of the existence of traces, and many arguments for traces have been convincingly refuted (Kaplan and Zaenen, 1989, Sag and Fodor, 1994, Sag, 1998, 2010, Dalrymple et al., 2007, among many others). However, little attention in this debate has been paid to patterns of nested and crossing dependencies: in many languages, intersecting long-distance dependencies must be nested, not crossing, and there have been few attempts to describe such patterns without appeal to traces. Here we provide the basis of an account which combines functional and configurational constraints, refines the notion of f-command, and appeals to the DIRECT ASSOCIATION HYPOTHESIS (Pickering and Barry, 1991, Pickering, 1993) to constrain the relation between a filler and the within-clause position that is relevant for patterns of nesting and crossing.

The well-known prohibition in English against crossing dependences was observed in early work by Kuno and Robinson (1972), who provide the examples in (20).

(20) ?This is the knife that this salami is easy to cut _ with _.

Nested, grammatical: Kuno and Robinson (1972, 477)

From Quirky Case to Representing Space: Papers in Honor of Annie Zaenen.
Tracy Holloway King and Valeria de Paiva.

(21) *This is the salami that my knife is easy to cut __ with __.

Crossing, ungrammatical: Kuno and Robinson (1972, 477)

The prohibition seems to crucially involve not only a filler but also an apparent gap position: the gap corresponding to the first filler must follow the gap corresponding to the second filter in order for a nested configuration to arise, and cases where the gap for the first filler appears between the second filler and its gap are ruled out.

Interestingly, such a prohibition is not operative in all languages; Maling and Zaenen (1982) were among the first to show that languages vary in allowing crossing dependencies. In particular, Norwegian allows crossing dependencies, as (22) shows:

(22) Denne gaven her vil du ikke gjette hvem jeg fikk __ fra   __.
     this   gift   here will you not guess who I   got __ from __

'This gift, you cannot guess who I got __ from __.'

Norwegian: Maling and Zaenen (1982, 236)

This indicates that constraints on nesting/crossing are part of the grammar of some but not all languages and do not constitute a more general psycholinguistic generalisation about how language is processed. Even if it turns out that the genesis of such constraints is through grammaticisation of processing requirements, the grammar of languages like English must be assumed to differ from the grammar of languages like Norwegian in imposing a prohibition against crossing.

In the following, we discuss and provide the basis of an analysis of crossing dependencies in languages like English. Of course, other factors are also known to influence the acceptability of long-distance dependency structures. These include d-linking (Pesetsky, 1987), relative acceptability of the counterpart with resumptive or intrusive pronouns (Maling and Zaenen, 1982, Engdahl, 1982), and general processing constraints (Gibson, 2000). Although we focus on the syntactic aspects of the relevant constructions, it is important to keep in mind that non-syntactic factors can give rise to unacceptability in examples which otherwise meet syntactic requirements for grammaticality.

11.2 Patterns to account for

Crossing disallowed: English Fodor (1978) notes that only a nested reading is available for the *tough*-construction in (23), though either a nested or a crossing reading is pragmatically plausible.

(23) What are boxes easy to store __ in __?   Fodor (1978, 448)

Not all examples involve the *tough*-construction; Pesetsky (1982) notes the contrast between (24a) and (24b):

(24) a. What subject do you know who to talk to __ about __?

b. *Who do you know what subject to talk to __ about __?

(Pesetsky, 1982, 267)

Crossing allowed: Norwegian Maling and Zaenen (1982) and Christiansen (1982) show that Norwegian allows both nesting ((25a)) and crossing ((25b)).

(25) a. Hvilke malerier$_i$ har ikke Petter noen vegg$_j$ å henge opp
which paintings$_i$ has not Peter any wall$_j$ to hang up
__$_i$ på __$_j$
__$_i$ on __$_j$
'Which paintings doesn't Peter have any wall to hang up on?'
Norwegian: Christiansen (1982, 79)

b. Hvilken vegg$_j$ har ikke Petter noen malerier$_i$ å henge opp
which wall$_j$ has not Peter any paintings$_i$ to hang up
__$_i$ på __$_j$
__$_i$ on __$_j$
'Which wall doesn't Peter have any paintings to hang up on?'
Norwegian: Christiansen (1982, 79)

Christiansen (1982, 78) also shows that non-interrogative sentences can have both nested and crossing readings in topicalisation constructions.

Crossing dispreferred: Swedish In Swedish, dispreferences for crossing readings are stronger than in Norwegian, though both nested and crossing readings are allowed. In many cases, as described by Maling and Zaenen (1982), resumptive pronouns must be used instead of gaps in crossing dependencies. However, Engdahl (1982) reports on an experiment which showed that although nested dependencies are preferred, both nesting and crossing readings are available, and Engdahl (1986) shows that when no ambiguity is possible, no resumptive pronoun is necessary.[1]

---

[1] The availability of crossing dependencies is not related to the number of dependencies. Maling and Zaenen (1982) show that Swedish and Norwegian allow three or more gaps while Norwegian and Icelandic allow no more than two *crossed* gaps.

(26) Strömming är den här kniven omöjlig   att rensa _ med _
     Herring   is this here knife impossible to clean _ with _.

'Herring, this knife is impossible to clean with.'

Swedish: Engdahl (1986, 128)

Engdahl (1986) claims that the relative unacceptability of crossing dependencies is a tendency and not a firm rule, saying that "... when a sentence is strongly pragmatically biased toward one association pattern, as in [(26)], people tend to report this reading, and only this reading, whereas a significant number of people report multiple readings for sentences where both assignments are possible".

Engdahl (1982, 169 ff.) shows that in many fully acceptable "crossing" examples, the gaps are adjacent ((27)). (28) allows either a crossing or a nested reading, since pragmatics allows either resolution. We return to the status of examples with adjacent gaps in Section 11.6.

(27) Det här problemet minns   jag inte hur jag bör   lösa _ _
     This problem   remember I   not how I   should solve _ _.

'This problem, I don't remember how I ought to solve.'

Swedish: Engdahl (1986, 128)

(28) Den här slaven minns   jag inte vem sultanen   erbjöd _ _
     this here slave remember I   not who the.sultan offered _ _

'This slave, I don't remember who the sultan offered .'

Swedish: Engdahl (1982, 170)

11.3 Previous LFG analyses

In their trace-based analysis of intersecting dependencies in English, Kaplan and Bresnan (1982) rule out crossing dependencies by disallowing cases where only one end of a filler-trace dependency appears between the filler and the trace in another dependency. Taking the Scandinavian data into account, Kaplan and Bresnan propose that languages may specify the degree of crossing that is allowed; they claim that languages like Icelandic allow one degree of filler-trace crossing, but not higher degrees, since in cases of two or more crossing dependencies a resumptive pronoun must be used.

In current LFG, long distance dependencies are handled by functional uncertainty (Kaplan and Maxwell, 1988), a relation between f-structures which allows a displaced element to fill a grammatical function within the clause without requiring traces in the c-structure tree. In this setting, the question of whether traces must be posited rests on the analysis of constraints on certain constructions which are apparently stated in terms of linear order constraints involving traces, such as the nested vs. crossing dependencies examined here.

11.4   A simple but inadequate account

We first consider and reject a simple account of the prohibition against crossing dependencies which uses only *f-precedence*, a relation between two f-structures based on the relative position of their c-structure counterparts. When analyzing these dependencies, we refer to the phrase corresponding to the gap as the OPERATOR (in the syntactic sense, e.g. a displaced *wh*-phrase in focus position); for purposes of discussion, we also assume traces, represented in the following as T1 and T2, though our final proposal does not assume that traces exist.

In sentences with multiple filler-gap dependencies, three possible configurations must be accounted for (O1 and O2 are the operators):

(29)   a.   Non-overlapping (acceptable):   *O1 ... T1 ... O2 ... T2*

    b.   Nested (acceptable):   c.   Crossing (unacceptable):

       O1 ... O2 ... T2 ... T1   *O1 ... O2 ... T1 ... T2*

A standard way of capturing ordering constraints in LFG is by using f-precedence. Two definitions of f-precedence have been proposed, the $\forall\forall$ and the $\forall\exists$ versions shown in (30) and (31) respectively.[2] A third $\exists\forall$ definition of f-precedence is also in principle possible, as in (32).

(30) $\forall\forall$ f-precedence (Zaenen and Kaplan, 1995, (12)):

    For two f-structure elements f_1 and f_2, f_1 *f-precedes* f_2 if and only if all the nodes that map onto f_1 c-precede all the nodes that map onto f_2:

    $f_1 <_f f_2$ iff for all $n_1 \in \phi^{-1}(f_1)$ and for all $n_2 \in \phi^{-1}(f_2)$, $n_1 <_c n_2$

(31) $\forall\exists$ f-precedence (Bresnan, 1995, (12)):

    f_1 f-precedes f_2 if and only if $\phi^{-1}(f_1)$ and $\phi^{-1}(f_2)$ are nonempty and all c_1 in $\phi^{-1}(f_1)$ precede some c_2 in $\phi^{-1}(f_2)$.

---

[2]Bresnan (1995, (17)) provides an alternative version of definition (31) which makes reference to the rightmost node corresponding to an f-structure. For our purposes, the two versions proposed by Bresnan (1995) are interchangable.

(32) $\exists\forall$ f-precedence:

f_1 f-precedes f_2 if and only if $\phi^{-1}(f_1)$ and $\phi^{-1}(f_2)$ are nonempty and some c_1 in $\phi^{-1}(f_1)$ precedes all c_2 in $\phi^{-1}(f_2)$.

However, given the configurations in (29), none of these definitions correctly discriminates among the three cases: it is impossible to distinguish the acceptable nesting cases from the unacceptable crossing ones with $\forall\forall$ f-precedence, or the acceptable non-overlapping cases from the unacceptable crossing ones with $\forall\exists$ f-precedence. $\exists\forall$ f-precedence distinguishes none of the cases.

(33)	$\forall\forall$	$\forall\exists$	$\exists\forall$
No overlap	O1 f-precedes O2	O1 f-precedes O2	O1 f-precedes O2
Nested	no relation	O2 f-precedes O1	O1 f-precedes O2
Crossing	no relation	O1 f-precedes O2	O1 f-precedes O2

11.5 Redefining the problem

Schematically, we require that if two dependencies INTERSECT, then if operator O1 is SUPERIOR in the relevant sense to operator O2, then T2 must be SUPERIOR in the relevant sense to T1.

(34) a. Permitted: b. Disallowed:

       O1 ... O2 ... T2 ... T1   *O1 ... O2 ... T1 ... T2*

Bresnan (1995) points out that different superiority factors are relevant for weak crossover constraints in different languages, with some languages defining SUPERIORITY in terms of f-structure, and others as a c-structure relation. Below, we consider how to define INTERSECTION of dependencies, the nature of O1 and O2 and the SUPERIORITY relation between them, and the definition of SUPERIORITY for T1 and T2.

11.5.1 Operator superiority

Many of the English examples which best illustrate the prohibition against crossing dependencies involve so-called *tough*-movement. Dalrymple and King (2000) show that the *tough*-construction involves an *unpronounced* operator in the subordinate clause. This means that the classic nesting and crossing examples involve at least one nonovert operator, as shown in (35).

(35) Which violin is this sonata tough to play on?

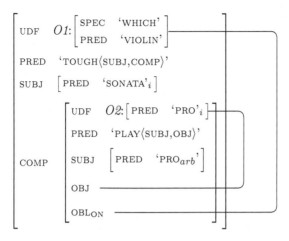

The operator $O2$ is the value of the UDF attribute (Unbounded Dependency Function: Asudeh 2010, 2012; see also Alsina 2008), and is also the object of *play*. There is no constituent in the c-structure that corresponds to $O2$. This means that the SUPERIORITY relation between operators cannot be defined in terms of position in the c-structure tree; the relevant relation must be *f-command*, a hierarchical relation defined at f-structure. The standard definition of f-command, shown in (36), works for many cases.

(36) F-command (original definition, to be replaced):

> f f-commands g if and only if f does not contain g, and all f-structures that contain f also contain g.   (Bresnan, 1982)

However, this definition does not always make the right predictions when two attributes share the same value, which is the situation we are interested in (R. Kaplan, p.c.; Dalrymple 2001). In (37), the f-structure f does not f-command the f-structure g, because there is an f-structure h that contains f but does not contain g.

(37) $\begin{bmatrix} \text{SUBJ} & f[\ ] \\ \text{OBJ} & g[\ ] \\ \text{XCOMP} & h\begin{bmatrix} \text{SUBJ} & \end{bmatrix} \end{bmatrix}$

Instead, we use the definition of f-command in (38).

(38) F-command (final definition):

f f-commands g if and only if:

$\neg(f \text{ GF}^*) = g$ (f does not contain g) and

$((\text{GF } f) \text{ GF}^+) = g$ (an f-structure whose value for some grammatical function GF is f also contains g). (Dalrymple, 2001)

Using this definition, we can define the relevant relation between the f-structure operators O1 and O2 as a special case of f-command which we call UDF-command, as in (39).

(39) F-command between operators:

Operator f UDF-commands operator g if and only if:

$\neg(f \text{ GF}^*) = g$ (f does not contain g) and

$((\text{UDF } f) \text{ GF}^* \text{ UDF}) = g$ (an f-structure whose value for the attribute UDF is f also contains an f-structure whose value for the attribute UDF is g).

We can now define the SUPERIORITY requirement for operators:

(40) If two dependencies INTERSECT, then if operator O1 UDF-**commands** operator O2, then T2 must be SUPERIOR to T1.

11.5.2 Intersecting dependencies

We next consider the definition of INTERSECTION between dependencies. We claim that O1 and O2 INTERSECT when they are in a MUTUAL F-COMMAND relation (general f-command, not UDF-command). In (35), the f-structure *O1* f-commands the f-structure *O2*, and *O2* also f-commands *O1*, since *O1* is the value of the OBL$_{\text{ON}}$ attribute in the COMP f-structure. We can, then, further specify our constraints by defining INTERSECTION as mutual f-command:

(41) If two dependencies **f-command each other**, then if operator O1 UDF-**commands** operator O2, then T2 must be SUPERIOR to T1.

11.5.3 Anchoring the dependencies

Finally, we turn to the definition of SUPERIORITY for the bottom of the dependency. At first glance, LFG's grammatical function (GF) hierarchy seems to give the right result for many of the cases.

(42) Proposal 1, to be discarded:

The f-structure corresponding to T2 (=O2) must be higher on the grammatical function hierarchy than the f-structure corresponding to T1 (=O1).

This produces the correct results for examples like *Which violin$_{O1}$ is this sonata tough O2 to play T2 on T1?*, because the *on*-marked oblique argument of *play* (*T1*) is lower than the object of *play* (*T2*) on the GF hierarchy. However, it does not work for equally-ranked obliques, as in (43), where there are two obliques, but only the nested reading is available.[3]

(43) Who$_{O1}$ is Bill easy *O2* to talk [to *T2*] [about *T1*]?

(modelled on Falk 2012, example 25)

The grammaticality of examples like (43) suggests that the nesting restriction has to do with linear order or f-precedence, not f-command or the grammatical function hierarchy. How can linear order constraints be imposed in a traceless theory of long-distance dependencies?

We appeal to the DIRECT ASSOCIATION HYPOTHESIS (Pickering and Barry, 1991, Pickering, 1993) to constrain the relation between T2 and T1. Pickering and Barry (1991) and Pickering (1993) propose that the apparent presence of traces arises from the retrieval and integration of a displaced constituent at the time of processing the predicate which subcategorises for the displaced item, which they call the subcategoriser.

(44) Direct Association Hypothesis (Pickering, 1993, 165): The filler is associated with the subcategoriser directly, without going via an empty category.

In many cases, the trace is assumed to appear immediately adjacent to the predicate (e.g., when it is the object), making it difficult to distinguish the purported position of the trace from the position of the predicate. Pickering and Barry (1991) and Pickering (1993) argue that where it is possible to distinguish the two, the predications of the Direct Association Hypothesis fare better than trace-based theories.

Adopting the Direct Association Hypothesis, we claim that the positions of the predicates subcategorising for the displaced items are crucially involved in constraints on nested/crossing dependencies. We refer to the relevant predicates as ANCHORS, and we say that a long-distance dependency is ANCHORED at its predicate. In (45), the anchor for *which violin* is *play*, and the anchor for the operator associated with *this sonata* is *on*.

---

[3] In his discussion of such examples, Pesetsky (1982) proposes that reanalysis has taken place, with the first preposition reanalysed as part of the verb; this reclassifies the first gap as an object and thus restores the required GF hierarchical relations between the two gap. We see no compelling evidence for reanalysis in these cases.

(45) *Which violin* is this sonata *O2* tough to   *play*   *on?*
     O1   *Anchor2 Anchor1*

We can now provide the final version of the constraint disallowing crossing dependencies:

(46) Nested dependencies, final version:

> If two dependencies **f-command each other**, then if operator O1 UDF-**commands** operator O2, then **the anchor for O1 must not f-precede the anchor for O2.**

We require that O1 does not f-precede O2 rather than that O2 f-precedes O1 because of the grammaticality of examples with shared anchors (§11.6). Due to space limitations, we leave the formal details of the anchoring relation and how it is established for future work.

11.6 Predictions: Shared Anchors

In the Swedish examples in (27) and (28), as well as in some Icelandic examples discussed by Maling and Zaenen (1982), the two gaps are adjacent and are arguments of the same verb. Such examples are claimed to be completely acceptable, although examples with crossing dependencies are otherwise somewhat degraded. In theories with traces, the traces are assumed to be in the same order as the canonical order of the overt NPs, and it is mysterious why they do not pattern with the other crossing cases in terms of acceptability.

On our analysis, these examples involve two operators anchored to the same predicate, and we correctly predict that these examples are grammatical even in a language where crossing dependencies are disallowed or dispreferred. This is because we disallow cases where the anchor of the earlier dependency precedes the anchor of the later dependency; when the dependencies are anchored to the same predicate, this constraint is not violated.

(47) þessum krakka hérna geter ðu   aldrei ímynað þér hvaða gjöf ég gaf
     this   boy   here can you never imagine   what gift I gave
     O1   *O2*   *Anchor1*
                                                Anchor2

Icelandic: Maling and Zaenen (1982, 236)

Unfortunately, it is difficult to come up with comparable examples in English to test our theory. We could try to construct examples with a double-object verb as the complement in a *tough*-construction, with extraction of one of the complements, but these examples seem quite bad, as in (48). However, it is difficult in general for double object verbs to appear as a complement in the *tough*-construction (though see Langendoen et al. 1973), as in (49), and so the source of the ungrammaticality in (48) is unclear.

(48) ??What kind of present is Bill tough to give?

(49) a. ??Bill is tough to give that kind of present.
     b. ??That kind of present is tough to give Bill.

11.7 Conclusion

We have proposed an account of the prohibition against crossing dependencies which combines f-structural and c-structural constraints and appeals to the Direct Association Hypothesis (Pickering and Barry, 1991, Pickering, 1993) in a traceless analysis of constraints on nested dependencies in LFG. By defining a notion of UDF-command and using the subcategorizing predicates to anchor the gaps, our account involves no significant extensions of the LFG formalism, does not require traces, and remains within the spirit of LFG.

This initial proposal leaves many avenues of exploration, the foremost of which is a formal account of how the anchoring relation is established and constrained. From the syntactic perspective, related phenomena such as superiority, resumptive pronouns, and restrictions on the number of crossing dependencies need to be addressed. From a broader perspective, pragmatic and processing constraints proposed on this topic should be reexamined.

Acknowledgments

Annie Zaenen's seminal and influential work on unbounded dependencies in Scandinavian is the basis upon which our proposals are built. For helpful comments on this work, we are grateful to Alex Alsina, Ash Asudeh, Yehuda Falk, Ron Kaplan, Prerna Nadathur, two anonymous reviewers, and audiences at: the workshop "Approaches to unbounded dependencies", Universitat Pompeu Fabra, March 2012 [funded by the grant "The syntax and information structure of unbounded dependencies", Ministerio de Ciencia e Innovación, Gobierno de España, PI Alex Alsina]; SE-LFG09 (9th South of England LFG Meeting), SOAS, March 2012; and the Syntax Working Group, University of Oxford, May 2012.

References

Alsina, Alex. 2008. A theory of structure-sharing: Focusing on long-distance dependencies and parasitic gaps. In M. Butt and T. H. King, eds., *On-line Proceedings of the LFG2008 Conference*.

Asudeh, Ash. 2010. Towards a unified theory of resumption. In A. Rouveret, ed., *Resumptive Pronouns at the Interfaces*. Amsterdam: John Benjamins.

Asudeh, Ash. 2012. *The Logic of Pronominal Resumption*. Oxford: Oxford University Press.

Bresnan, Joan. 1982. Control and complementation. In J. Bresnan, ed., *The Mental Representation of Grammatical Relations*, pages 282–390. Cambridge, MA: The MIT Press.

Bresnan, Joan. 1995. Linear order, syntactic rank, and empty categories: On weak crossover. In M. Dalrymple, R. M. Kaplan, J. T. Maxwell, and A. Zaenen, eds., *Formal Issues in Lexical-Functional Grammar*, pages 241–274. Stanford: CSLI Publications.

Christiansen, Kirsti Koch. 1982. On multiple filler-gap dependencies in Norwegian. In E. Engdahl and E. Ejerhed, eds., *Readings on Unbounded Dependencies in Scandinavian Languages*, pages 77–98. Stockholm: Almqvist and Wiksell.

Dalrymple, Mary. 2001. *Lexical Functional Grammar*, vol. 34 of *Syntax and Semantics*. New York: Academic Press.

Dalrymple, Mary, Ronald M. Kaplan, and Tracy Holloway King. 2007. The absence of traces: Evidence from weak crossover. In J. Grimshaw, J. Maling, C. Manning, J. Simpson, and A. Zaenen, eds., *Architectures, Rules, and Preferences: A Festschrift for Joan Bresnan*. Stanford: CSLI Publications.

Dalrymple, Mary, Ronald M. Kaplan, John T. Maxwell, III, and Annie Zaenen, eds. 1995. *Formal Issues in Lexical-Functional Grammar*. Stanford: CSLI Publications.

Dalrymple, Mary and Tracy Holloway King. 2000. Missing-object constructions: Lexical and constructional variation. In M. Butt and T. H. King, eds., *On-line Proceedings of the LFG2000 Conference*.

Engdahl, Elisabet. 1982. Restrictions on unbounded dependencies in Swedish. In E. Engdahl and E. Ejerhed, eds., *Readings on Unbounded Dependencies in Scandinavian Languages*, pages 151–174. Stockholm: Almqvist and Wiksell.

Engdahl, Elisabet. 1986. *Constituent Questions*. Dordrecht: Kluwer Academic Publishers.

Falk, Yehuda N. 2012. Superiority effects. MS, The Hebrew University of Jerusalem.

Fodor, Janet Dean. 1978. Parsing strategies and constraints on transformations. *Linguistic Inquiry* 9:427–473.

Gibson, Edward. 2000. The dependency locality theory: A distance-based theory of linguistic complexity. In A. Marantz, Y. Miyashita, and W. O'Neil, eds., *Image, Language, Brain*, pages 95–126. Cambridge, MA: The MIT Press.

Kaplan, Ronald M. and Joan Bresnan. 1982. Lexical-Functional Grammar: A formal system for grammatical representation. In J. Bresnan, ed., *The Mental Representation of Grammatical Relations*, pages 173–281. Cambridge, MA: The MIT Press. Reprinted in Dalrymple et al. (1995, 29–130).

Kaplan, Ronald M. and John T. Maxwell, III. 1988. An algorithm for functional uncertainty. In *Proceedings of the 12th International Conference on Computational Linguistics (COLING88)*, Budapest, vol. 1, pages 297–302. Reprinted in Dalrymple et al. (1995, 177–197).

Kaplan, Ronald M. and Annie Zaenen. 1989. Long-distance dependencies, constituent structure, and functional uncertainty. In M. Baltin and A. Kroch, eds., *Alternative Conceptions of Phrase Structure*, pages 17–42. Chicago University Press. Reprinted in Dalrymple et al. (1995, 137–165).

Kuno, Susumu and Jane J. Robinson. 1972. Multiple WH-questions. *Linguistic Inquiry* 3(4):463–487.

Langendoen, D. Terence, Nancy Kalish, and John Dore. 1973. Dative questions: A study of the relation of acceptability to grammaticality of an English sentence type. *Cognition* 2(4):451–478.

Maling, Joan and Annie Zaenen. 1982. A phrase structure account of Scandinavian extraction phenomena. In P. Jacobson and G. K. Pullum, eds., *The Nature of Syntactic Representation*, pages 229–282. Dordrecht: D. Reidel.

Pesetsky, David. 1982. *Paths and Categories*. Ph.D. thesis, MIT.

Pesetsky, David. 1987. Wh-in-situ: Movement and unselective binding. In E. Reuland and A. ter Meulen, eds., *The Representation of (In)definiteness*. Cambridge, MA: The MIT Press.

Pickering, Martin. 1993. Direct association and sentence processing: A reply to Gorrell and to Gibson and Hancock. *Language and Cognitive Processes* 8(2):163–196.

Pickering, Martin and Guy Barry. 1991. Sentence processing without empty categories. *Language and Cognitive Processes* 6(3):229–259.

Sag, Ivan A. 1998. Without a trace. MS, Stanford University.

Sag, Ivan A. 2010. English filler-gap constructions. *Language* 86(3):486–545.

Sag, Ivan A. and Janet D. Fodor. 1994. Extraction without traces. In *Proceedings of the Thirteenth West Coast Conference on Formal Linguistics*. Stanford: CSLI Publications.

Zaenen, Annie and Ronald M. Kaplan. 1995. Formal devices for linguistic generalizations: West Germanic word order in LFG. In *Linguistics and Computation*, CSLI Lecture Notes, number 52. Stanford: CSLI Publications. Reprinted in Dalrymple et al. (1995, 215–239).

Part III

Semantics and Beyond

12

Representing Paths of Motion in VerbNet

JENA D. HWANG, MARTHA PALMER, AND ANNIE ZAENEN

12.1 Introduction

Rich, explicit semantic representations are necessary elements in the automatic interpretation and processing of natural text. VerbNet, a lexical resource that incorporates both semantic and syntactic information, has been used in various tasks in Natural Language Processing (NLP) including semantic role labeling (Swier and Stevenson, 2004) and creation of conceptual graphs (Hensman and Dunnion, 2004). Furthermore, the detailed semantic predicate information that VerbNet provides in its verb classes has been used to derive appropriate inferences from natural texts (Zaenen et al., 2008). Thus, whether it is for text-specific semantic representations or for inferencing, it is important that VerbNet's representation be explicit, unambiguous and consistent. Consider the following examples:

(1) a. The horse jumped *in the paddock*.

b. The horse jumped *into the neighbor's garden*.

In both sentences, the italicized prepositional phrases refer to a location of a sort. The unmistakable difference here is that the phrase in the first sentence refers to a location that remains static over the course of the event, while the phrase in the second sentence refers to the location at which the horse has arrived by the end the event. Additionally, the implication present in the second sentence, though lacking in the first, is that of the change of location: at the beginning of the event the horse

From Quirky Case to Representing Space: Papers in Honor of Annie Zaenen.
Tracy Holloway King and Valeria de Paiva.
Copyright © 2013, CSLI Publications.

is located in an unknown location and by the end of the event it has moved to the neighbor's garden.

In a study by Zaenen et al. (2008), the authors seek to extract such inferences relating to the pre- and post-states of change of location from VerbNet predicate information. Their general conclusion is that even though many of the VerbNet classes contain information leading to a path interpretation, VerbNet is limited in that not all VerbNet classes of change of location code for path information and is inconsistent in its representation across classes. That is, when comparing classes that do contain the desired path information for inference making, the information is not necessarily consistent across all of VerbNet, making the inferencing difficult.

The purpose of this paper is to evaluate the current status of Verb-Net's representation of path phrases to identify the existing inconsistencies and limitations, and finally, to suggest a more explicit and semantically informed representation for paths of motion in VerbNet. Unifying the current path representations into a single established representation is becoming critical as we are also now attempting to identify and classify constructions that involve paths of motion. Studies such as the one in Hwang et al. (2010) show the separation of caused motion from non-caused motion usages in text is possible with high accuracy. Consequently, it calls for an explicit representation of path that can then be associated with the caused motion usages.

12.1.1 VerbNet Background

VerbNet (Kipper et al., 2008) is a lexical resource that expands on the verb classification of Levin (1993). In accordance with Levin's work, VerbNet's classification of verbs is based on the hypothesis that verbs that are realized in similar syntactic environments will share in their semantics. That is, VerbNet class membership is determined by shared meaning and shared syntactic alternation. Thus, a class is characterized by (1) a set of semantic roles shared by all members in the class, (2) syntactic frames in which the verbs occur, and (3) the semantic representation of the event (designated by E). Additionally, VerbNet's class definition is hierarchical in nature; meaning that a member can either be associated at the most general level of class description or at one of the more semantically specific subclass levels. Take as an example the *put-9.1* class[1] shown in example 2. The *put-9.1* class includes verbs of putting, such as *arrange* and *position* and is associated with the thematic roles: Agent, Theme, Destination.

---

[1] The question mark in front of the semantic representation means that in that given sentence the role is not instantiated

(2)

class: put-9.1	
Roles	AGENT, THEME, DESTINATION
Members	arrange, position, situate, etc.
Frame	NP V NP PP.DESTINATION
Ex(ample) **Syn(tax)** **Sem(antics)**	*I put the book on the table.* AGENT V THEME DESTINATION cause(Agent,E) motion(during(E),Theme) not(Prep(start(E),Theme,Destination)) Prep(end(E),Theme,Destination)
subclass: put-9.1-1	
Members	bury, deposit, embed, etc.
Frame	NP V NP
Ex **Syn** **Sem**	*I stashed the book.* AGENT V THEME cause(Agent,E) motion(during(E),Theme) not(Prep(start(E),Theme,?Destination)) Prep(end(E),Theme,?Destination)

The subclass *put-9.1-1* and its member verbs (i.e., *bury, deposit*) inherits all of the roles and frames associated with its parent class *put-9.1*. Additionally, the subclass defines a more specific frame (i.e., NP V NP) that does not apply to the parent class. Each of the syntactic frames in this class is defined by both syntactic and semantic representations.

12.1.2 Goals

For the purposes of our study we hope to address the issues of representing paths or elements of paths involved in physical changes of location. First, we seek to distinguish the representation of a static location from a path of motion. That is, we want to be able to distinguish arguments denoting the path of motion (see ex. 1b) from constituents that encode locative information about where an event occurs (see ex. 1a). Second, we want to be able to account for all the pieces of a path of motion: *source* – where the moving entity is at the beginning of the event, *trajectory* – the path over which the moving entity travels, and *destination* – where the moving entity is at the end of the event. Third, we aim for a representation that is guided by semantics rather than syntax. Consider the following two sentences:

(3) a. The horse jumped *the fence.*

  b. The horse jumped *over the fence.*

Both phrases in italics, despite their differing syntactic functions, semantically are the same. They refer to the trajectory over which *the horse* travels. A successful semantic representation of path of motion should treat the two phrases in the same manner, in such a way that the same motion inference available to one is available to the other. Finally, what we seek is an explicit representation that supports proper inferencing and reasoning based on what we know about motion and change of location (Zaenen et al., 2008, 2010). For example, given sentence 1b we want to be able to conclude that the horse is outside *the neighbor's garden* at the beginning of the event and is located inside *the neighbor's garden* at the end of the event.

12.2 Current VerbNet Treatment of Path of Motion

There currently is no established or consistent manner representing path information of change of location verbs in VerbNet. However, we observe that there are a number of general tendencies in how VerbNet currently handles the path of motion. We will focus on specific predicates (i.e., location(), Prep(), via() and direction()) and what we perceive as inconsistencies in their current usage.

12.2.1 Predicate location()

In general, for classes in which the realized piece of the path refers to either endpoint of the change of location, VerbNet makes use of the location() predicate in conjunction with the motion() predicate to represent path information. Consider the *slide-11.2* class:

(4)

slide-11.2	
Roles	Agent, Theme, Source, Destination
Frame	NP V PP.source
Ex **Syn** **Sem**	*The book slid from the table onto the floor.* Theme V Source Destination motion(during(E), Theme) location(start(E), Theme, Source) location(end(E), Theme, Destination)

The specification of path in terms of location() allows for VerbNet to specify that the Theme is at the specified location at the start of the event (i.e., *the table*), is set in motion during (i.e., *during(E)*) the event, and is located at Destination (i.e., *the floor*) by the end of the event. However, it is not always the case that only change of location type events will have location() predicates marked as the start or end of an event. In the example sentence in (5), the predicate location() is used as a means of indicating that the decoration (i.e., Theme; *the name*) is made on the ring (i.e., Destination) and does not indicate that there was a change of location that occurred over the course of the event.

(5)

illustrate-25.3	
Ex	*The jeweler decorated the ring with the name.*
Syn	Agent V Destination Theme
Sem	cause(E, Agent) created_image(result(E), Theme) location(end(E), Theme, Destination))

Even if we were to say that change of location happens only for classes that have the `motion()` predicate along with a `location()` predicate, it is not a reliable measure as there are classes such as *banish-10.2* (e.g., *The king deported the general to the isle.*) that fail to specify the predicate `motion()` in their frames.

12.2.2 Predicate Prep()

If the sentence expresses the trajectory of the motion, rather than the starting or ending location, VerbNet currently tends to favor the use of the `Prep()` accompanied by the `motion()` predicate as seen in example 6:

(6)

run-51.3.2		
Roles	Agent, Theme, Location	
Frame	NP V PP.location	
	Ex	*The horse jumped over the fence.*
	Syn	Theme V Location
	Sem	motion(during(E), Theme) Prep(E, Theme, Location)

The most obvious problem is that unlike the `location()` predicate that represents the location of an event, the `Prep()` predicate, on its own, does not represent a specific meaning. That is, given the `Prep()` predicate alone, it is difficult to determine what relationship Theme and Location have with each other and how they relate to event *E*. Even if we set this problem aside, this representation of path is somewhat problematic since the same predicate `Prep()` is used to represent a static location of an object such as *in the corner* in the sentence *"The statue stood in the corner"* (*spatial_configuration-47.6*), which is unlike the trajectory `Prep()` as used in example 6. The way to distinguish such instances is seemingly to look for the `motion()` predicate along with the `Prep()`. However, such a heuristic is not fail-safe either. Consider example 7 as a comparison to example 6, in which the representation (e.g., the use of the `Prep()` in the presence of `motion()`) seems to look

much like the representation we see in (6). However, unlike (6), the
Prep() in the *swarm-47.5.1* class refers to a static location in which
the motion occurs.

(7)

swarm-47.5.1	
Ex	*Bees are swarming in the garden.*
Syn	Theme V Location
Sem	exist(during(E), Theme)
	motion(during(E), Theme)
	Prep(during(E), Theme, Location)

Finally, unlike the location() predicate, which we have seen in the
previous section, and via() and direction() predicates, which we
will see in the following section, Prep() is a variable predicate that
gets instantiated by a specific preposition. Our intent is to replace this
with predicates such as via() or direction() that have argument slots
of prepositions, thus avoiding second order logic.

12.2.3 Predicates via() and direction()

Less frequent representations of the path of motion are the direction()
and the via() predicates. Like location() and Prep(), they are used
in conjunction with the motion() predicate. The following is an example of the use of the direction() predicate:

(8)

run-51.3.2	
Roles	Agent, Theme, Location
Frame	NP V NP.location
Ex	*The horse jumped the stream.*
Syn	Theme V Location
Sem	motion(during(E), Theme)
	via(during(E), Theme, Location)

Although Location roles in examples 6 and 8 specify the trajectory
along which the Theme moves, the creators of this class chose to treat
(8) as a case of via() instead of Prep() as seen in (6). The motivation
behind this treatment was likely a syntactic one – the Location in
(6) is found in a prepositional phrase, while the same role appears
as the noun phrase in (8). The predicate via() appears in two other
classes, *vehicle-51.4.1* (e.g., *She skated the canals.*) and *nonvehicle-
51.4.2* (e.g., *She rowed the canals.*); both of which are also classes where
the syntactic frame in which the path of motion appears is taken into
account in the creation of the semantic frames.

The direction() predicate is generally found to represent the meaning of the trajectory in a given path of motion as seen in example 9. This representation is comparable to the one for (6). One advantage this representation has over the use of Prep() is that while with Prep() the actual preposition is instantiated from the context, the direction() specifies that the THEME is directed towards the LOCATION during the event. Outside of this factor, it is not clear that VerbNet needs to distinguishes the path information in (9) from that in (6).

(9)

escape-51.1	
Roles	THEME, LOCATION
Frame	NP V PP.OBLIQUE
Ex	*The prisoners advanced across the field.*
Syn	THEME V OBLIQUE
Sem	motion(during(E),Theme)
	direction(during(E),Prep_Dir^2,Theme,Oblique)

12.2.4 Semantic Roles

VerbNet, as discussed above, currently does not have an established method of representing the path of motion. The representations for source, trajectory and destination are currently spread over several different representations, and they are generally specific to the needs of the class in which they are found. Furthermore, another difficulty in representing path of motion comes from the fact that VerbNet classes do not contain the necessary semantic roles to properly represent the path of motion. For example, consider the *run-51.3.2* class seen in example 6. Currently this class specifies AGENT, THEME and LOCATION, allowing for sentences such as *The horse jumped over the river* or *The horse jumped onto the shore*. However, when more than one piece of the path of motion is realized, these roles are no longer adequate.

(10) a. The horse jumped from the rock over the river.

b. The horse jumped from the rock over the river onto the shore.

For complete representations of sentences 10a and 10b, we would need three semantic roles: source, trajectory and destination. A majority of the classes of motion have at least one of these three roles. A number of classes such as *slide-11.2* (see ex. 4) and *pour-9.5* currently assign up to two semantic roles for the path of motion. Other classes of verbs that readily take motion paths such as *push-12* do not specify any of the roles above.

12.3 Proposed Path Predicate

For a consistent and semantically informed VerbNet representation of path of motion, we propose a single `path()` predicate accompanied by a consistent inclusion of a `motion()` predicate:

Roles	SOURCE, TRAJECTORY, DESTINATION
Semantics	motion(during(E), THEME)
	path(E, Source, Trajectory, Destination)

The proposed predicate includes the event E that links the path to the E of the `motion()` predicate, and by association, the THEME in motion. Additionally, the `path()` predicate includes all three roles that indicate the different parts of the path of motion, namely, the SOURCE, TRAJECTORY and DESTINATION roles. The `path()` predicate would allow for the representation of all possible combinations in the expression of path, which thus far has not been possible in VerbNet. Here is the revised view of the *run-51.3.2* class:

(11)

run-51.3.2 *(revised)*
Roles:
AGENT THEME SOURCE TRAJECTORY DESTINATION
Frame: NP V PP.TRAJECTORY
The horse jumped over the river. motion(during(E),Theme) path(E, ?Source, Trajectory, ?Destination)
Frame: NP V NP.TRAJECTORY
The horse jumped the river. motion(during(E),Theme) path(E,?Source, Trajectory, ?Destination)
Frame: NP V PP.SOURCE PP.DESTINATION
The horse jumped from the rocks onto the shore. motion(during(E),Theme) path(E, Source, ?Trajectory, Destination)

The `path()` predicate, thus, would replace both the `Prep()` (see ex. 6) and the `via()` (see ex. 8). With the replacement of `Prep()`, we are achieving a more semantically explicit representation of the path. The replacement of `via()` allows us to represent the semantics of the trajectory independently of the constituent's syntactic expression.

Additionally, as seen in the examples above, not all roles in the `path()` predicate have to be instantiated in the sentence, which are allowed under representation VerbNet's semantic representation. These uninstantiated roles or *null instantiated complements* (Fillmore, 1986) are syntactically unexpressed but, nonetheless, semantically essential. For example, even though SOURCE and DESTINATION are not expressed in *"Horse jumped the river"*, the semantics of these roles are still implicit in the sentence. Recognizing the existence of uninstantiated roles allows us to make semantically implicit information explicit in the representation. (Palmer et al., 1986).

Furthermore, the path usage of the `location()` predicate (as opposed to the static location usage as shown in ex. 5) and the `direction()` predicate would be united under the same representation.

(12) a.

slide-11.2 *(revised from ex. 4)*	
Ex	*The book slid from the table onto the floor.*
Sem	motion(during(E), Theme)
	path(E, Source, ?Trajectory, Destination)

   b.

escape-51.1 *(revised from ex. 9)*	
Ex	*The prisoners advanced across the field.*
Sem	motion(during(E),Theme)
	path(E, ?Source, Trajectory, ?Destination)

Finally, the advantage of a consistent and explicit representation of path of motion is that we get the desired change of location inferences for free. In other words, in the sentence in example 4, the inference we want to retrieve is that the *the book* is *on the table* before the event begins and is no longer there at the end of the event. In the same way, *the book* is not *on the floor* before the event, but is there at the end of the event. Currently, VerbNet generally, albeit inconsistently, handles this by using the `start()` and `end()` predicates to show where the THEME is located at the specified point in time. Take the *banish-10.2* class as an example:[3]

(13) a. *"The king banished the general from the army."*
       cause(Agent, E)
       location(start(E), Theme, Source)
       not(location(end(E), Theme, Source))

   b. *"The king deported the general to the isle."*
       cause(Agent, E)
       location(start(E), Theme, ?Source)
       location(end(E), Theme, Destination)

---

[3]It is not by omission that `motion()` is not present in this example. This class does not currently include it, although it should as a class expressing change of location.

Even in a single VerbNet class we see that the representation is incomplete and inconsistent. In (13a), only the Source location is marked as being true at the beginning of the event but not at the end of the event. In (13b), both Source location and Destination are represented, but neither of them are marked as not being true at the other points in time. For a complete representation of all possible inferences we would have had to specify:

location(start(E), Theme, Source)
location(end(E), Theme, Destination)
not(location(start(E), Theme, Destination))
not(location(end(E), Theme, Source))

By having separate roles for Source, Trajectory, and Destination roles, we can make a generalization that for every instance of a `path()` predicate the entity in motion will be (1) located at the source at the beginning (and *only* at the beginning) of the event, (2) located over the specified trajectory during (and *only* during) the event, and (3) located at the destination at the end (and *only* at the end) of the event.

12.4   Final Considerations and Conclusion

In this paper, we have presented the current status of VerbNet semantic representations with respect to verbs expressing change of location. Currently, VerbNet has no consistent way of handling the path of motion required for representing change of location. Moreover, semantic predicates that currently represent path of motion are not exclusive to path of motion, making the identification and extraction of change of location verbs difficult. We have therefore proposed new predicates that can be used to represent the verbs that specify path information.

There still remain outstanding issues and linguistically interesting considerations that will require our attention. These include, although are not limited to, the possibility of additional path elements (e.g., *"The horse trotted towards the stables"*), possible need for recognizing verbs that imply but do not strictly entail motion (e.g., *"She urged her mother into the basement"*) and the need for allowing for multiple and semantically varied trajectories (e.g., *"The hamster ran over the table, under the fridge and across the kitchen floor"*). Even so, the representation we have proposed in this paper will take us a step further towards to making paths more semantically explicit and meaningful, and more consistent across all relevant classes, allowing for easier inferencing.

The next step to our study is the implementation of this representation in VerbNet. We noted at the beginning of this paper that we hope to limit the scope of what we mean by "motion" to physical changes of location. However, defining a clear boundary between the physical and the abstract or metaphorical will be no small task. Because VerbNet classes do not make a distinction between abstract and physical meanings of verbs (e.g., *throw-17.1* includes both *Steve threw the ball into the box* and *Steve threw light into the corners of the room*) we cannot avoid abstract or metaphorical expressions of change of location. However, if we try to expand our predicate representations to also include more abstract changes, such as change of state, then they may no longer be appropriate for simple changes of location.[4]

Another implementation challenge is the possibility of semantic coercion. In other words, verbs such as *rumble* in the *sound_emission-43.2* class or *shiver* in the *body_internal_states-40.6* class do not intrinsically carry or readily allow the semantics of motion. However, there are attested usages such as *The truck rumbled past* or *I shivered into the driver's seat*, where the semantics of directed motion is coerced by the virtue of the addition of the path phrase. Thus, the direct inclusion of a path of motion representation in the classes such as *sound_emission-43.2* and *body_internal_states-40.6* would not be representative of the class in question. However, for such classes we envision that a frame that defines the path of motion representation should be linked to the class as a means of signalling that such a construction (and its corresponding semantic representation) is also available for these classes (Hwang et al., 2010, Bonial et al., 2011).

Acknowledgements

We gratefully acknowledge the support of DARPA/IPTO funding under the GALE program, DARPA/CMO Contract No. HR0011-06-C-0022 and the National Science Foundation Grants NSF-1116782, A Bayesian Approach to Dynamic Lexical Resources for Flexible Language Processing. Any opinions, findings, and conclusions or recommendations expressed in this material are those of the authors and do not necessarily reflect the views of the National Science Foundation.

References

Bonial, Claire, Susan Windisch Brown, Jena D. Hwang, Christopher Parisien, Martha Palmer, and Suzanne Stevenson. 2011. Incorporating coercive constructions into a verb lexicon. In *Proceedings of the ACL 2011 Workshop on Relational Models of Semantics*. Portland, Oregon.

---

[4]We also expect challenges posed by verbs that specify path but do not indicate changes in location as exemplified by the sentence *A river runs from Palo Alto to Menlo Park*.

Fillmore, Charles J. 1986. Pragmatically controlled zero anaphora. *Berkeley Linguistics Society* 12:95–107.

Hensman, Svetlana and John Dunnion. 2004. Automatically building conceptual graphs using VerbNet and WordNet. In *Proceedings of the 2004 international symposium on Information and communication technologies (ISICT '04)*.

Hwang, Jena D., Rodney D. Nielsen, and Martha Palmer. 2010. Towards a domain independent semantics: Enhancing semantic representation with construction grammar. In *Proceedings of the NAACL HLT Workshop on Extracting and Using Constructions in Computational Linguistics*, pages 1–8. Los Angeles, California: Association for Computational Linguistics.

Kipper, Karin, Anna Korhonen, Neville Ryant, and Martha Palmer. 2008. A large-scale classification of English verbs. *Language Resources and Evaluation Journal* 42(1):21–40.

Levin, Beth. 1993. *English Verb Classes and Alternations: A Preliminary Investigation*. University of Chicago Press.

Palmer, Martha, Deborah Dahl, Rebecca Passonneau, Lynette Hirschman, Marcia Linebarger, and John Dowding. 1986. Recovering implicit information. In *Proceedings of the Sixth Annual Meeting of the Association for Computational Linguistics*. New York.

Swier, Robert S. and Suzanne Stevenson. 2004. Unsupervised semantic role labelling. In *Proceedings of the 2004 Conference on Empirical Methods in Natural Language Processing (EMNLP 2004)*, pages 95–102. Barcelona, Spain.

Zaenen, Annie, Danny Bobrow, Lucas Champollion, Cleo Condoravdi, and Liz Coppock. 2010. From language to reasoning: A case study. *Linguistic Issues in Language Technology (LiLT)* 4(1).

Zaenen, Annie, Cleo Condoravdi, and Danny Bobrow. 2008. The encoding of lexical implications in VerbNet predicates of change of locations. In *Proceedings of the Sixth International Conference on Language Resources and Evaluation (LREC'08)*. Marrakech, Morocco: European Language Resources Association (ELRA).

13

You Will Be Lucky To Break Even

Lauri Karttunen

There is a substantial body of literature on the semantics of English verbal complement constructions starting with Kiparsky and Kiparsky (1970) and Karttunen (1971a, 1973), including Rudanko (1989, 2002), Nairn et al. (2006), Egan (2008) and Karttunen (2012). These studies have developed a semantic classification of verbs and verb-noun collocations that take clausal complements. They focus on constructions that give rise to implied commitments that the author cannot disavow without being incoherent or without contradicting herself. For example, (1a) presupposes that Kim had not rescheduled the meeting, while (1b) entails that she did not and presupposes that she intended to reschedule it.

(1) a. Kim forgot that she had not rescheduled the meeting.

b. Kim forgot to reschedule the meeting.

Factive constructions like *forget that X* involve presuppositions; implicative constructions like *forget to X* give rise to entailments and may carry presuppositions.

Presuppositions persist under negation, in questions and *if*-clauses. Questions and *if*-clauses do not yield any entailments about the truth of embedded complements but negations of some types of implicative sentences have entailments. For example, the simple negation (without any focus intonation) of (1b), *Kim did not forget to reschedule the meeting*, entails that Kim did reschedule the meeting and presupposes, as (1b) does, that it was her intention to do so.

It is well-known that there are factive adjective constructions (Norrick, 1978) such as *be pleased that X* but there is no systematic study yet

From Quirky Case to Representing Space: Papers in Honor of Annie Zaenen.
Tracy Holloway King and Valeria de Paiva.
Copyright © 2013, CSLI Publications.

of implicative adjective constructions. This paper makes a start with one such case, the *be lucky to X* and its sister constructions *be unlucky to X*, *be fortunate to X*, and *be unfortunate to X*.

We show that *be lucky to X* has a regular meaning of a two-way implicative construction (Section 13.1) and an idiomatic sense limited to the future tense that suggests that X probably will not happen (Section 13.3). We show (Section 13.2) that the construction is not factive, contrary to the ensconced view in recent literature, and propose a way to understand and reconcile the opposing intuitions. Most of the example sentences in the paper were collected with Google searches.[1]

13.1 *Be lucky to X* is a two-way implicative

Table 1 presents a few examples of two-way implicative verbs and verbnoun collocations from Karttunen (1971a, 1973, 2012). Two-way implicative constructions yield an entailment both in positive and negative contexts. The $++ \mid --$ signature indicates that *manage to X* and *use the occasion to X* yield a positive entailment about X in positive contexts and a negative entailment in negative contexts. The $+- \mid -+$ signature indicates that *fail to X* and *waste the opportunity to X* give us a negative entailment about X under positive polarity, and vice versa.

$++ \mid --$ implicatives	$+- \mid -+$ implicatives
manage to X	fail to X
remember to X	forget to X
use the occasion to X	squander the chance to X
have the chutzpah to X	waste the opportunity to X

TABLE 1 Examples of two-way implicative constructions

The examples of *be lucky to X* in (2) and (3) show that the the construction has the same implicative signature as *manage to X* and *use the occasion to X*, $++ \mid --$.

(2) a. A family of eight is lucky to be alive after flames destroyed their home.

  b. India has been lucky to witness several eclipses over the past two years.

  c. He thought Fraser had been lucky to come home in one piece.

The sentences in (2) entail that the complement clause is true, the examples in (3) have a negative entailment.

---

[1]The exceptions are (1), (6), (7), and (8) that were made up by the author.

(3) a. Anyway, I was not lucky to get a table on this trip. Maybe next time.

b. Pakistan has not been lucky to have genuine leaders after the demise of the Quaid-i-Azam.

c. At thirty-one, Esther had not been lucky to find a man to marry her.

The examples in (4) show the interaction of *be lucky to X* with some other two-way implicatives.

(4) a. I was really lucky to manage to recover some files.

b. She had been lucky to forget to wear her watch yesterday.

c. I still have not been lucky to manage to get my orchids to flower again.

(4a) entails that the innermost complement clause is true. In (4b) and (4c), *forget to* and *not* flip the polarity to yield a negative entailment.

The negative examples in (3) and (4) feature the ordinary *not*, the examples in (5) contain a metalinguistic *not* (Karttunen and Peters, 1979, Horn, 1985).

(5) a. He is not lucky to be alive, he is blessed.

b. The girl is NOT lucky to have 2 mums, she needs a father figure.

c. Cody is not lucky to get to go to Cornell. Cornell is lucky to have him!

In all the examples in (5), the complement clause of *lucky* is presumed to be true. The author is not in disagreement about the objective facts. The point of metalinguistic negation is to assert that it is inappropriate to use the construction *be lucky to X* to describe the situation, contrary to what someone might have said or thought. In the case of (5c), it is understood that Cody is going to Cornell, the issue is whether it is Cody or Cornell that can be said to be lucky.

13.2 *Be lucky to X* is not factive

Given the examples in (3) it is obvious that *be lucky to X* is not a factive construction although it has been erroneously classified as such by Karttunen (1971a) and many later authors. Norrick (1978) and Barker (2002) cite Wilkinson (1976). If *be lucky to X* were factive, the X complements in (3) would be presupposed to be true but in fact the sentences in (3) entail that the complement clauses are false. Norrick and Barker make the wrong call because they fail to consider any *lucky* examples with negation. Wilkinson (1976) classifies *be lucky to X* as factive but correctly identifies *be lucky enough to X* as implicative because of its behavior under negation (p. 173, fn. 13).

Let us consider two kinds of conversational situations, A and B, to help us understand how the illusion of *be lucky to X* being factive might arise. In situation A the participants in the conversation have not talked about X, the truth or falsity of X is not self-evident, X is not part of the "common ground" of the conversation. If we hear (6) in such a situation, without any previous knowledge about Kim's finances,

(6) Kim was not lucky to have a well-paying job. She needed more money.

we conclude that Kim did not have a well-paying job because *be lucky to X* is a $++ \mid --$ implicative construction. The same may be true of some of the other EVALUATIVE adjectives listed by Barker (2002).

If we replace *lucky* in (6) by an EMOTIVE adjective such as *content*, the conclusion is different.

(7) Kim was not content to have a well-paying job. She needed more money.

The construction *be content to X* is factive: it presupposes X. If Kim having a well-paying job is not yet in the common ground, it becomes part of it in (7) by ACCOMMODATION (Karttunen, 1974, Stalnaker, 1974, Lewis, 1979). But there is no accommodation in the case of (6): it does not add to the common ground the assumption that Kim has a well-paying job, in fact it entails the opposite. The accommodation test shows that an emotive adjective such as *content* is factive, an evaluative adjective such as *lucky* is not factive.

The other type of conversational situation, B, for *be lucky to X* is a situation where X being true is part of the common ground, already accepted by the discourse participants at least for the sake of the conversation. This is the kind situation for the examples of metalinguistic negation in (5). In the B type situation (6) has to be understood as not contradicting that Kim had a well-paying job but the presupposition that she was lucky to have it.

The difference between A and B type situations is relevant not only for the interpretation of negation, it also carries on to questions. In an A type situation the question

(8) Was Cody lucky to get into Cornell?

is a genuine question about whether Cody got into Cornell with the presupposition that it would have been a good thing for Cody. In a B situation where we already know that Cody got into Cornell, (8) becomes a question about whether getting into Cornell was lucky for

Cody in some sense of *lucky*. Did Cody get in on his merits or because of some fortuitous sequence of events that he cannot take any credit for? Or, given what we know about how the future unfolded or might have unfolded, was getting to Cornell overall a good thing for Cody or not?

13.3 The idiom *will be lucky to X*

Although *be lucky to X* can be a two-way implicative in all of its tense forms, in the future tense, and only in the future tense, it may have another, idiomatic, interpretation.

(9) Wong Kwan will be lucky to break even.[2]

Without special emphasis on any of the words, (9) entails that Wong Kwan is not likely to break even. It is possible to read (9) differently, to interpret it as a positive prediction about Kwan's return on investments but that requires a non-standard stress pattern, *Wong Kwan WILL be lucky to break even*. But without a special emphasis on *will* and with emphasis on *lucky*, (9) favors the idiomatic interpretation, a pessimistic prognostic on Wong Kwan's financial future. As we will see in Section 13.4, this idiomatic reading of *will be lucky to X* is also subject to several other conditions.

A sample of idiomatic *will be lucky to X* examples picked from Google searches is shown in (10).

(10) a. Without a track record, they will be lucky to get anyone to listen to, much less steal, their ideas.
 b. Scientists claim that we will be lucky to have 50 more years before turtles and tortoises are extinct.
 c. Relative or not if anyone ever lays an inappropriate hand on my kids they will be lucky to be left breathing afterwards.
 d. I think they will be lucky to not get the wooden spoon.
 e. The Raiders will be lucky to win six games in 2012.

It is possible to strengthen *lucky* to *quite lucky*, *very lucky* and *extremely lucky* without losing the idiomatic meaning, examples in (11).

(11) a. You will be quite lucky to find a place that allows ONE dog, let alone two.

---

[2]This example comes from *FactBank* (Saurí and Pustejovsky, 2009). It is the only example in FactBank that contains the adjective *lucky* with a clausal complement. FactBank annotates the veridicality of each predicate on a seven-point scale: CT+ (certainly true), PR+ (probably true), PS+ (possibly true), unmarked, PS− (possibly false), PR− (probably false) and CT− (certainly false). FactBank tags *break* in (9) as PR− (probably false). This is correct but not of much use without additional *be lucky to X* judgments in other tenses, under negation, interrogatives, etc.

   b. With the worst starting QB in the league throwing to the worst wide receiving corps in the league, they will be very lucky to win 6 games.

   c. If you hit moguls at high speed you will be very lucky to stay standing.

   d. Yeah we will be extremely lucky to get either of those guys.

   e. The bank will be very lucky to reach even that diminished level again in the immediate future.

When *lucky* in *will be lucky to X* is strengthened towards *extremely lucky*, the likelihood of X gets correspondingly diminished.

As we will see in Section 13.4, *lucky enough* is incompatible with the idiomatic reading and *so lucky* is biased against it. In section 13.5 we give examples to show that *almost lucky* is also incompatible with the idiomatic reading.

In all of the examples in (9)–(11) the infinitival complement could be replaced by an *if*-clause. *Wong Kwan will be lucky to break even* and *Wong Kwan will be lucky if he breaks even* are paraphrases. In languages such as French and German the infinitival complement translates to an *if*-clause. This is nicely demonstrated by the earliest instance of the *will be lucky to X* idiom we have found so far. It appears in a 1813 book *Memoirs of the kings of Spain of the House of Bourbon*, Volume 3, by William Coxe. On page 307 we find the passage:

(12) This measure appeared a death blow to the authority of Philip; when the news was communicated at Versailles, marshal Villars could not refrain from exclaiming, "Adieu, court of St. Ildefonso; you will be lucky to be assured of a regular supply of your daily meals!"

But of course le maréchal de Villars did not say that. He spoke French. Coxe gives the original exclamation in a footnote: *"Adieu, la cour de St. Ildefonso. Elle sera heureuse si son dîner et son souper sont bien assurés."* The infinitival complement in (12), *to be assured of a regular supply of your daily meals*, is a translation of an *if*-clause in French: *si son dîner et son souper sont bien assurés*.[3] The word *si* is *if* in French.

---

[3] Coxe translates *son dîner et son souper* as *your daily meals*. Translating this phrase as *dinner and supper* would have been misleading. In the Versailles court *dîner* was at lunch time and *souper* a meal late in the evening, not interchangeable words for the same meal. Coxe could have translated *elle sera heureuse si* literally as *it will be lucky if* but he chose the idiomatic English *you will be lucky to* instead. Choosing *you* instead of *it* to address the court of St. Ildefonso adds a nice touch. Chapeau, M. Coxe !

Thanks to http://books.google.com/ngrams/ for the discovery of this example.

All the examples in (9)-(12) are future affirmative sentences containing *will* with proper names, definite NPs, or pronominal subjects. These are all crucial enabling features of the idiomatic reading. Switching from affirmative to negative makes a difference.

(13) Wong Kwan will not be lucky to break even.

(9) implies that Wong Kwan is not likely to break even; (13) entails that he will not break even. It is a stronger statement than (9). Switching from the future to the past tense also has an unexpected side effect. (14) entails that Wong Kwan broke even, not that he might not have broken even.

(14) Wong Kwan was lucky to break even.

In (13) and (14) *be lucky to X* can only have its literal meaning of a $++ \mid --$ implicative construction.

13.4 The brittleness of the idiom

There are many environments where the idiomatic sense of *will be lucky to X* is not present at all. It is possible only when there is uncertainty about whether the complement will be true even though that is not a sufficient condition. In the following examples only the literal interpretation is possible because it is known, expected or independently implied that X will in fact be true.

(15) a. Wherever she ends up, they will be lucky to have her.

b. The college that you choose will be lucky to have you as student.

c. California is the largest state in the US. This means you will be lucky to have several schools offering RN programs.

d. Obviously, the more leads you will be lucky to get the higher your profits will become.

Sentences with indefinite subject NPs seem to admit only the literal interpretation.[4]

(16) a. Some man will be lucky to receive your love some day.

b. A few people will be lucky to have permanent reduction in as little as only three treatments.

---

[4]The indefinite NPs that disallow the idiomatic reading all seem to be INTERSECTIVE quantifiers; Keenan (1987), Section 6.3 in Peters and Westerståhl (2006).

The idiomatic reading is possible if *someone* is used to refer to a specific individual: *I was about to hang up when I heard you call me a* HOPA. *Someone [= you] will be lucky to avoid a sexual harassment suit.*

    c. Very few people will be lucky to have a job once the financial armageddon settles upon us.

    d. Another woman will be LUCKY to have you in her life.

But universally quantified subject NPs are compatible with the idiom.

(17) a. A case of Mid-East meets Mid-West and everyone will be lucky to get out alive.

    b. Everyone will be lucky to even look at them, let alone purchase one.

    c. The looming slump/recession means everyone will be lucky to even get close to – or at best match nevermind exceed – this year's sales.

    d. Police officials in Virginia Beach and Newport News insist this isn't about generating revenue, that everyone will be lucky to break even.

The presence of negative polarity items favors the idiomatic reading.

(18) a. Motorola will be lucky to get another dime from me ever again.

    b. In fact you will be lucky to see any traffic at all.

Replacing the negative polarity items in (18b), *any* by *some* and *at all* by *at least* takes away the idiomatic reading.

(19) In fact you will be lucky to see at least some traffic.

Any adverbial modification of *will be lucky to X* takes away the idiomatic reading. Removing the adverb restores it in (20).

(20) a. (Perhaps) you will be lucky to find your buyer in a simple passer-by or your next-door neighbour.

    b. (Maybe) you will be lucky to stalk the elusive eland or find a hive of wild honey.

    c. If you employ a farm and permit a field take care of itself, you will (always) be lucky to have virtually any crop from it.

    d. You will (sometimes) be lucky to find an editor who can also typeset your completed book.

It appears that *lucky enough* is compatible only with the literal interpretation.

(21) a. She will be lucky enough to escape her own execution.

    b. The road to recovery will be long, but she will be lucky enough to walk it with the love and support of so many around her.

    c. This will be Ponder's first start against Detroit, but he will be lucky enough to face their defense without the suspended Ndamukong Suh.

   d. You will be lucky enough to receive a signed copy of the completed EP before anyone else!

Although the *very lucky* and *extremely lucky* are fine in the examples in (11) that feature the idiomatic reading, *will be so lucky to X* favors the literal interpretation, some examples in (22).

(22) a. You will be So Lucky to have these boots from Naughty Monkey.

   b. When in need, they will be so lucky to receive the level of care that saved Mr. Savov's life against the odds.

   c. The women who are attending this Sunday's salon will be so lucky to have been touched by Amy. It's not a promise, it's a fact.

   d. My future boyfriend will be so lucky to have me cooking yummy food like this every day.

Here *so* is an empathetic intensifier unlike the detached *very* and *extremely*. Somehow that makes a difference. Examples with *so lucky* that have the idiomatic sense such as (23a) and (23b) are hard to find.

(23) a. However, in the real world you will be so lucky to even get three quarters of the information required.

   b. You will be so lucky to find a guy that doesn't play Call of Duty and if you do he is probably taken already.

13.5 Two interpretations of *be almost lucky*

Because *almost X* is a counteractive, one expects *almost be lucky to X* to have only the literal interpretation entailing not X. That prediction is correct for a few examples of this pattern found on the web (24).

(24) I have to head to work right now. You almost were lucky to get to talk to the cool cat that is me.

If *almost* goes between the copula and *lucky*, two patterns emerge. The examples in (25) work like (24), no idiomatic interpretation, negative entailment.

(25) a. I was almost lucky to take a chick for lunch but she turned me down.

   b. I was almost lucky to escape stretch marks the 2nd time but I ended up getting a couple small ones a week or so before Aiden was born.

   c. The last plate, I was almost lucky to guess what it was, is Suman Panna Cotta.

The second pattern is also based on the literal interpretation but with a positive entailment.

(26) a. Mitch Heard was almost lucky to have such an easily satirized last name.

    b. I think I was almost lucky to have been forced to embrace my own psychopathology early.

    c. I sometimes think that Fred was almost lucky to die when he did.

The contrast between (25) and (26) might be correlated with a difference in stress, *ALMOST lucky* in (25) but *almost LUCKY* in (26). In (25) *almost* has wide scope over the complement clause as it clearly does in (24); in (26) it is a modifier of *lucky*.

13.6 Sister adjectives: *unlucky, fortunate, unfortunate*

All the findings in the previous sections about *be lucky to X* generalize to *be unlucky to X, be fortunate to X* and *be unfortunate to X*. They can all have the idiomatic "X is not likely" interpretation under the same conditions as *be lucky to X*; otherwise they too are $++ \mid --$ implicative constructions. (27) gives examples with the idiomatic reading.

(27) a. We will be unlucky to encounter rain, but it is certainly possible.

    b. Yields are so pathetically low today that you will be fortunate to get much of a yield at all.

    c. She will be unfortunate to get six months in jail, usually she is put on parole and released.

All the examples in (27) imply that the complement clause X is not likely.

The idiomatic readings of *lucky* and *unlucky* mirror each other in a predictable way.

(28) a. You will be lucky to receive a C in this course.

    b. You will be unlucky to receive a C in this course.

The two examples in (28) agree in that the addressee is not likely to get a C. (28a) suggests that the grade might be a D; (28b) suggests that the grade will be a B or an A.

The examples in (29) and (30) only have the literal $++ \mid --$ interpretation.

(29) a. He was unlucky to miss out on an Academy Award nomination.

  b. I have been fortunate to have followed my passion for most of my life.

  c. We were unfortunate to have lived in the path of two tornados.

(30) a. I had not been unlucky to be near twin towers on 9/11 but once was at major accident on highway.

  b. For those clinicians who have not been fortunate to study with Dr. Faye, his technique DVDs are truly a blessing.

  c. I have not been unfortunate to pick an absolutely dismal game yet.

(29c) entails that we lived in the path of two tornados and presupposes that it was a misfortune. (30c) entails that I have not picked an absolutely dismal game and presupposes that, if I had, it would have been a misfortune.

13.7 Conclusion

This investigation started from the simple observation in *FactBank* that *Wong Kwan will be lucky to break even* implies that most likely Wong Kwan will not break even. The example taught us that *be lucky to X* can have an idiomatic 'most likely not X' reading in the future tense. It appears to be a new discovery.[5] We gave ample evidence to show that in its literal sense *be lucky to X* is an implicative construction, not factive as has been sometimes claimed. In the literal sense *Wong Kwan will be lucky to break even* entails that he will break even with the presupposition that it will be a lucky outcome for Kwan.

We found a complex set of structural features that enable or disable the idiomatic reading of *be lucky to X*. They include: tense, negation, type of subject, negative polarity items, and adverbial modification. We know that the distinction between generic and non-generic sentences also plays a role but we have not worked that out yet. There are undoubtedly many non-structural features that favor or disfavor the idiomatic reading such as whether the sentence is embedded in a context that triggers the expectation of good news or bad news. These contextual features are now the subject of an ongoing investigation at CSLI as part of DARPA's Machine Reading project. We will report on the results in a future joint paper by all the members of the Language and Natural Reasoning group at CSLI.

---

[5]There is the well-known sarcastic expression *I should be so lucky* that means, roughly, 'there is no chance that it will happen.' It comes to English from Yiddish and seems unrelated to the idiomatic sense of *will be lucky* this paper is about.

Acknowledgements

Thanks to Daniel G. Bobrow, Elizabeth Traugott and my fellow participants in the Natural Language and Reasoning group at CSLI (Cleo Condoravdi, Miriam King Connor, Marianne Naval, Stanley Peters, Tania Rojas-Esponda and Annie Zaenen) for their help on the content and style of this presentation. Thanks also to Daniel Lassiter and Christopher Potts for their help on the judgments about *will be so lucky to X*, to Herbert Clark for raising the issue of *unlucky*, and to the other members of the audience for their comments and suggestions at the presentation of this work at the *SemFest* meeting at Stanford on March 16, 2012. Special thanks to Laurence Horn and Craige Roberts for the contrarian view (p.c.) that *be lucky to X* is a factive construction because the crucial negative examples in (3) and (4) in their dialect presuppose that the complement is true instead of implying falsehood as they clearly do on Google. For Horn and Roberts, the implicative reading requires replacing *lucky* by *lucky enough*. Because the examples in (3) come from websites outside of the US, it is possible that there is a systematic difference between "US English" and "World English" in whether *be lucky to X* is a factive or a two-way implicative construction in its literal sense.

The author gratefully acknowledges the support of Defense Advanced Research Projects Agency (DARPA) Machine Reading Program under Air Force Research Laboratory (AFRL) prime contract no. FA8750-09-C-0181. Any opinions, findings, and conclusions or recommendations expressed in this material are those of the author and do not necessarily reflect the view of DARPA, AFRI, or the US government.

References

Barker, Chris. 2002. The dynamics of vagueness. *Linguistics and Philosophy* 25(1):1–36.

Beaver, David I. and Bart Geurts. 2011. Presupposition. In E. N. Zalta, ed., *The Stanford Encyclopedia of Philosophy*. Stanford University, summer 2011 edn.

Egan, Thomas. 2008. *Non-finite complementation: A usage-based study of infinitive and -ing clauses in English*. Rodopi.

Geis, Michael L. and Arnold M. Zwicky. 1971. On invited inferences. *Linguistic Inquiry* 2(4):561–566. http://www.jstor.org/stable/4177664.

Grice, Paul H. 1989. *Studies in the Way of Words*. Harvard University.

Horn, Laurence. 1985. Metalinguistic negation and pragmatic ambiguity. *Language* 61(1):121–174.

Horn, Larry. 2003. Implicature. In L. Horn and G. Ward, eds., *Handbook of Pragmatics*. Blackwell.

Karttunen, Lauri. 1971a. Implicative verbs. *Language* 47:340–358.

Karttunen, Lauri. 1971b. The logic of English predicate complement constructions. http://www2.parc.com/istl/members/karttune/publications/-english_predicate.pdf French translation: "La logique des constructions anglaises á complément prédicatif" *Langages* 8:56–80, 1973.

Karttunen, Lauri. 1973. La logique des constructions anglaises à complément prédicatif. *Langages* 8:56–80.

Karttunen, Lauri. 1974. Presupposition and linguistic context. *Theoretical Linguistics* 1(1):181–194.

Karttunen, Lauri. 2007. Word play. *Computational Linguistics* 33:443–467.

Karttunen, Lauri. 2012. Simple and phrasal implicatives. In **SEM 2012*, pages 124–131. Association for Computational Linguistics.

Karttunen, Lauri and Stanley Peters. 1979. Conventional implicature. In C.-K. Oh and D. A. Dinneen, eds., *Syntax and Semantics, Volume 11: Presupposition*, pages 1–56. Academic Press.

Karttunen, Lauri and Annie Zaenen. 2005. Veridicity. In G. Katz, J. Pustejovsky, and F. Schilder, eds., *Annotating, Extracting and Reasoning about Time and Events*, no. 05151 in Dagstuhl Seminar Proceedings. Internationales Begegnungs- und Forschungszentrum (IBFI), Schloss Dagstuhl, Germany. <http://drops.dagstuhl.de/opus/volltexte/2005/314> [date of citation: 2005-01-01].

Keenan, Edward. 1987. A semantic definition of 'indefinite NP'. In E. Reuland and A. ter Meulen, eds., *The Representation of (In)definiteness*, pages 286–317. MIT Press.

Kiparsky, Paul and Carol Kiparsky. 1970. Fact. In M. Bierwisch and K. E. Heidolph, eds., *Progress in Linguistics*, pages 143–173. Mouton.

Lewis, David K. 1979. Scorekeeping in a language game. *Journal of Philosophical Logic* 8(1):339–359.

Nairn, Rowan, Cleo Condoravdi, and Lauri Karttunen. 2006. Computing relative polarity for textual inference. In *ICoS-5*, pages 67–76.

Norrick, Neal R. 1978. *Factive adjectives and the theory of factivity*. Niemeyer.

Peters, Stanley and Dag Westerståhl. 2006. *Quantifiers in Language and Logic*. Oxford University Press.

Pichotta, Karl. 2008. Processing paraphrases and phrasal implicatives in the Bridge question-answering system. Undergraduate Honors Thesis, Symbolic Systems Program, Stanford University.

Potts, Christopher. 2005. *The Logic of Conventional Implicatures*. Cambridge University Press.

Rudanko, Juhani. 1989. *Complementation and Case Grammar*. State University of New York Press.

Rudanko, Juhani. 2002. *Complements and Constructions. Corpus-Based Studies on Sentential Complements in English in Recent Centuries*. University Press of America.

Rudanko, Juhani. 2011. Unexpected and innovative uses of constructions: Is there a need to supplement a dictionary with constructional information? In *Proceedings The Fifth International Conference on Historical Lexicography and Lexicology (ISHLL 5)*, pages 1–10.

Saurí, Roser and James Pustejovsky. 2009. Factbank 1.0. Linguistic Data Consortium.

Stalnaker, Robert. 1974. Pragmatic presuppositions. In M. Munitz and P. Unger, eds., *Semantics and Philosophy*, pages 197–213. New York University Press.

Thomason, Richmond. 1990. Accommodation, meaning, and implicature: Interdisciplinary foundations for pragmatics. In P. Cohen, J. Morgan, and M. Pollack, eds., *Intentions in Communication*, pages 325–363. MIT Press.

Wilkinson, Robert. 1970. Factive complements and action complements. In *CLS 6*, pages 425–444.

Wilkinson, Robert W. 1976. Modes of predication and implied adverbial complements. *Foundations of Language* 14(2):153–194.

14

On Presenting Something in English and Hungarian

Tibor Laczkó

14.1 Introduction

In this paper[1] I present an analysis of the English verb *present* as used in constructions like *present something to somebody* and *present somebody with something*. I systematically compare it with its two Hungarian counterparts, with particular attention to the partially different behavior of their derived nominal equivalents. In Section 2, I summarize my analysis in Laczkó (1991) in the classical framework of Lexical-Functional Grammar (LFG), then in Section 3 I outline my modified account couched in the version of the Lexical Mapping Theory (LMT) component of LFG proposed by Ackerman (1992) and Zaenen (1993). This is followed by some concluding remarks in Section 4.

---

[1] I gratefully acknowledge the inspiration I have received for the analysis developed here from Annie Zaenen's work in this particular domain of grammar. I am also thankful to two anonymous reviewers for their very helpful comments. Naturally, all remaining errors are my sole responsibility. The research reported here has been supported, in part, by OTKA (Hungarian Scientific Research Fund, grant number: K 72983), by the Research Group for Theoretical Linguistics of the Hungarian Academy of Sciences and the University of Debrecen, and by the TÁMOP 4.2.1./B-09/1/KONV-2010-0007 project, which is implemented through the New Hungary Development Plan, co-financed by the European Social Fund and the European Regional Development Fund, and the Research Group for Theoretical Linguistics of the Hungarian Academy of Sciences at the University of Debrecen.

14.2 The pre-LMT analysis

Rappaport (1983) is probably the most influential paper on (event) nominalization in English in the classical framework of LFG.[2] The essence of this approach is that the semantic identity of verbs and the nouns derived from them should not be captured in terms of the (constituent) structural isomorphism of the two predicate types; instead, it should be analyzed in terms of shared argument structure. Consequently, the systematic behavioral differences between the two types should not be captured in terms of differences between verbs and nouns with respect to their governing and case-assigning properties in the context of general principles of Government and Binding Theory (GB). Rappaport (1983) points out several empirical and theory-internal problems with Kayne's (1981) GB analysis along these lines. She claims that the greatest problem for Kayne's analysis is the existence of derived nominals with two complements, as in (1a), as opposed to (1b).

(1) a. John's presentation of a medal to Mary

    b. *John's presentation of Mary with a medal

    c. John presented a medal to Mary.

    d. John presented Mary with a medal.

Kayne has to assume two different, and otherwise syntactically unmotivated, representations for verbal predicates with two internal arguments. This can be taken to be a brute force way of ensuring that certain verbal predicates in a particular configuration have nominal counterparts in the corresponding (isomorphic) NP configuration, whereas other verbal predicates in the other configuration do not have such nominal counterparts. In Rappaport's (1983) approach, the partial difference between verbal and nominal predicates can be feasibly captured by dint of the following two basic assumptions. (i) Nominal predicates can only assign semantically restricted grammatical functions to their arguments.[3] (ii) This grammatical function assignment must always

---

[2] The paper appeared in a volume entitled *Papers in Lexical Functional Grammar*, edited by Annie Zaenen, Lori Levin, and Malka Rappaport (Levin et al. 1983). Not only this paper but also other papers in the volume, including a paper coauthored by Annie, were so influential that twenty-five years later the book was reissued as *Lexical Semantics in LFG* (Butt & King 2008), and the introduction to this reissue was cowritten by Annie.

[3] It is to be noted that I and some other researchers assume that at least in Hungarian the POSS grammatical function is semantically unrestricted; see, for instance, Laczkó (1995,2004), Komlósy (1998), and Chisarik & Payne (2003). However, this issue is irrelevant from the perspective of this paper.

respect the principle of thematic constancy, i.e. the grammatical functions must match the semantic roles of the arguments they are associated with. Verbal predicates are exempt from both constraints: they can assign unrestricted functions (SUBJ and OBJ), and they may assign restricted functions in violation of the thematic constancy principle. Rappaport's explanation for the contrast between (1a) and (1b) is that in the former, the assignment of the two OBL functions respects thematic constancy: OBL_{TH} is assigned to the theme argument (*of a book*), and OBL_{GO} is assigned to the goal argument (*to Mary*), while in the latter, there are mismatches. The reason why (1d) is grammatical, as opposed to (1b), is that the assignment of semantically restricted grammatical functions does not necessarily have to obey the constancy principle in the verbal domain.

In Laczkó (1991) I make a comparison between these English constructions and their Hungarian counterparts.[4] Consider the following Hungarian examples and compare them with their English translations, which are identical to the English examples in (1).[5]

(2) a. egy érme   oda-ajándékoz-ás-a Máriá-nak János által
        a   medal.NOM to-present-DEV-3SG Mary-DAT John by
        'John's presentation of a medal to Mary'

     b. Mária   meg-ajándékoz-ás-a   egy érmé-vel   János által
        Mary.NOM PERF-present-DEV-3SG a   medal-with John by
        '*John's presentation of Mary with a medal'

     c. János   (oda-)ajándékoz-ott egy érmé-t   Máriá-nak.
        John.NOM to-present-PAST.3SG a   medal-ACC Mary-DAT
        'John presented a medal to Mary.'

     d. János   meg-ajándékoz-ta   Máriá-t   egy érmé-vel.
        John.NOM PERF-present-PAST.3SG Mary-ACC a   medal-with
        'John presented Mary with a medal.'

The contrast is between the grammatical Hungarian construction in (2b) and its ungrammatical English counterpart in (1b). In the paper, I

---

[4]Note that this 1991 paper is based on a presentation five years earlier: Conference in English and American Studies at Attila József University, Szeged, 1986.

[5]In the glosses, DEV stands for the nominalizing suffix. As the glosses show, the Hungarian verb is combined with preverbs; in (2a) and (2c) the preverb is *oda* glossed as *to*, meaning something like 'to there', and in (2b) and (2d) it is *meg* which is the par excellence perfectivizing preverb in Hungarian, glossed as PERF. Also note that *oda* is optional and *meg* is obligatory. (Rarely another preverb is also used in this construction type: *neki* 'to, against'.) It is also important to point out that in Hungarian there can only be one possessor constituent within a noun phrase. It is for this reason that in the Hungarian examples in (2a) and (2b) the agent is expressed by a postpositional phrase corresponding to the English *by*-phrase.

assume that Rappaport's (1983) thematic constancy generalization also holds within the domain of Hungarian noun phrases and I claim that the contrast can be explained by postulating that, although the situations described by the relevant constructions are very similar, and also there are straightforward parallels between the corresponding grammatical functions in the two languages, in Hungarian the two (formally also different) predicates do not share the same argument structure as regards the semantic roles of some of their arguments. Consider Table 1, summarizing my generalizations.

Situation in both languages: x gives y to z as a present				
English	*present₁*	<SUBJ	OBJ	OBL_GO>
		ag	th	go
		x	y	z
	present₂	<SUBJ	OBL_INST	OBJ>
		ag	th	go
		x	y	z
Hungarian	*(oda-)ajándékoz*	<SUBJ	OBJ	OBL_GO>
		ag	th	go
		x	y	z
	meg-ajándékoz	<SUBJ	OBL_INST	OBJ>
		ag	inst	th
		x	y	z

TABLE 1 A classical LFG analysis of *present* and its Hungarian counterparts

I assume that in Hungarian the (obligatory) presence of the perfectivizing preverb causes the semantic change that affects the semantic roles of two arguments. This change in the semantic roles of the relevant arguments makes the Hungarian derived nominal construction grammatical even from the perspective of Rappaport's (1983) thematic constancy principle. In support of my analysis, in the paper I also discuss another contrast between certain English and Hungarian predicates. Compare the following Hungarian examples and their English translations.

(3) a. János   közelít-ett   a ház felé.
     John.NOM approach-PAST.3SG the house towards
     'John was approaching the house.'

    b. János   meg-közelít-ette   a ház-at.
     John.NOM PERF-approach-PAST.3SG the house-ACC
     'John approached the house.'

(4) a. János   közelít-és-e   a   ház   felé
John.NOM approach-DEV-3SG the house towards
'John's approach to the house'

    b. a   ház   meg-közelít-és-e   János által
the house.NOM PERF-approach-DEV-3SG John by
'John's approach of the house' (ungrammatical in English)

The parallel I draw should be straightforward: the appearance of the perfectivizing preverb *meg* results in a semantic role change: a goal becomes a theme.

In Laczkó (1991) I also deal with several predicates of the *spray*, *load* type in both English and Hungarian, and I show that they behave similarly in the two languages. Consider the following very often cited English examples.

(5) a. He loaded the hay (on the cart).

    b. his loading of the hay (on the cart)

(6) a. He loaded the cart (with the hay).

    b. his loading of the cart (with the hay)

In Hungarian we find exactly the same patterns. My generalization about the omissibility of arguments in this domain (holding for both languages) is that only a non-theme argument can be optional.

I also point out that there are at least three *spray*, *load* predicates in English which can be combined with the prefix *be-*, and the resulting predicate will no longer have the well-known alternation, cf.:

(7) a. He sprinkled water on the flowers.

    b. He sprinkled the flowers with water.

(8) a. *He besprinkled water on the flowers.

    b. He besprinkled the flowers with water.

I suggest that this English prefix has a function very similar to that of perfectivizing *meg* in Hungarian. Its appearance triggers the theme (re)interpretation of an argument which "originally" is a goal.

Now I would like to make the following remarks on my analysis in Laczkó (1991).

(A) My description of the function of the *be-* prefix in English is not consistent. At one point I claim that its function is to turn the goal argument of a verb like *sprinkle* into a theme argument. However, at an earlier point I assume and exemplify that such a predicate (even without *be-*) has to be analyzed as being polysemous, and the two homophonous versions have partially different argument structures (cf. (7a) and (7b)). I think this is the correct approach, and in this light the appropriate generalization about *be-* is that it overtly (morphologically) reinforces (endorses) the theme interpretation of an otherwise goal-like argument to the exclusion of the other interpretation.

(B) My generalization that if a predicate has two internal arguments then only the non-theme argument can be optional is strongly supported by the English nominalization facts in the light of Rappaport's (1983) thematic constancy principle (i.e. if the derived nominal's argument is expressed by a prepositional phrase, then it must be a theme because such a prepositional phrase encodes the OBL$_{TH}$ grammatical function).

(C) Now I have found additional evidence in favor of assuming that in the relevant cases the preverb *meg* can be taken to affect argument structure. Its essence is as follows. In Hungarian, particle verb constructions are typically telic (and the telicizing function is attributed to the particle).[6] When they are used in progressive (non-perfect) aspect, the particle (aka the preverb) has to follow the verb (while in neutral sentences, it obligatorily immediately precedes the verb). It is a generally accepted generalization in the Hungarian generative literature that if the sole role of the preverb in a particle verb construction is telicization, then, in a sentence with a progressive interpretation, it usually does not show up, not even postverbally. Consider the following examples.

(9) a. ír   b. meg-ír
     write   PERF-write
     'write (atelic)'   'write something (telic)'

(10) a. János   ír-ta   (??meg) a   level-et,   amikor ...
      John.NOM write-PAST.3SG   PERF the letter-ACC when ...
      'John was writing the letter when...'

     b. János   rak-ta   ??(meg) a   szeker-et (széná-val),
      John.NOM load-PAST.3SG   PERF the cart-ACC hay-with

      amikor ...
      when ...
      'John was loading the cart (with hay) when ...'

As (9) shows, in the case of the *ír* ~ *meg-ír* pair, the only function of the preverb *meg* is telicization. It is for this reason that in the progressive sentence in (10a) its occurrence is rather strongly dispreferred (although marginally acceptable). By contrast, in the case of *meg-rak* 'load' we have the opposite scenario: the absence of the preverb is strongly dispreferred (and it is only marginally acceptable). The most natural and

---

[6] For an LFG (implementational) analysis of Hungarian, English and German particle verbs, see Forst et al. (2010).

straightforward explanation for this contrast is that in (10b) the preverb is not only a mere telicizer: it exerts an additional semantic effect on the argument structure of the input verb.

(D) The analysis in Laczkó (1991) is couched in a pre-LMT and pre-Proto-Roles LFG framework, using the classical (quite widely criticized) semantic role labels. This makes the approach marked in the well-known sense: its essence is relabelling certain arguments with respect to their semantic roles: goal ⟶ theme; theme ⟶ instrument-like secondary theme. In the next section I will briefly discuss the key issues from an LMT perspective. I will point out that the version of LMT that I use (based on Ackerman (1992), Zaenen (1993) and Ackerman & Moore (2012)) provides an appropriate mechanism for capturing the relevant phenomena in a more principled fashion.

(E) In Laczkó (1991) I seek to account, in a more or less descriptive manner, for a contrast between English *present* and Hungarian *(oda)ajándékoz* ~ *megajándékoz*, see (1), (2), and Table 1 above. However, I do not address a more general and substantial question: what may be the reason for this contrast? This question is all the more valid, because in English, too, the "semantic-role-changing" dual pattern is available: see the famous group of *spray, load* verbs. A closer look at the nature and meanings (uses) of these verbs in the two languages readily provides us with a straightforward answer: although the verb forms themselves do contain the 'gift' meaning element, the Hungarian verbs are absolutely unambiguous, while the English verb is multiply ambiguous. It is a further, and not at all insignificant, difference that while in English there is conversion (that is, the form of the input noun and that of the output verb are identical morphologically), in Hungarian there is noun ⟶ verb derivation by dint of suffixation (that is, a verbal suffix is added to the noun stem). This facilitates the identification of the 'gift' meaning element in the Hungarian verb forms.

Hungarian monolingual explanatory dictionaries give only one meaning or definition, roughly the same as we have indicated in Table 1 in the description of the background situation: 'x gives y to z as a present'; see Juhász (1972), for instance. By contrast, *present* is massively (and polysemously) ambiguous. For example, in Hornby (1982), an English monolingual explanatory dictionary, one finds the following main meanings: (i) give/offer/submit; (ii) introduce formally; (iii) show/reveal; (iv) produce.[7] It is meaning (i) that is involved in the construction under investigation. It is my conviction that the contrast between *present*

---

[7]It is for this reason that the title of this paper is (deliberately) multiply ambiguous.

and *(oda)ajándékoz* ∼ *megajándékoz* can be explained by these afore-mentioned differences between these English and Hungarian verbs.

I think that this approach is strongly supported by the fact that in English there is a verb that is much closer to the Hungarian *(oda)ajándékoz* ∼ *megajándékoz* pair: *gift* used as a verb.[8] Its form is really nominal and in this case, too, conversion takes place (compare this with the Hungarian nominal stem serving as input to noun ⟶ verb suffixal derivation). When *gift* is clearly used as a verb (for instance, when it occurs in a typical verbal position and (very often) it is inflected as a verb (for instance, when a verbal suffix like *-ed* or *-ing* is attached to it)) then the conversion effect and the presence of the 'gift' meaning component are absolutely obvious. It is also quite natural (following from the etymology of the word: *give* ⟶ *gift*) that as a verb it is typically used to express the 'x gives y to z as a present' sense from the perspective in which the given object is interpreted as the theme of the event. The real question is whether there is evidence for the use of the word *gift* as a verb in such a way that the receiver of the gift is interpreted as the theme of the event, undergoing a kind of a change of state: by receiving the gift (s)he has become richer in the relevant sense. The most efficient way of testing whether the use of this "converted" verb in this special interpretation is possible or not is as follows. We need to check whether it can be nominalized in such a way that the construction clearly suggests that the recipient is really viewed as the theme of the event. Despite the fact that, as I mentioned above, the verbal use of the word *gift* extremely strongly brings about the other interpretation of the situation, in which the theme is the entity undergoing a change of possession, even a short browsing exercise (Google search) on the internet provides evidence that the verb can be used in this alternative sense. In (11) I give two randomly selected examples in which (as is even much more evident from the context) the nominalized form (*gifting*) is clearly used in the sense we are after: the argument expressed by the *of* prepositional phrase is the recipient of the gifting event and it is interpreted as the theme, which is straightforwardly borne out by the fact that it can be realized by this particular prepositional phrase. Compare the examples in (11) with (1b).[9]

---

[8]Note that this verb would also disambiguate the title of the paper: *On Gifting Something in English and Hungarian*.

[9]The link to (11a), which is a title, is http://sarahoual.com/2011/07/13/wedding-weekend-the-gifting-of-the-maids/, and the relevant context is this: "What would each of them love? They're all so freaking different. I could get them each something different..." The link to (11b) is http://www.spiritgivengifts.com/.

(11) a. Wedding Weekend: The Gifting of the 'Maids
b. the reality of God's love for, and gifting of everyone

14.3 An LMT approach

In Laczkó (2000) I develop a more comprehensive and more detailed analysis of the relationships between the argument structure of verbal predicates and that of derived nominal predicates. I point out the advantages of Lexical Mapping Theory as outlined, for instance, in Bresnan & Zaenen (1990) and Bresnan (1991) and then I show that the account of Hungarian *spray, load* verbs developed by Ackerman (1992) elegantly avoids the problem of associating distinct and discrete semantic role labels to arguments. He applies Dowty's (1991) Proto-Agent and Proto-Patient properties to calculate the intrinsic classification of arguments in terms of the $[\pm r]$ and $[\pm o]$ features.[10] Furthermore, he distinguishes what he calls morphosyntactic and morpholexical processes. The former result in (partial) reassignment of grammatical functions but they leave argument structure (including the semantic roles of the arguments) intact. In Ackerman's approach passivization and the dative shift belong here.[11] By contrast, morpholexical rules are capable of affecting argument structure, in addition to the (partial) reassignment of grammatical functions. According to Ackerman, the alternation in the lexical forms of Hungarian *spray, load* verbs is such a process.

Ackerman's (1992) solution can be naturally extended to the treatment of the Hungarian *(oda)ajándékoz ~ megajándékoz* verb pair. Compare my original analysis in Laczkó (1991) and the new one along these lines in Table 2, which also compares them with the analyses of *present$_1$* and *present$_2$*. The basic idea is that the same gifting situation can be viewed from two significantly different perspectives: either the gift can be interpreted as the most affected participant in the situation (this is grammatically expressed when we use *(oda)ajándékoz*) or the recipient of the gift can be taken to be significantly affected (this is grammatically expressed when we use *megajándékoz*). Affectedness is a crucial Proto-Patient property; therefore, it will result in the $[-r]$ intrinsic specification of the argument in question: the gift in the former case and the recipient in the latter, and, thus, it is this argument that is

---

[10]Zaenen (1993), in her analysis of Dutch participles, proposes the same combination of Dowty's proto-properties and LFG's LMT. For the most recent discussion of combining these two approaches, see Ackerman & Moore (2012).

[11]It is noteworthy that Bresnan's (1991) treatment of ditransitive verbs like *cook* (cf. *cook somebody something* and *cook something for somebody)* is essentially along the lines of a morpholexical process, although she does not explicitly address (the details and consequences of) this issue.

Situation in both languages: x gives y to z as a present			
lang.	verb	pre-LMT account	LMT account
Eng.	$present_1$	SUBJ OBJ OBL$_{GO}$ $< \quad x \quad y \quad z \quad >$ ag th go	$< \quad x \quad y \quad z \quad >$ $[-o] \ [-r] \ [-o]$
	$present_2$	SUBJ OBL$_{IN}$ OBJ $< \quad x \quad y \quad z \quad >$ ag th go	$< \quad x \quad y \quad z \quad >$ $[-o] \ [-r] \ [-o]$
Hun.	$(oda-)ajándékoz$	SUBJ OBJ OBL$_{GO}$ $< \quad x \quad y \quad z \quad >$ ag th go	$< \quad x \quad y \quad z \quad >$ $[-o] \ [-r] \ [-o]$
	$meg\text{-}ajándékoz$	SUBJ OBL$_{IN}$ OBJ $< \quad x \quad y \quad z \quad >$ ag inst th	$< \quad x \quad y \quad z \quad >$ $[-o] \ [-o] \ [-r]$

TABLE 2 A special LMT analysis of *present* and its Hungarian counterparts

mapped onto the OBJ grammatical function in LMT. Given that Hungarian is an asymmetrical language in Bresnan & Moshi's (1990) sense, this means that the other argument can only receive the $[-o]$ specification, and this results in its mapping onto an OBL function.

The crucial point here is that this approach does not employ discrete semantic roles, and, thus, it is not forced to postulate that the two alternative predicates require the relabeling of the arguments with different semantic roles.[12]

I would like to add that this analysis is independently supported by the behavior of a particular Hungarian participle, which the traditional descriptive literature calls perfective, and which I call passive (in an extended sense).[13] In Laczkó (1995, 2005), the crucial generalization in my LMT style analysis is that in Hungarian the -*t*/-*tt* participial suffix can only be attached to a verb, whether transitive or intransitive, which has a $[-r]$ argument (a theme argument in the pre-LMT approach), and its attachment *triggers* or *endorses* the mapping of that argument onto the SUBJ grammatical function. In the case of a transitive input verb, standard passivization takes place (the suffix suppresses the high-

---

[12] It is especially problematic that when in the discrete semantic roles approach the "receiver" argument is associated with the theme role, it is rather hard to associate the gift, that is, the "original theme" argument, with a well-motivated discrete and individual semantic role. Given the form of the constituent in question, an instrument-like role is, perhaps, the most likely candidate, but it is easy to see that this argument is quite far from being a canonical instrument.

[13] For a recent descriptive grammatical approach, see Keszler (2000).

est [−o] argument), and, thus, the [−r] argument is mapped onto SUBJ (triggering). The sole [−r] argument of an intransitive input verb continues to be mapped onto SUBJ (endorsement). This approach has been partially motivated by Bresnan's (1982) theme condition on participle ⟶ adjective conversion in English and Zaenen's (1993) LMT analysis of certain Dutch participles. Compare (2c) and (2d) with (12a) and (12b), respectively.[14]

(12) a. egy Máriá-nak János által (oda-)ajándékoz-ott érme
    a   Mary-DAT John by   to-present-PART   medal
    'a medal presented to Mary by John'

   b. a   János által egy érmé-vel   meg-ajándékoz-ott Mária
      the John by   a   medal-with PERF-present-PART Mary
      'Mary presented by John with a medal'

The relevance of the obvious parallels between the examples is that, for the participle forming rule to be applicable, in the argument structures of the two verbal predicates we have to assume that the [−r] feature is assigned precisely to the argument whose [−r] status I postulated in my analysis of the nominalization processes involving these two predicates.

14.4   Concluding remarks

In this paper I have outlined an LFG-LMT analysis of the following English and Hungarian verbal predicates: *present* ∼ *gift* and *(oda)ajándékoz* ∼ *megajándékoz*.[15] Space limitations prevent me from elaborating, in a systematic and detailed manner, on the consequences and ramifications of my analysis, and I have to confine myself to two general observations.

1. Languages may differ considerably as to the ways in which they employ predicates to reflect the perspective from which a particular situation is viewed. For instance, in English *approach* exclusively requires a "goal" second argument (in a generalized and neutral sense), whereas in Hungarian it has two (morphologically) distinct counterparts, one requiring (and encoding) a "goal" and another requiring (and encoding) a "theme".[16]

2. Whether a particular verb form is capable of encoding different

---

[14]Note the homophony of the past tense marker and the participial suffix.

[15]As I pointed out in passing, some aspects of my approach have been directly influenced by Annie's work, for which I am most grateful. This paper can also be partially seen as a small present that I have gifted Annie with.

[16]The contrast between *present* in English and *(oda)ajándékoz* ∼ *megajándékoz* in Hungarian is essentially of the same nature.

perspectives on a situation may depend on external factors like (massive) polysemy, as shown by the contrast between the verbs *present* and *gift* in the relevant sense.

References

Ackerman, Farrell. 1992. Complex predicates and morpholexical relatedness: Locative alternation in Hungarian. In I. Sag and A. Szabolcsi, eds., *Lexical Matters*, pages 55–84. CSLI Publications.

Ackerman, Farrell and John Moore. 2012. Proto-properties in a comprehensive theory of argument realization. In T. H. King and V. de Paiva, eds., *From Quirky Case to Representing Space: Papers in Honor of Annie Zaenen*. CSLI On-line Publications.

Bresnan, Joan. 1982. The passive in lexical theory. In J. Bresnan, ed., *The Mental Representation of Grammatical Relations*, pages 3–86. The MIT Press.

Bresnan, Joan. 1991. Monotonicity and the theory of relation changes in LFG. *Language Research* 26:637–652.

Bresnan, Joan. 2001. *Lexical-Functional Syntax*. Basil Blackwell.

Bresnan, Joan and Lioba Moshi. 1990. Object asymmetries in comparative Bantu syntax. *Linguistic Inquiry* 21:147–185.

Bresnan, Joan and Annie Zaenen. 1990. Deep unaccusativity in LFG. In K. Dziwirek, P. Farrell, and E. Mejías-Bikandi, eds., *Grammatical Relations: A Cross-Theoretical Perspective*, pages 45–57. CSLI Publications.

Butt, Miriam and Tracy Holloway King, eds. 2008. *Lexical Semantics in LFG*. CSLI Publications.

Chisarik, Erika and John Payne. 2003. Modelling possessor constructions in LFG: English and Hungarian. In M. Butt and T. H. King, eds., *Nominals: Inside and Out*, pages 181–199. CSLI Publications.

Dowty, David R. 1991. Thematic proto-roles and argument selection. *Language* 67:547–619.

Forst, Martin, Tracy Holloway King, and Tibor Laczkó. 2010. Particle verbs in computational LFGs: Issues from English, German, and Hungarian. In M. Butt and T. H. King, eds., *Proceedings of the LFG '10 Conference*, pages 228–248. CSLI On-line Publications. ISSN 1098-6782, http://cslipublications.stanford.edu/LFG/15/ index.shtml.

Hornby, A. S., ed. 1982. *Oxford Advanced Learner's Dictionary of Currrent English*. Oxford University Press.

Juhász, József, István Szőke, Gábor O. Nagy, and Miklós Kovalovszky, eds. 1972. *Magyar Értelmező Kéziszótár [Concise Hungarian Explanatory Dictionary]*. Akadémiai Kiadó.

Kayne, Richard. 1981. Unambiguous paths. In J. Koster and R. May, eds., *Levels of Syntactic Representation*, pages 143–183. Foris.

Keszler, Borbála, ed. 2000. *Magyar Grammatika [Hungarian Grammar]*. Nemzeti Tankönyvkiadó.

Komlósy, András. 1998. A nomen actionis argumentumainak szintaktikai funkcióiról [On the syntactic functions of the arguments of the nomen actionis]. Manuscript. Budapest: Institute for Linguistics, Hungarian Academy of Sciences.

Laczkó, Tibor. 1991. On the relationship between semantic roles and grammatical functions. In B. Korponay and P. Pelyvás, eds., *Studies in Linguistics. Volume 1*, pages 42–51. Lajos Kossuth University.

Laczkó, Tibor. 1995. *The Syntax of Hungarian Noun Phrases: A Lexical-Functional Approach*. Peter Lang.

Laczkó, Tibor. 2000. A magyar igei predikátumok és deverbális főnévi predikátumok argumentumszerkezetéről: Lexikális-funkcionális megközelítés [On the argument structure of Hungarian verbal predicates and deverbal nominal predicates: A lexical-functional approach]. In I. Kenesei, ed., *Igei vonzatszerkezet a magyarban [Verbal Argument Structure in Hungarian]*, pages 67–126. Osiris Kiadó.

Laczkó, Tibor. 2004. Grammatical functions, LMT, and control in the Hungarian DP revisited. In M. Butt and T. H. King, eds., *Proceedings of the LFG '04 Conference*. CSLI On-line Publications. ISSN 1098-6782, http://www-csli.stanford.edu/publications/LFG2/lfg04.html.

Laczkó, Tibor. 2005. Nominalization, participle-formation, typology and lexical mapping. In C. Piñón and P. Siptár, eds., *Approaches to Hungarian: Volume 9: Papers from the Düsseldorf Conference*, pages 205–230. Akadémiai Kiadó.

Levin, Lori, Malka Rappaport, and Annie Zaenen, eds. 1983. *Papers in Lexical-Functional Grammar*. Indiana University Linguistic Club.

Rappaport, Malka. 1983. On the nature of derived nominals. In L. Levin, M. Rappaport, and A. Zeanen, eds., *Papers in Lexical-Functional Grammar*, pages 113–142. Indiana University Linguistic Club.

Zaenen, Annie. 1993. Unaccusativity in Dutch: Integrating syntax and lexical semantics. In J. Pustejovsky, ed., *Semantics and the Lexicon*, pages 129–161. Kluwer.

15

A Semantic Account of Contextual Valence Shifting

LIVIA POLANYI AND MARTIN HENK VAN DEN BERG

15.1 Introduction

Beginning with Turney (2002) and Pang and Lee (2002)'s seminal work in classifying documents in terms of the positive or negative opinions expressed in the text, research in Sentiment Analysis has been a focus of computational natural language processing research. The interest in sentiment analysis is application driven. Businesses need to know how their products are being received; consumers rely on the opinions expressed in reviews of movies, hotels and other goods and services to choose what to buy; political analysts as well as politicians care keenly about how policies or individuals are viewed, while government agencies are similarly concerned with the attitudes expressed by persons or organizations. The explosive growth of social media since 2010 has fueled interest in sentiment even further, as efforts to mine the attitudes revealed in postings on social sites have increased. Commercial companies as well as open source systems that provide sentiment analytic services have only proliferated since 2008 when at least twenty companies were known to be operating in this area (Bo and Pang, 2008)

Despite the commercial frenzy, from a scientific perspective, providing a satisfactory account of the intent of a writer or speaker to express positive or negative opinions of an entity remains a challenging open research problem. Workshops and symposia associated with major conferences in a number of computational fields are held frequently. A recent version of Wiebe's online bibliography (2012) lists over five hundred publications including several dissertations like Wilson (2008) and Somasundaran (2010) as well as at least one full length monograph (Pang and Lee 2008).[1]

Despite the progress that has been made, even if one concentrates only on the deployment of lexical items used to express positive or negative sentiment, and excludes such issues as intonation, gesture, facial expression or punctuation, their typographical proxies, or indirect rhetorical devices such as irony, litotes or hyperbole, devices that may be of less interest to a theoretical linguist, one is still confronted with a number of complex issues that need to be solved in order for fully satisfactory computational sentiment analytic systems to be built. Chief among these: foundational problems arise for symbolic theoretical linguistic analyses as annotating a lexicon for positive or negative sentiment remains a large stumbling block. Some of these difficulties originate in the nature of the lexicon itself: as a string of phonemes makes its way through history, its core meaning might change or, while some meaning core may stay intact, various senses of the term may themselves have different connotations expressing differing polarities. Thus, the term, *hussy*, encountered in early texts carries a neutral connotation while in a contemporary text, the term is only negative. From a synchronic perspective, different senses of a word or a term applied in different domains may differ in sentiment — i.e. *lightweight* is a positive property for a camera while labeling a theoretical argument as *lightweight* expresses a negative evaluation. Even within a domain, a term might have a negative connotation in one context and a positive connotation in another: a camera described as *light* referring to its weight is being praised, while a camera that produces images that are *light* is being criticized. Machine learning methods involving collocation are often employed to try to address these problems with often very disappointing results.

However, the lexicon per se, is not the main focus here. Rather, we will build upon and generalize the approach to sentiment first sketched in Polanyi and Zaenen (2006) that introduced the notion of *contextual valence shifters* including general negation, modals, presuppositions and irony. In that paper, it was demonstrated that simple views of sentiment assigned by a value associated with the lexical item were inadequate because valence shifters reverse or nullify core sentiment values when deployed in context.

In the present paper, we will propose that viewing sentiment assignment from the perspective of semantic scope phenomena provides

---

[1]See Liu (2010) for an excellent overview of the field.

a unified account of a variety of context valence shifting phenomena first proposed in Polanyi and Zaenen. We will argue that entities or events are assigned sentiment by sentiment carrying expressions that have scope over them at any level of linguistic structure, and that if there is more than one expression that assigns a sentiment to a given entity or event, the assigned sentiment will be that of the expression with the widest scope, even if there is a conflict between the different sentiment carrying expressions and/or the inherent sentiment of the target. Taking the position that discourse syntax subsumes sentential syntax and encodes semantic scope relations as do negation, reported speech, modality, etc. we will demonstrate how sentiment context shifting operates in discourse after a brief discussion of sentiment conflict resolution at the sentential and sub-sentential levels.

15.2 Sentiment as a Semantic Scope Phenomena

Within the sentence, semantic scope is expressed using syntactic embedding and is normally directly derived from it. Sentential sentiment assignment is a semantic phenomenon that is informed by syntactic structure at the sentence level and below. Just as the adjective in an Adjective Phrase such as *red house* restricts the meaning of the noun that it modifies, the *house* referred to by the term *beautiful house* receives a positive interpretation because the NP *house* is within the scope of *beautiful* which has a positive valence. Similarly, *The cat purred* is interpreted as a positive event — *purr* having a positive connotation — and *The cat purred sweetly* is even more positive, the positive connotation of *purr* being intensified by *sweetly* which has scope over the verb. More interestingly, just as a negation has scope over its target and can thus negate the sentiment of a term in its scope, i.e. *not kind* has negative sentiment despite *kind* being positively valenced, a conflict in valence within an Adjective Phrase between the noun and its modifier results in a phrase bearing the valence of the adjective. For example, if we assume the word *kitten* normally has positive associations, *vicious kitten* eliminates the possibility of a positive interpretation altogether. Similarly, the Adverbial Phrase *the dangerous lovely summer evening* is negatively valenced, as is the sentence *The lovely young lady whined throughout the wonderful evening* and the adverbial quantifying expression *Every lousy evening the kitten purrs*.

Scope interaction within other parts of speech and phrases may similarly influence attitude calculations. While negation or the use of antonyms usually shifts valence, this is not always the case. For example, *faint praise* is not *real* praise, and therefore is not positive and, in the phrase *although he is a brilliant mathematician* the term *although* blocks the positive evaluation, preparing the reader for a negative continuation. Similarly, in the sentence *The friendly dog does not like the horrible cat*, *dog* is in the scope of *friendly*, *cat* is in the scope of *horrible*, and the whole predication is in the scope of the negation.

Wilson et al. (2005), Moilanen and Pullum (2007), Choi and Cardie (2008), Moilanen et al. (2010) and Nakagawa et al. (2010), often working within a Machine Learning paradigm, concentrated on sentential and sub-sentential phenomena and proposed approaches based on sentential syntax which can be characterized as claiming that sentential constituents c-commanded by a dominating constituent will inherit the sentiment of the dominating constituent. While we agree that these approaches capture important linguistic behavior at the sentence level, they cannot account for the phenomena of contextual valence shifting in general because they are necessarily bounded at the sentence level and contextual sentiment assignment occurs at the discourse level as well. And it is to the discourse level to which we next turn our attention.

15.3   Overview of the LDM

We will use the *Linguistic Discourse Model* (LDM) (Polanyi 1983, 2003; Polanyi and Scha 1984; Scha and Polanyi 1988; Polanyi and van den Berg 1999; Polanyi et al. 2004a, 2004b; Prüst et al. 1994; van den Berg 1996) to assign a structural representation to texts containing sentiment bearing expressions and show how the dominance relations exposed in the discourse level representation enables assignment of the proper sentiment to entities encoded in constituent phrases.

LDM takes as input sequences of propositional signals and outputs a structural and semantic representation of its input. The data structure that is created through the parsing process is called a Discourse Parse Tree (DPT). It is an Open Right Tree that only allows attachment of input along the right edge and is designed to capture the discourse history of an Interaction. The DPT is not structure preserving but allows for insertion of new nodes between two existing nodes on the Right Edge of the Tree.

The LDM consists of four elements: a set of discourse units, a set of relations that hold among units, a data structure in the form of an Open Right Tree that represents the history of the emergent discourse and a set of semantic interpretations created through discourse processing.

15.3.1   Content and Function Units

In the LDM, we have adopted the distinction from linguistics between (i) function terms that encode relations among elementary or constructed units that encode propositional information and (ii) proposition encoding units themselves which characterize linguistic units at the discourse level.[2]

Function Units encode information about how previously occurring (or possibly subsequent) linguistic gestures relate structurally, semantically, interactionally or rhetorically to other units in the discourse or to information in or out of the context in which the discourse takes place. They include terms such as *for example, however, but, so, anyway, good bye, yes,* as well as vocatives, interjections, hesitation and back channel markers, connectives as well as coordinating and subordinating conjunctions. Preposed adjectival and adverbial clauses with wide discourse scope are also classified as functional units.

Discourse Units are content encoding units. Complex Discourse Constituent Units (DCUs) are formed from recursive sequencing and embedding of elementary content encoding units called Basic Discourse Units (BDU). *The BDU is semantic construct that projects onto the discourse level the interpretation of a verb based structure that is able to carry both content and indexical information.*

The **feature structure** of a BDU contains both all surface structure information that the BDU expresses including how that information is expressed (e.g. the words used, the order of the terms and placement of constituents in the string, the full syntactic parse) and a rich representation of semantic information including a specification of all pertinent context indices (e.g. temporality, modality, polarity, genericity, as well as sentiment source and target, stylistic information and various dimensions of Point of View in addition to interaction, speech event and text or genre unit information). The propositional meaning of the BDU is also represented. Performance information that typographical details such as script, font size, bolding, etc. for written text is also available at the node. Because BDUs have information about their context of interpretation, they are able to act as an anchor for subsequent units that either will be interpreted relative to the same context or to another context depending on the information in that new unit.

15.3.2 Discourse Parsing with the LDM

Discourse parsing under the LDM involves an analysis of the incoming string and attaching the resulting structure to the emerging *Discourse Parse Tree* (DPT). The DPT is an Open Right Tree data structure of *Discourse Constituent Units* (DCUs) that provide a record of the his-

---

[2]Some verbal structures such as gerunds or nominalizations that do not carry contextual information because they derive their temporal and modal interpretation from other sentential units are not BDUs.

tory of a discourse up to that attachment. The terminal nodes of the tree are the BDUs. The BDUs have features that encode all relevant linguistic information for discourse derived from the syntactic and semantic analysis of the corresponding string, as well as information from the utterance context. Larger DCUs have the same set of features, with values calculated from the corresponding features of their constituents.

If the incoming string is a simple sentence, sub-sentential unit or fragment, the string will correspond to one BDU. If it has a more complex syntactic structure, it will be composed of more than one BDU, and the sentence will give rise to its own, small discourse tree. The result of this analysis is referred to as the incoming DCU, or simply DCU if no confusion is possible.

In the LDM, there is no special status to BDUs, except for being the minimal units that all larger units are constructed from. In fact, all nodes in the Discourse Parse Tree are first class citizens: all content nodes, terminals and constructed nodes alike have computable content and can combine freely with each other. There is no theoretic distinction between BDUs, the terminal nodes of the tree, discourse nodes created through re-analysis of the sentential structure of a sentence as a DPT consisting of BDUs, and nodes constructed via discourse attachment rules.

To attach the incoming DCU to the tree, the parsing process involves selecting where to attach on the right edge of the tree, the Attachment Point (AP), and how to attach to it, the Discourse Relation. In the following three sections, we will briefly discuss the possible discourse relations and the attachment process.

15.3.3 Discourse Relations (DPT)

We distinguish three main types of discourse attachment relations:

- *Subordination* (elaborations, interruptions)
  At attachment, a new Subordination node is created with an extension that inherits all information present at the subordinating (usually left) daughter. The incoming subordinated DCU is attached to the tree as the right daughter of a newly created Subordination Node.

- *Coordination* (lists, narratives)
  At attachment, either a new Coordination node is created with an extension that inherits all information common to all child nodes, or the incoming DCU is added to an already existing Coordination node.

- *N-Ary* (if/then, question/answer sequences, etc.)
  This covers a number of specific, language specific constructions, many of which, but not all, are sentence internal. The extension of an n-ary node is constructed out of all information present at all child nodes.

Once a node is no longer on the Right Edge, it is no longer accessible.

15.4 Discourse Structure and Sentiment

From the perspective of discourse analysis, sentiment which is a *valuation relation* between a *participant* having the sentiment and the *entity (action, etc.)* the sentiment is attributed to is one of many modal indices in the feature set. For example, (1) and (2) illustrate how implicature-canceling by the contrast relation applies to sentiment just as it applies to other contrasting features:

(1) John has a really great voice, but I do not like his singing.

(2) I admit that John has a really great voice. You would be surprised, however, how bad his singing is.

Example (1) expresses a negative sentiment valuation of the speaker to John's singing, even though the antecedent has the (canceled) presupposition that John would sing well. Of course, the contrast has to be between the sentiments expressed. For example, in the case of

(3) Mary loved the concert but John hated it.

the opinions of two different people are contrasted. In this case, the inherited value is the two valuation relations: MARY-LOVING-CONCERT and JOHN-HATING-CONCERT.

Calculation of the overall sentiment of (part of) a text is determined by the general rules of discourse construction. So in the case of coordinations, comparable sentiment values can, in a first approximation, be added up using simple arithmetic:

In example (4):

(4) My sister got married last month and I needed a place to stay for the wedding. Anyway, I found this great little hotel. It had a clean, comfortable bed. It also had the greatest view of the city.

The construction of the coordinated list of positive characteristics of the hotel located on the right edge of the DPT involved the inheritance up to that coordination node of the positive sentiment in the semantics of *clean* (+) *comfortable* (+) and *greatest view* (+). This constructed List DCU with its three + terms, is subordinated to *great little hotel* (++) with the positive valence of the sentiment carrying term in each subordinated DCU along with the hotel related term licensing the assignment of the Subordination relation. In these cases, the presence of the $+++$ valences of the subordinated DCU reinforces the $++$ valence of the dominating node. This really was a great little hotel!

15.4.1 Sentiment Inheritance (down)

Now let us consider a case in which sentiment bearing DCUs dominate or evaluate non-sentiment bearing DCUs and thereby express the author's or speaker's opinion towards information with no overt marking in the dominated sentences. Consider (5) and (6), a minimal pair of texts. The only difference between them is that the first two sentences in (5) contain negative sentiment terms, and in (6) positive terms.

(5) (1) I had a **horrible** day at work yesterday. (2) Super **ghastly**. (3) My boss was in and out of my office all day. (4) He kept asking for last month's sales figures. (5) He kept saying over and over that he couldn't believe them. (6) You should have seen the expression on his face. (7) Now, I know what's going to happen with my raise.

(6) (1) I had a **wonderful** day at work yesterday. (2) Super **fantastic**. (3) My boss was in and out of my office all day. (4) He kept asking for last month's sales figures. (5) He kept saying over and over that he couldn't believe them. (6) You should have seen the expression on his face. (7) Now, I know what's going to happen with my raise.

FIGURE 1 Structure for (5) and (6)

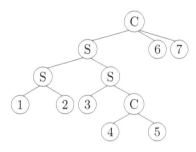

Both (5) and (6) have the same structure, since they differ only in the valence that the author assigns to the experience of day in the first two nodes. Yet, although the text never indicates explicitly at the sentence level what those sales figures were like, we have no trouble understanding that the figures the boss examined in (5) were pretty terrible, while the figures the boss in (6) examined were pretty wonderful. The speaker is confident of her raise in (5) and probably fearful for her job in (6).

The negative interpretation of the first text and the positive interpretation of the second can be understood only with reference to the discourse as a whole. The sentiment in the description of the day is, in each text, inherited from the sentiment expressed explicitly in the DCUs dominating the identically phrased elaborations of what went on at the office.

15.4.2 Sentiment Inheritance (up)

Elaborations provide more detail about an entity. In the following example, a hotel is mentioned, followed by a subordination that gives more detail about some aspects of that hotel (e.g. the rooms, the view).

(7) (1) In Granada, I found a hotel. (2a) The room was very clean, (2b) the service was excellent and (2c) the breakfast room had a great view of Alhambra.

(8) (1) In Granada, I found a hotel. (2a) The room was not clean, (2b) the service was poor and (2c) the breakfast room had a lousy view of a neighboring gas station.

Because the hotel is the sum of its parts, and we can assume, all else being equal, that the subordinated lists (7.2a–c) and (8.2a–c) express that the author of (7) liked and the author of (8) did not like the hotel. This is shown in Figure 2.

Note that it is easy to cancel the implicatures of the subordinate clauses by adding more information, for example, by following (7) with *Still, I hated staying there* or (8) with *I did love the stay there, though, because I met my future wife in the entry hall*. In this case the opinions of the room, service and breakfast are still the same, but do not carry over to the hotel as a whole.

15.5 Conclusion

In conclusion, then, our argument is simple: discourse syntax encodes semantic scope exactly as sentential syntax encodes scope. Sentiment assignment is a semantic phenomenon. By viewing the interpretation of sentiment both within and beyond the sentence as respecting the well-known semantic rules for interpretation based on scopal relations, we have provided a uniform account of contextual valence assignment.[3]

---

[3] While Asher and his colleagues (Asher et al. 2008a,b) have recently implemented a sentiment analysis component using the S-DRT framework that can handle dis-

FIGURE 2 Structures for (7) and (8)

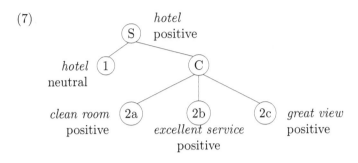

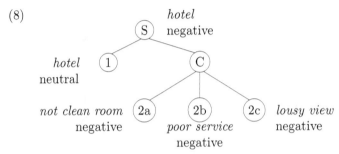

References

Afantenos, Stergos D. and Nicholas Asher. 2010. Testing SDRT's right frontier. In *COLING*, pages 1–9.

Asher, Nicholas. 1993. *Reference to Abstract Objects in Discourse*. Kluwer Academic Publishers.

Asher, Nicholas, Farah Benamara, and Yvette Yannick Mathieu. 2008a. Distilling opinion in discourse: A preliminary study. In *COLING (Posters)*, pages 7–10.

Asher, Nicholas, Farah Benamara, and Yvette Yannick Mathieu. 2008b. Categorizing opinion in discourse. In *ECAI*, pages 835–836.

Asher, Nicholas and Alex Lascarides. 2003. *Logics of Conversation*. Cambridge University Press.

Choi, Yejin and Claire Cardie. 2008. Learning with compositional semantics as structural inference for subsentential sentiment analysis. In *EMNLP*, pages 793–801.

Grosz, Barbara and Candace Sidner. 1986. Attention, intentions and the structure of discourse. *Computational Linguistics* 12:175–204.

course level sentiment, they confined their efforts to the practical and did not point out any of the semantic issues underlying their practical efforts.

Hatzivassiloglou, Vasileios and Kathleen McKeown. 1997. Predicting the semantic orientation of adjectives. In *EACL '97 Proceedings of the Eighth Conference on European Chapter of the Association for Computational Linguistics*, pages 174–181.

Liu, Bing. 2010. Sentiment analysis and subjectivity. In N. Indurkhya and F. Damerau, eds., *Handbook of Natural Language Processing, Second Edition*. Chapman and Hall.

Marcu, Daniel. 2000. *The Theory and Practice of Discourse Parsing and Summarization*. MIT Press.

Maxwell, John and Ronald M. Kaplan. 1993. The interface between phrasal and functional constraints. *Computational Lingusitics* 19:571–589.

Moilanen, Karo and Stephen Pulman. 2007. Sentiment composition. In *Proceedings of the Recent Advances in Natural Language Processing International Conference*, pages 378–382.

Moilanen, Karo, Stephen Pulman, and Yue Zhang. 2010. Packed feelings and ordered sentiments: Sentiment parsing with quasi-compositional polarity sequencing and compression. In *Proceedings of the 1st Workshop on Computational Approaches to Subjectivity and Sentiment Analysis (WASSA 2010) at the 19th European Conference on Artificial Intelligence (ECAI 2010)*, pages 36–43.

Nakagawa, Tetsuji, Kentaro Inui, and Sadao Kurohash. 2010. Dependency tree-based sentiment classification using crfs with hidden variables. In *Human Language Technologies: The 2010 Annual Conference of the North American Chapter of the ACL*, pages 786–794.

Pang, Bo and Lillian Lee. 2008. Opinion mining and sentiment analysis. *Foundations and Trends in Information Retrieval* 2:1–135.

Pang, Bo, Lillian Lee, and Shivakumar Vaithyanathan. 2002. Thumbs up? sentiment classification using machine learning techniques. In *Proceedings of EMNLP 2002*, pages 79–86.

Polany, Livia and Martin H. van den Berg. 1999. Logical structure and discourse anaphora resolution. In *Proceedings of the ACL99 Workshop on the Relationship Between Discourse/Dialogue Structure and Reference*.

Polanyi, Livia. 1983. On the recursive structure of discourse. In K. Ehlich and H. van Riemsdijk, eds., *Connectedness in Sentence, Discourse and Text*, pages 141–178. Tilburg University.

Polanyi, Livia. 1985. A theory of discourse structure and discourse coherence. In P. D. Kroeber, W. H. Eilfort, and K. L. Peterson, eds., *Papers from the General Session at the 21st Regional Meeting of the Chicago Linguistics Society*, pages 306–322.

Polanyi, Livia. 2003. The linguistic structure of discourse. In D. Schiffrin, D. Tannen, and H. Hamilton, eds., *Handbook of Discourse Analysis*. Wiley-Blackwell.

Polanyi, Livia, Chris Culy, Martin H. van den Berg, G. Lorenzo Thione, and David Ahn. 2004b. A rule based approach to discourse parsing. In *Proceedings SigDial 04*, pages 108–117.

Polanyi, Livia and Remko Scha. 1984. A syntactic approach to discourse semantics. In *Proceedings of the 10th International Conference on Computational Linguistics*, pages 413–419.

Polanyi, Livia, Martin H. van den Berg, Chris Culy, G. Lorenzo Thione, and David Ahn. 2004a. Sentential structure and discourse parsing. In *ACL2004 - Workshop on Discourse Annotation*.

Polanyi, Livia and Annie Zaenen. 2006. Contextual valence shifters. In J. G. Shanahan, Y. Qu, and J. Wiebe, eds., *Computing Attitude and Affect in Text*. Springer Verlag.

Prasad, Rashmi, Nikhil Dinesh, Alan Lee, Eleni Miltsakaki, Livio Robaldo, Aravind Joshi, and Bonnie Webber. 2008. The penn discourse treebank 2.0. In *Proceedings of LREC 2008*.

Prüst, Hub, Remko Scha, and Martin H. van den Berg. 1994. Discourse grammar and verb phrase anaphora. *Linguistics and Philosophy* 17:261–327.

Scha, Remko and Livia Polanyi. 1988. An augmented context free grammar for discourse. In *Proceeding of the 12th International Conference on Computational Linguistics*, pages 573–577.

Shaikh, Mostafa Al Masum, Helmut Prendinger, and Mitsuru Ishizuka. 2007. Assessing sentiment of text by semantic dependency and contextual valence analysis. In *Proceeedings 2nd International Conference Affective Computing and Intelligent Interaction*.

Somasundaran, Swapna. 2010. *Discourse-Level Relations for Opinion Analysis*. Ph.D. thesis, Department of Computer Science, University of Pittsburgh.

Somasundaran, Swapna, Janyce Wiebe, and Josef Ruppenhofer. 2008. Discourse level opinion interpretation. In *The 22nd International Conference on Computational Linguistics (COLING-2008)*, pages 801–808.

Turney, Peter D. 2002. Thumbs up or thumbs down? Semantic orientation applied to unsupervised classification of reviews. In *Proceedings of the 40th Annual Meeting of the Association for Computational Linguistics*, pages 417–424.

Turney, Peter D. and Michael L. Littman. 2003. Measuring praise and criticism: Inference of semantic orientation from association. *ACM Transactions on Information Systems (TOIS)* 21:315–346. (NRC 46516).

van den Berg, Martin H. 1996. Discourse grammar and dynamic logic. In P. Dekker and M. Stokhof, eds., *Proceedings of the Tenth Amsterdam Colloquium*. ILLC/Department of Philosophy, University of Amsterdam.

Wiebe, Janyce. 2012. Sentiment and opinion bibliography http://www.cs.pitt.edu/ wiebe/subjectivity.bib. On-line bibliography.

Wilson, Theresa. 2008. *Fine-Grained Subjectivity Analysis*. Ph.D. thesis, Intelligent Systems Program, University of Pittsburgh.

Wilson, Theresa, Janyce Wiebe, and Paul Hoffmann. 2005. Recognizing contextual polarity in phrase- level sentiment analysis. In *Proceedings of the 2005 Joint Conference on Human Language Technology and Empirical Methods in Natural Language Processing*, pages 347–354.

Wolf, Florian and Edward Gibson. 2005. Representing discourse coherence: A corpus-based study. *Computational Linguistics* 31:249–287.

16

Two Maps of Manhattan

HINRICH SCHÜTZE

16.1 Representations of meaning

What should an adequate formal theory of the meaning of linguistic expressions look like? The most serious contender in terms of coverage of phenomena (linguistic and semantic) and languages is perhaps traditional formal semantics, including Montague semantics (Chierchia and McConnell-Ginet, 1991), discourse representation theory (Kamp and Reyle, 1993) and file change semantics (Heim, 2008, Karttunen, 1976), to name a few older incarnations. It provides elegant explanations for negation, quantification, conditionals and many other phenomena. However, there is an arguably equally large set of phenomena that I would argue it has difficulty with: vagueness, uncertainty, prototypicality, embodiment (Zadeh, 1965, Rumelhart et al., 1986, McClelland et al., 1986, Lakoff, 1987, Barsalou, 2008).

Because I was frustrated with these perceived shortcomings of formal semantics, I became interested in statistical approaches to semantics in 1990/91. It was at this point that Annie Zaenen introduced me to the information access group at Xerox PARC. Her motivation probably was that nobody at Stanford linguistics would have been able to supervise a thesis on statistical approaches, and therefore I should consider collaborating with statisticians like Jan Pedersen and John Tukey. This introduction did a great service to me. I would not have been able to complete my PhD and then make my living as an academic without the supportive and interdisciplinary environment that I enjoyed at PARC for many years.

The contrast between the two polar opposites I have just introduced

From Quirky Case to Representing Space: Papers in Honor of Annie Zaenen.
Tracy Holloway King and Valeria de Paiva.
Copyright © 2013, CSLI Publications.

– formal semantics and statistical semantics or, more generally, symbolic and statistical approaches – has become a cliché in computational linguistics. The view of semantics and meaning that I would like to argue for is that meaning is heterogeneous and that semantic theory will always consist of distinct modules that are governed by different principles. The main argument for this view is that human experience of the world is highly heterogeneous; thus, the theory of the representation of this experience could plausibly have the same property.[1]

Prominent and frequently studied domains of "semantic heterogeneity" are time, space, motion, causation, number and color. We can hardly survive in the world without an adequate understanding of these domains and without the ability to communicate effectively about them. Because these domains pose interesting challenges to semanticists, there is a long tradition of work on them in theoretical linguistics.

My hypothesis is that the human cognitive system has unique representation and processing mechanisms for each of these domains, and that in turn the linguistic encoding of each domain will have different properties in human language. If this hypothesis is correct, the alignment between different modes of human experience and different semantic domains can guide our linguistic and cognitive theories.

One could perhaps object that representation and processing could differ cognitively without affecting language and, in particular, without affecting semantics. However, there is evidence that linguistic organizing principles are correlated with general cognitive organizing principles. A nice example of this are the Thaayorre people who conceptualize space in terms of absolute compass directions and this is directly reflected in the linguistic encoding of their language (Boroditsky, 2011). So part of the heterogeneity hypothesis is that differences in cognitive representation and processing translate into linguistic and semantic differences between modes/modalities – not necessarily, but frequently, and that therefore semantics is also heterogeneous.

One small project in this vein was the only time Annie and I directly worked together. Stanley Peters and Annie hired me as a student researcher in 1990/91 to look into the linguistics of particular types of relative spatial linguistic expressions (cf. Wunderlich and Herweg (1991)). For example, "left" in "the left door of the car" is usually resolved with respect to the standard orientation of the car – the direction of travel; but in some circumstances it can refer to the door that is positioned to the left of the speaker or the hearer. The set of doors identified by

---

[1]There is an interesting parallel to the skepticism expressed by Dupré (1993) about the plausibility of a grand unified theory of science. I do not explore this parallel in this contribution.

"doors open to the left" when a train enters a terminus station is distinct from the set of doors referred to by the same phrase after the train has left the terminus and is entering the next station.

These are the types of "domain-specific" phenomena that may require domain-specific semantic theories. I regret that I never contributed anything to Annie and Stanley's project because I became excited about statistical semantics at the same time and focused all my energy on publishing in this emerging subfield (Schütze, 1992b, 1993, 1995). However, the phenomena we investigated in the project have stayed with me as examples of the complexity of semantics and the impossibility of reducing meaning to a single simplistic unified notion.

16.2 An example

I will not provide a detailed argument for heterogeneous semantics in this paper. In general, arguments for the non-existence of something – in our case a unified grand theory of semantics – are difficult. Instead, I will provide an example and hope that the reader will view the heterogeneity of meaning elements needed in this case as evidence that semantics is heterogeneous.

The example I have chosen is Manhattan and its neighborhoods. I will use the abbreviations in Table 1.

Abbreviation	Neighborhood
BaPaCi	Battery Park City
Che	Chelsea
Chi	Chinatown
EaHa	East Harlem
EaVi	East Village
FiDi	Financial District
GrVi	Greenwich Village
Ha	Harlem
LiIt	Little Italy
LoEaSi	Lower East Side
No	Noho
So	Soho
Tr	Tribeca
UpEaSi	Upper East Side
UpWeSi	Upper West Side
WaHe	Washington Heights

TABLE 1 Abbreviations used for Manhattan neighborhoods

Table 2 lists a small number of facts or propositions that could be formal semantics representations of the meaning of some linguistic expressions about these neighborhoods.

1   subarea_of(SoHo, Lower_Manhattan)
2   south_of(SoHo, NoHo)
3   eastern_boundary(Upper_West_Side, Central_Park)
4   tourist_destination(Little_Italy)
5   latino_neighborhood(East_Harlem)
6   located_in(World_Trade_Center, Financial_District, 1974, 2001)
7   historic_ethnic_neighborhood(Little_Italy)
8   historic_ethnic_neighborhood(Chinatown)
9   name_is_of_Dutch_origin(Greenwich_Village)
10   name_is_of_Dutch_origin(Harlem)

TABLE 2 Facts about Manhattan neighborhoods

The first three (1-3) could also be read off of a map of Manhattan. For example, Figure 1 shows that SoHo (So) is located south of NoHo (No). However, the two ways of representing this piece of knowledge – propositional vs. on a map – may not be cognitively equivalent as representation can make a difference in ease of access and processing. Propositional representations are a mainstay of much of the work in symbolic artificial intelligence (McCarthy, 1993) and theoretical and applied semantics (Van Benthem, 1986, Bobrow et al., 2007).

Facts 4–6 are more complex than the simple "map" facts 1–3. They capture complex conceptual knowledge, including temporal relativization (fact 6), that symbolic formalisms are best equipped to handle.

Facts 7–10 are intended as examples of features that are prominent versus those that are not. Chinatown and Little Italy are often perceived as similar neighborhoods because they share a number of prominent characteristics, including the fact that they are historic ethnic neighborhoods. Greenwich Village and Harlem also share a number of characteristics, including the fact that their names are derived from Dutch (Greenwijck and Haarlem); but in this case these characteristics are not salient and the two neighborhoods are not perceived as similar. This is the type of inference that is difficult to do in a purely symbolic system because graded phenomena like salience cannot be naturally handled without weights, probabilities, confidences or similar indicators of grading.

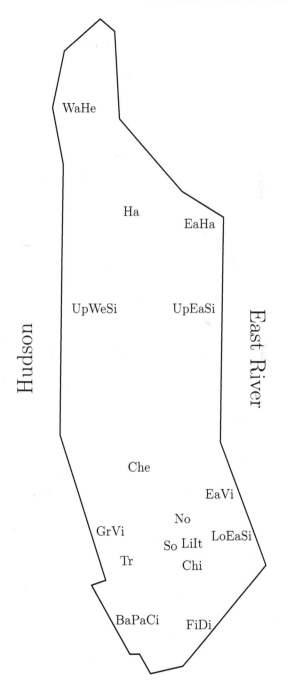

FIGURE 1 A map of Manhattan

Figure 2 is a multidimensional scaling (MDS) of the 16×16 similarity matrix of the 16 neighborhoods shown in Table 1.

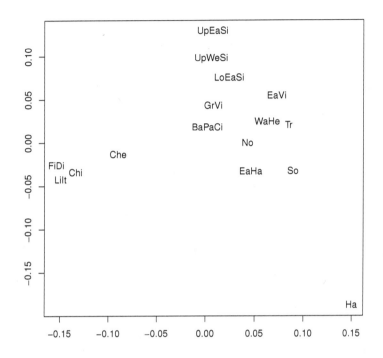

FIGURE 2   Multidimensional scaling (MDS) of Manhattan neighborhods based on word space similarities

Following roughly the approach pursued by Schütze (1992a, 1998) at PARC in the early nineties, each neighborhood was first represented in a high-dimensional word space. To simplify the computations, I ran a Google search on each neighborhood and took as contexts the top 100 hits – using both titles and snippets – that were returned (instead of looking for mentions of the neighborhood in a corpus). The average number of words per context was 35, including a fair number of tokens that could have been cleaned in more careful preprocessing: URLs, truncated title words like "Hypno...", meta-information like "cached", etc. The weight of a neighborhood vector on the dimension corresponding to a word w was calculated as $1 + \log f_w$ where f_w is the number of times w occurred in the contexts. The similarity between two neighborhoods is defined as the cosine of their vectors. Multidimensional scaling is an approximative technique for depicting the similarity relationships between objects in a high-dimensional space in lower dimensionality.

It is clear that Figure 2 conveys a type of information that is not symbolic. Similarity and dissimilarity are often used for semantic processing in statistical natural language processing (Manning and Schütze, 1999). The upscale residential areas Upper East Side (UpEaSi) and Upper West Side (UpWeSi) are neighbors in the uppermost part of the figure even though they are not adjacent geographically. Conversely, the geographical neighbors Upper East Side (UpEaSi) and East Harlem (EaHa) are not adjacent on the MDS map, which is a reflection of their disparity in a number of important properties. The quality of Figure 2 is somewhat hampered by the fact that it represents a distribution of contexts as a single point, its mean or centroid. More accurate and complex statistical inferences can be made when the distribution of contexts as a whole is taken into account, e.g., by clustering the contexts (Schütze, 1998). Despite its shortcomings, hopefully Figure 2 is a sufficiently clear contrast to Table 2 to make the point that these two formal ways of approaching semantics have different strengths and weaknesses.

In addition to the two by now traditional symbolic and statistical meaning representations, there is also "domain-specific" semantics here – in this case space. Figure 1 is a simplified version of a conventional geographic map of Manhattan. We see that the 16 selected neighborhoods cover Manhattan in a geographically very uneven way. We can infer that starting in Chelsea (Che), it takes a long time to walk to Washington Heights (WaHe) and a much shorter time to walk to Greenwich Village (GrVi). We also see which neighborhoods border the rivers and on what side. All of this spatial information is directly and naturally encoded in the map representation. We can of course also represent it in a "non-map" way, but the natural representation is a map and is arguably closer to cognitive reality than propositions or similarity spaces.

16.3   Unified and non-unified theories of meaning

There is no particularly deep insight in the three sketches of representations of Manhattan I have presented. The example is simply meant as an illustration of the fact that each of them is good at representing certain types of meaning and bad at representing others.

Symbolic representations are good at representing the type of information shown in Table 2. However, there is no satisfactory treatment of uncertainty, similarity and probability in these frameworks.

Statistical representations are good at handling uncertainty, similarity and probability. However, to the extent that a probabilistic model is a parameterized structure, a non-symbolic probabilistic approach is impossible: all statistical models have a symbolic core. This is also true for neural networks whose symbolic core is a structure consisting of neurons and their connections. We need symbolic categories and relations between them for any type of semantics.

Finally, there is evidence that special domains like space, time and color have given rise to *specialized cognitive processing and representation capabilities*. In the case of space, these capabilities include the ability to remember paths and to create internal maps that let us plan and act appropriately when we encounter a particular spatial layout in a novel way; for example, we know that the door that is on our right as we walk towards the dining car will be on our left on the way back.

These considerations suggest that it will be difficult to come up with a grand unified theory that explains all semantic phenomena.

16.4 Outlook

To summarize, we have explored the hypothesis that semantics is heterogeneous because human experience consists of heterogeneous modalities that are encoded by human languages in diverse and modality-specific ways. For the example of Manhattan, we have looked at three types of semantic knowledge people have about a geographic area: propositional formulas, similarity judgments and the spatial representation of the area. This example was designed to convey the intuition that different types of semantic knowledge are fundamentally different and cannot be unified in one grand theory.

If we accept semantic heterogeneity, then two questions arise. First, without a unifying formal model, how do the heterogeneous modalities interface with each other? Increasingly complex NLP systems provide one answer to this question. My impression is that in these systems interaction is implemented in an ad-hoc and manually optimized way. For example, the IBM question answering system Watson (Ferrucci et al., 2010) has many heterogeneous modules that each contribute information useful for solving a Jeopardy task. The final design of the components that integrate this information into the Jeopardy answer seems to have been the result of careful and time-intensive fine tuning.

Another answer as to how different modalities interact could come from research on the brain. Many areas of the brain are specialized for particular modalities: vision, sound, motion, etc. The neural activities in these areas interface with each other for complex tasks like eye-hand coordination and the control of whole-body actions like walking and reaching. Thus, a detailed model of neural processing in the brain may also turn out to be a model of how different modules of a heterogeneous theory of semantics interface with each other. However, our understanding of how the brain works will probably remain too rudimentary for a while to shed light on this issue.

The second question that arises if we accept semantic heterogeneity is how we can investigate the nature of semantic representations and how language is mapped to them. Grand theories have the advantage of being more easily falsified since a few phenomena that they do not cover suffice for falsification. If semantics is heterogeneous, then we have to develop distinct theories for different domains – which is much harder.

One way to approach the problem is psychological and (more recently) brain imaging research. Maybe methodological advances will be so great that at some point all the answers will come from these fields. I doubt it.

An alternative approach is linguistics. Language is a window into the mind and linguists have always exploited the great diversity of human languages to make inferences about how we process and represent meaning.

When I look back at Annie's work so far, I see this as one of the threads in her research over the years. It certainly was an important element in the space project that she and Stanley led and that I participated in. Her work on unaccusativity and quirky case (Zaenen et al., 1985, Zaenen, 1993) is relevant here because it investigates the grammatical means languages use to express the participants of an event or action. Her work on animacy (Zaenen et al., 2004) addresses the syntactic and morphological encoding of this important semantic category, with implications for mental representation and processing as well as for computational linguistics. The work at PARC on textual inference she contributed to (Zaenen et al., 2005) makes a convincing case that there are crisp logical phenomena that are not subject to probabilites and relativization by context and world knowledge.

My hope is that we can continue this type of deep linguistic analysis and will eventually be able to put forward formal models of semantics – even if they are not part of a grand unified theory – that are both linguistically and cognitively adequate and computationally powerful in NLP applications.

Acknowledgments

I would like to thank the reviewers of this contribution for their questions and their constructive feedback.

References

Barsalou, Lawrence W. 2008. Grounded cognition. *Annual Review of Psychology* 59(1):617–645.

Bobrow, Daniel G., Bob Cheslow, Cleo Condoravdi, Lauri Karttunen, Tracy Holloway King, Rowan Nairn, Valeria de Paiva, Charlotte Price, and Annie Zaenen. 2007. PARC's bridge and question answering system. In *Grammar Engineering Across Frameworks*, pages 46–66. CSLI Publications.

Boroditsky, Lera. 2011. How language shapes thought. *Scientific American* 304(2):62–65.

Chierchia, Gennaro and Sally McConnell-Ginet. 1991. *Meaning and Grammar*. The MIT Press.

Dupré, John. 1993. *The Disorder of Things*. Harvard University Press.

Ferrucci, David A., Eric W. Brown, Jennifer Chu-Carroll, James Fan, David Gondek, Aditya Kalyanpur, Adam Lally, J. William Murdock, Eric Nyberg, John M. Prager, Nico Schlaefer, and Christopher A. Welty. 2010. Building watson: An overview of the DeepQA project. *AI Magazine* 31(3):59–79.

Heim, Irene. 2008. File change semantics and the familiarity theory of definiteness. In P. Portner and B. H. Partee, eds., *Formal Semantics*, pages 223–248. Blackwell.

Kamp, Hans and Uwe Reyle. 1993. *From Discourse to Logic. Introduction to Modeltheoretic Semantics of Natural Language, Formal Logic and Discourse Representation Theory*. Kluwer.

Karttunen, Lauri. 1976. Discourse referents. In J. D. McCawley, ed., *Syntax and Semantics*, vol. 7, pages 363–385. Academic Press.

Lakoff, George. 1987. *Women, Fire, and Dangerous Things*. The University of Chicago Press.

Manning, Christopher D. and Hinrich Schütze. 1999. *Foundations of Statistical Natural Language Processing*. MIT Press.

McCarthy, John. 1993. Notes on formalizing context. In *Proceedings of the 13th international joint conference on Artifical intelligence - Volume 1*, pages 555–560.

McClelland, James L., David E. Rumelhart, and the PDP Research Group, eds. 1986. *Parallel Distributed Processing. Explorations in the Microstructure of Cognition. Volume 2: Psychological and Biological Models*. The MIT Press.

Rumelhart, David E., James L. McClelland, and the PDP research group, eds. 1986. *Parallel Distributed Processing. Explorations in the Microstructure of Cognition. Volume 1: Foundations*. The MIT Press.

Schütze, Hinrich. 1992a. Dimensions of meaning. In *ACM/IEEE Conference on Supercomputing*, pages 787–796.

Schütze, Hinrich. 1992b. Word sense disambiguation with sublexical representations. In C. Weir, S. Abney, R. Grishman, and R. Weischedel, eds., *Workshop Notes of the AAAI Workshop on Statistically-Based NLP Techniques*, pages 109–113. AAAI.

Schütze, Hinrich. 1993. Word space. In *Advances in Neural Information Processing Systems*, pages 895–902.

Schütze, Hinrich. 1995. Distributional part-of-speech tagging. In *Conference of the European Chapter of the Association for Computational Linguistics*, pages 141–148.

Schütze, Hinrich. 1998. Automatic word sense discrimination. *Computational Linguistics* 24(1):97–124.

Van Benthem, Johan F.A.K. 1986. *Essays in Logical Semantics*. Studies in Linguistics and Philosophy. D. Reidel.

Wunderlich, Dieter and Michael Herweg. 1991. Lokale und Direktionale. In A. von Stechow and D. Wunderlich, eds., *Semantik. Ein internationales Handbuch der zeitgenössischen Forschung*, pages 758–785. de Gruyter.

Zadeh, Lotfali Askar. 1965. Fuzzy sets. *Information and Control* 8:338–353.

Zaenen, Annie. 1993. Unaccusativity in Dutch: Integrating syntax and lexical semantics. In J. Pustejovsky, ed., *Semantics and the Lexicon*, pages 129–161. London: Kluwer.

Zaenen, Annie, Jean Carletta, Gregory Garretson, Joan Bresnan, Andrew Koontz-Garboden, Tatiana Nikitina, M. Catherine O'Connor, and Tom Wasow. 2004. Animacy encoding in English: Why and how. In *Proceedings of the 2004 ACL Workshop on Discourse Annotation*, pages 118–125.

Zaenen, Annie, Lauri Karttunen, and Richard Crouch. 2005. Local textual inference: Can it be defined or circumscribed? In *Proceedings of the ACL Workshop on Empirical Modeling of Semantic Equivalence and Entailment*, EMSEE '05, pages 31–36.

Zaenen, Annie, Joan Maling, and Hoskuldur Thrainsson. 1985. Case and grammatical functions: The Icelandic passive. *Natural Language and Linguistic Theory* 3:441–483.

Part IV

Annie Zaenen: Curriculum Vitae and Bibliography

17

Curriculum Vitae and Bibliography

Annie Zaenen

Education[1]

1961 **Kandidatuur in Romance Philology**, *Rijksuniversiteit Gent*, Gent, Belgium 'with great distinction'

1967 **Licentie in Philosophy**, *Rijksuniversiteit Gent* Gent, Belgium 'with great distinction'

1980 **Ph.D. in Linguistics**, *Harvard University*, Cambridge, MA, Dissertation title: *Extraction Rules in Icelandic*

Grants and Scholarships

1968 **N.F.W.O. doctoral dissertation grant**, *National Foundation for Scientific Research*, Belgium

1974 **Frank Boas Scholarship for Graduate Study**, *Harvard University*

1980 **Postdoctoral Fellowship**, *Center for Cognitive Science*, M.I.T.

1984 **Faculty Summer Research Grant**, *Cornell University*

---

[1]The editors would like to thank Lauri Karttunen for providing the CV and bibliography for this section.

From Quirky Case to Representing Space: Papers in Honor of Annie Zaenen.
Tracy Holloway King and Valeria de Paiva.
Copyright © 2013, CSLI Publications.

Experience

Research and Managerial Experience

1965–68	**Research Associate**, *Centre de Recherches et d'Information Socio-Politiques*, Brussels
Sum. '72	**Research Assistant**, *Prof. H. Weiss (C.U.N.Y.)*, Zaire
1978–80	**Research Associate**, *Prof. J. Maling*, (N.S.F. Grant 78-16522) "Investigations in Comparative Germanic Syntax", Brandeis University
1980–81	**Postdoctoral Fellow**, *Center for Cognitive Science*, M.I.T.
1982–83	**Research Affiliate LFG-project**, *Center for Cognitive Science*, M.I.T.
1985–93	**Staff member**, *Xerox-PARC*, ISTL, formerly: System Sciences Laboratory; formerly: Intelligent Systems Laboratory
1985–	**Member**, *Center for the Study of Language and Information*
1993–99	**Area Manager**, *MLTT*, RXRC-Grenoble
1999–2000	**Scientific Programme Coordinator**, *RXRC-Grenoble*
1993–2000	**Participant European Projects**, *Compass, Eagles, Trindi*
1995–2000	**Project leader ParGram**, *XRCE-Grenoble*
2001–2011	**Principal Scientist**, *NLTT*, ISL, PARC
2008–2010	**Acting Area Manager**, *NLTT*, ISL, PARC

Teaching Positions

1963–64	**Lecturer in Ethics**, *Normaalschool*, Brugge, Belgium
1972	**Substitute Teaching Assistant in Psycholinguistics**, *Institut de Psychologie*, Université de Genève Spring semester
1972–74	**Teaching Assistant in Philosophy**, *R.U.G.*, Belgium
1975–78	**Teaching Fellow in French**, *Harvard University*, intermediate and advanced level
1977	**Teaching Fellow for Introduction to Linguistics**, *Harvard University*, fall semester
1978–79	**Lecturer in Linguistics**, *University of Pennsylvania*
1979	**Teaching Fellow for Introduction to Transformational Syntax**, *Harvard University*, fall semester
1981–83	**Lecturer in Linguistics**, *Harvard University*

1983–84	Assistant Professor in Linguistics and French Language and Linguistics, *Cornell University*
1985–1994	Consulting Professor in Linguistics, *Stanford University*
2001–	Consulting Professor in Linguistics and Symbolic Systems, *Stanford University*

Visiting Appointments

1986	Summer School in Linguistics, *Munich, Germany*
1987	LSA Summer School in Linguistics, *Stanford University*
1987	University of Stuttgart, *Germany*
1988	Summer School on the Lexicon, *Pisa, Italy*
1989	ILTEC, *Lisbon, Portugal Course in LFG*
1991	LSA Summer School, *UCSC Santa Cruz, CA*
1993	Paris 7, France, *Course in LFG*
1994	Summer School, *Prague, Czechoslovakia*, Lectures on LFG
1995	Elsnet Summer School, *Edinburgh, Scotland*, Variation and Universals in Syntax
1998	University of Pennsylvania, *Spring semester*, Bantu Syntax
2005	LSA Summer School, *M.I.T.*
2006	ESSLI, *Malaga, Spain*
2007	LSA Summer School, *Stanford University*
2011	LSA Summer School, *University of Colorado Boulder*

Books and Edited Volumes

1985	Extraction Rules in Icelandic, *Annie Zaenen*, Garland Publishers

Edited volumes:

1990	Modern Icelandic Syntax, *Joan Maling and Annie Zaenen, editors*, Academic Press. Volume 24 of *Syntax and Semantics*
1995	Formal Issues in Lexical-Functional Grammar, *Mary Dalrymple, Ronald M. Kaplan, John T. Maxwell III, and Annie Zaenen, editors*, CSLI Publications
1996	Survey of the State of the Art in Human Language Technology, *Ronald A. Cole, Editor in Chief, Joseph Mariani, Hans Uszkoreit, Annie Zaenen and Victor Zue, editors*, Oxford University Press
2008	Architectures, Rules and Preferences: Variations on Themes by Joan W. Bresnan, *Annie Zaenen, Jane Simpson, Tracy Holloway King, Jane Grimshaw, Joan Maling, and Chris Manning, editors*, CSLI Publications

Bibliography

Zaenen, Annie. 1967. Is Das Kapital een wetenschappelijk werk? *Studia Philosophica Gandensia* 5.

Zaenen, Annie and F. Vandamme. 1970. Review of Dirven et al.: Transformationele generatieve grammatica. *Communication and Cognition* 3.

Zaenen, Annie. 1973. The understanding of relative clauses by Dutch-speaking children (ages 4-9). *Communication and Cognition* 6(3/4).

Zaenen, Annie. 1974. Preface to the special issue on language learning. *Communication and Cognition* 7(2).

Zaenen, Annie and Jessie Pinkham. 1976. The discovery of another island. *Linguistic Inquiry* 7(4):652–664.

Maling, Joan and Annie Zaenen. 1978. The nonuniversality of a surface filter. *Linguistic Inquiry* 9(3):475–497.

Zaenen, Annie. 1979. Infinitival complements in Dutch. In *CLS 15*, pages 378–389. Chicago, IL: Chicago Linguistic Society.

Maling, Joan and Annie Zaenen. 1981. Germanic word order and the format of surface filters. In F. Heny, ed., *Binding and Filtering*, pages 255–278. London, UK: Croom Held.

Zaenen, Annie. 1981. Characterizing binding domains. In *Occasional Paper 17*. Cambridge, MA: Center for Cognitive Science, M.I.T.

Zaenen, Annie, Elisabet Engdahl, and Joan M. Maling. 1981. Resumptive pronouns can be syntactically bound. *Linguistic Inquiry* 12(4):679–682.

Bresnan, Joan, Ronald M. Kaplan, Stanley Peters, and Annie Zaenen. 1982. Cross-serial dependencies in Dutch. *Linguistic Inquiry* 13(4):613–635.

Zaenen, Annie and Joan M. Maling. 1982a. A phrase-structure account of Scandinavian extraction phenomena. In P. Jacobson and G. Pullum, eds., *The Nature of Syntactic Representation*. Dordrecht, Holland: Reidel.

Zaenen, Annie and Joan M. Maling. 1982b. Resumptive pronouns in Swedish. In E. Ejerhed and E. Engdahl, eds., *Readings on Unbounded Dependencies in Scandinavian Languages*, Acta Universitatis Umensis. Stockholm, Sweden: Almqvist and Wiksell.

Clements, George N., James McCloskey, Joan Maling, and Annie Zaenen. 1983. String-vacuous rule application. *Linguistic Inquiry* 14(1):1–17.

Zaenen, Annie. 1983a. On syntactic binding. *Linguistic Inquiry* 14(3):469–504.

Zaenen, Annie. 1983b. Verb-first clauses in Icelandic, successive cyclic Wh-movement and syntactic binding. In L. Tasmowski and D. Willems, eds., *Current Research in Syntax*, Acta Universitatis Umensis. Ghent, Belgium: Communication and Cognition.

Perlmutter, David M. and Annie Zaenen. 1984. The indefinite extraposition construction in Dutch and German. In D. M. Perlmutter and C. G. Rosen, eds., *Studies in Relational Grammar*, vol. 2, pages 171–216. Chicago, IL: University of Chicago Press.

Zaenen, Annie. 1984. Double objects in Kikuyu? In *Cornell Working Papers in Linguistics*, vol. 5, pages 199–206. Ithaca, NY: Department of Modern Languages and Linguistics, Cornell University.

Zaenen, Annie and Lauri Karttunen. 1984. Morphological non-distinctiveness and coordination. In *ESCOL*, vol. 1, pages 309–320. Columbus, OH: Department of Linguistics, Ohio State University.

Zaenen, Annie, Höskuldur Thráinsson, and Joan Maling. 1984. Passive and oblique case. In *Working Papers in Scandinavian Syntax*. Trondheim, Norway: Linguistics Department, University of Trondheim.

Maling, Joan and Annie Zaenen. 1985. Preposition stranding and oblique case. In *Cornell Working Papers in Linguistics*, pages 149–161. Ithaca, NY: Department of Modern Languages and Linguistics, Cornell University.

Kaplan, Ronald M. and Annie Zaenen. 1988. Functional uncertainty and functional precedence in Continental West Germanic. In H. Trost, ed., *Österreichische Artifical Intelligence-Tagung*, vol. 176 of *Informatik-Fachberichte*, pages 114–123. Berlin, Germany: Springer Verlag.

Kaplan, Ronald M., Klaus Netter, Jürgen Wedekind, and Annie Zaenen. 1989. Translation by structural correspondences. In *EACL*, pages 271–281.

Kaplan, Ronald M. and Annie Zaenen. 1989. Long-distance dependencies, constituent structure, and functional uncertainty. In M. Baltin and A. Kroch, eds., *Alternative Conceptions of Phrase Structure*, pages 17–42. Chicago, IL: Chicago University Press.

Dalrymple, Mary, John Maxwell III, and Annie Zaenen. 1990. Modeling syntactic constraints on anaphoric binding. In *Coling'90*, pages 72–76.

Kaplan, Ronald M. and Annie Zaenen. 1990. Functional precedence and constituent structure. In C. Huang and K. Chen, eds., *ROCLING II*, pages 19–40. Taipei, Taiwan: Academia Sinica.

Zaenen, Annie and Joan Maling. 1990. Unaccusative, passive and quirky case. In J. Maling and A. Zaenen, eds., *Modern Icelandic Syntax*, vol. 24 of *Syntax and Semantics*, pages 171–216. New York, NY: Academic Press.

Zaenen, Annie, Joan Maling, and Höskuldur Thráinsson. 1990. Case and grammatical functions: The Icelandic passive. In J. Maling and A. Zaenen, eds., *Modern Icelandic Syntax*, vol. 24 of *Syntax and Semantics*, pages 95–136. New York, NY: Academic Press.

Bever, Thomas G., Steven Jandreau, Rebecca Burwell, Ron Kaplan, and Annie Zaenen. 1991. Spacing printed text to isolate major phrases improves readability. *Visible Language* 25(1):74–87.

Bresnan, Joan and Annie Zaenen. 1991. Deep unaccusativity in LFG. In K. Dziwirek, P. Farrell, and E. M. Bikandi, eds., *Grammatical Relations:*

A Cross-theoretical Perspective, pages 45–57. Stanford, CA: CSLI Publications.

Dalrymple, Mary and Annie Zaenen. 1991. Modeling anaphoric superiority. In *International Conference on Current Issues in Computational Linguistics*, pages 235–247. Penang, Malaysia.

Wescoat, Michael T. and Annie Zaenen. 1991. Lexical Functional Grammar. In F. G. Droste and J. E. Joseph, eds., *Linguistic Theory and Grammatical Description: Nine Current Approaches*, vol. 75 of *Current Issues in Linguistic Theory*, pages 103–136. Amsterdam, Holland: John Benjamins Publishing Company.

Karttunen, Lauri, Ronald M. Kaplan, and Annie Zaenen. 1992. Two-level morphology with composition. In *Coling'92*, pages 387–396. Nantes, France.

Nunberg, Geoffrey and Annie Zaenen. 1992. Systematic polysemy in lexicology and lexicography. In *Euralex II*, pages 387–396. Tampere, Finland.

Goldberg, Adele E. and Annie Zaenen. 1993. Review of Grimshaw, Argument Structure. *Language* 69(4):807–816.

Jackendoff, Ray, Joan Maling, and Annie Zaenen. 1993. Home is subject to principle A. *Linguistic Inquiry* 24(1):173–177.

Zaenen, Annie. 1993. Unaccusatives in Dutch and the syntax-semantics interface. In J. Pustejovsky, ed., *Semantics and the Lexicon*, pages 129–161. Dordrecht, Holland: Kluwer Academic Publishers.

Zaenen, Annie. 1994. Unaccusativity in Dutch: integrating syntax and lexical semantics. In J. Pustejovsky, ed., *Semantics and the Lexicon*, vol. 49 of *Studies in Linguistics and Philosophy*, pages 129–162. Dordrecht, Holland: Kluwer.

Zaenen, Annie and Elisabet Engdahl. 1994. Descriptive and theoretical syntax in the lexicon. In B. T. S. Atkins and A. Zampolli, eds., *Computational Approaches to the Lexicon*, pages 181–212. Oxford, UK: Oxford University Press.

Zaenen, Annie and Geoff Nunberg. 1994. Communication technology, linguistic technology and the multilingual individual. In T. Andernach, M. Moll, and A. Nijholt, eds., *Proceedings of the Fifth CLIN Meeting*. Parlevink Research Group, Centre for Telematics and Information Technology of the University of Twente, Enschede, Holland.

Bauer, Daniel, Frédérique Segond, and Annie Zaenen. 1995. Locolex: the translation rolls of your tongue. In *ACH-ACCL*, pages 6–8. Santa Barbara, CA.

Zaenen, Annie and Ronald M. Kaplan. 1995. Formal devices for linguistic generalizations: West Germanic word order in LFG. In M. Dalrymple, R. M. Kaplan, J. T. M. III, and A. Zaenen, eds., *Formal Issues in Lexical Functional Grammar*, pages 215–239. Stanford, CA: CSLI Publications.

Segond, Frédérique and Annie Zaenen. 1996. Cherche linguiste informaticien désespérément. *Traitement Automatique des Langues* 37(1):7–16.

Zaenen, Annie. 1996. Contrastive dislocation in Dutch and Icelandic. In E. Anagnostopoulou, H. V. Riemsdijk, and F. Zwarts, eds., *Materials on Left Dislocation*, pages 119–148. Amsterdam, Holland: John Benjamins Publishing Company.

Zaenen, Annie and Mary Dalrymple. 1996. Les verbes causatifs "polymorphiques": les prédicats complexes en français. *Langages* 30(122):96–122.

Juilliard, Laurent and Annie Zaenen. 1997. Les outils de recherche documentaire de Callimaque. In F. Renzetti, ed., *Stratégies informationnelles et valorisation de la recherche scientifique publique*, Collection Sciences de l'information. Série Recherches et documents. Paris, France: ADBS.

Nunberg, Geoff and Annie Zaenen. 1997. La polysémie systématique dans la déscription lexicale. *Langue française* 113:12–23.

Larsson, Staffan and Annie Zaenen. 2000. Document transformations and information states. In *1st SIGdial Workshop on Discourse and Dialogue*, pages 112–120. Hong Kong, China: Association for Computational Linguistics

Trouilleux, François, Éric Gaussier, Gabriel G. Bès, and Annie Zaenen. 2000. Coreference resolution evaluation based on descriptive specificity. In *LREC*. Athens, Greece: ILSP.

Tutin, Agnes, François Trouilleux, Catherine Clouzot, Éric Gaussier, Annie Zaenen, Stephanie Rayot, and Georges Antoniadis. 2000. Annotating a large corpus with anaphoric links. In *DAARC2000*, pages 28–38. Lancaster, UK.

Larsson, Staffan, Agnes Sandor, David Traum, and Annie Zaenen. 2001. Text and dialogue. In *The TRINDI Book*, pages 261–296. Gothenburg, Sweden: University of Gothenburg.

Frank, Anette and Annie Zaenen. 2002. Tense in LFG: syntax and morphology. In H. Kamp and U. Reyle, eds., *How We Say When it Happens: Contributions to the Theory of Temporal Reference in Natural Language*, pages 17–52. Tübingen, Germany: Niemeyer.

Zaenen, Annie. 2002a. Musings about the impossible electronic dictionary. In M.-H. Corréard, ed., *Lexicography and Natural Language, A Festschrift in Honour of B. T. S. Atkins*, pages 230–244. Grenoble, France: EURALEX.

Zaenen, Annie. 2002b. A review of Polysemy: theoretical and computational approaches, edited by Yael Ravin and Claudia Leacock (Oxford University Press; 2000). *International Journal of Lexicography* 15(3):238–242.

Zaenen, Annie and Ronald M. Kaplan. 2002. Subsumption and equality: German partial fronting in LFG. In M. Butt and T. H. King, eds., *Proceedings of the LFG'02 Conference*, pages 408–426. Stanford, CA: CSLI Publications.

Riezler, Stefan, Tracy Holloway King, Richard Crouch, and Annie Zaenen. 2003. Statistical sentence condensation using ambiguity packing and stochastic disambiguation methods for Lexical-Functional Grammar. In *HLT-NAACL*, pages 118–125. Ann Arbor, Michigan: Association for Computational Linguistics.

Kaplan, Ronald M. and Annie Zaenen. 2003a. Things are not always equal. In A. Gelbukh, ed., *Computational Linguistics and Intelligent Text Processing*, vol. 2588 of *Lecture Notes in Computer Science*, pages 3–24. Berlin, Germany: Springer.

Kaplan, Ronald M. and Annie Zaenen. 2003b. West-Germanic verb clusters in LFG. In P. Seuren and G. Kempen, eds., *Verb Constructions in German and Dutch*, pages 127–150. Amsterdam, Holland: John Benjamins Publishing Company.

Zaenen, Annie and Ronald M. Kaplan. 2003. Stylistic inversion in French: equality and inequality in LFG. In C. Beyssade, O. Bonami, P. Cabredo-Hofherr, and F. Corblin, eds., *Empirical Issues In Syntax and Semantics*, vol. 4, pages 190–205. Paris, France: Presses Universitaires de Paris Sorbonne.

Crouch, Richard, Tracy Holloway King, John T. Maxwell III, Stefan Riezler, and Annie Zaenen. 2004. Exploiting F-structure input for sentence condensation. In M. Butt and T. King, eds., *Proceedings of the LFG'04 Conference*. CSLI Publications, Stanford, CA.

King, Tracy Holloway and Annie Zaenen. 2004. F-structures, information structure, and discourse structure. In M. Butt and T. King, eds., *Proceedings of the LFG'04 Conference*. CSLI Publications, Stanford, CA.

Polanyi, Livia and Annie Zaenen. 2004a. Contextual lexical valence shifters. In *Proceedings of the AAAI Spring Symposium on Exploring Attitude and Affect in Text: Theories and Applications*.

Polanyi, Livia and Annie Zaenen. 2004b. Contextual valence shifters. In J. G. Shanahan, Y. Qu, and J. Wiebe, eds., *Computing Attitude and Affect in Text: Theories and Applications (AAAI Spring Symposium Series)*, pages 1–10. Berlin, Germany: Springer.

Zaenen, Annie, Jean Carletta, Gregory Garretson, Joan Bresnan, Andrew Koontz-Garboden, Tatiana Nikitina, M. Catherine O'Connor, and Tom Wasow. 2004. Animacy encoding in English: Why and How. In B. Webber and D. K. Byron, eds., *ACL 2004 Workshop on Discourse Annotation*, pages 118–125. Barcelona, Spain: ACL.

Bobrow, Danny, Cleo Condoravdi, Richard Crouch, Valeria de Paiva, Ronald M. Kaplan, Lauri Karttunen, Tracy Holloway King, John Maxwell III, and Annie Zaenen. 2005. A basic logic for textual inference. In S. Harabagiu, D. Moldovan, S. Narayanan, C. Manning, D. Bobrow, and K. Forbus, eds., *Papers from the AAAI Workshop on Inference for Textual Question Answering*, pages 31–36. Pittsburg,PA: AAAI.

Karttunen, Lauri and Annie Zaenen. 2005. Veridicity. In G. Katz, J. Pustejovsky, and F. Schilder, eds., *Annotating, Extracting and Reasoning about Time and Events*, Dagstuhl Seminar Proceedings. Dagstuhl, Germany: Internationales Begegnungs- und Forschungszentrum für Informatik (IBFI), Schloss Dagstuhl, Germany.

Zaenen, Annie. 2005a. Review of Berman, Topics in the Clausal Syntax of German. *Journal of Germanic Linguistics* 17(1):68–75.

Zaenen, Annie. 2005b. Unaccusativity. In K. Brown, ed., *The Encyclopedia of Language and Linguistics, 2nd Edition*, pages 127–150. Cambridge, UK: Cambridge University Press.

Zaenen, Annie, Lauri Karttunen, and Richard Crouch. 2005. Local textual inference: Can it be defined or circumscribed? In *Proceedings of the ACL Workshop on Empirical Modeling of Semantic Equivalence and Entailment*, pages 31–36. Ann Arbor, Michigan: Association for Computational Linguistics.

Butt, Miriam and Annie Zaenen. 2006. Introduction to lexical semantics in LFG. In M. Butt and T. H. King, eds., *Lexical Semantics in LFG*. Palo Alto, CA: CSLI Publications.

Snider, Neal and Annie Zaenen. 2006. Animacy and syntactic structure: Fronted NPs in English. In M. Butt, M. Dalrymple, and T. H. King, eds., *Inteliigent Linguistic Architectures*, pages 323–338. Palo Alto, CA: CSLI Publications.

Zaenen, Annie. 2006. Mark-up: Barking up the wrong tree. *Computational Linguistics* 32(4):577–580.

Bobrow, Daniel, Bob Cheslow, Cleo Condoravdi, Tracy Holloway King, Lauri Karttunen, Rowan Nairn, Valeria de Paiva, Lottie Price, and Annie Zaenen. 2007a. PARC's Bridge Question Answering System. In T. H. King and E. M. Bender, eds., *Proceedings of the GEAF07 Workshop*, pages 26–45. Stanford, CA: CSLI Publications.

Bobrow, Daniel, Richard Crouch, Tracy Holloway King, Cleo Condoravdi, Lauri Karttunen, Rowan Nairn, Valeria de Paiva, and Annie Zaenen. 2007b. Precision-focused textual inference. In *Proceedings of the ACL-PASCAL Workshop on Textual Entailment and Paraphrasing*, pages 16–21. Prague: Association for Computational Linguistics.

Zaenen, Annie. 2007. Syntaxis – Op zoek naar een theorie en een methodologie. In S. Hertmans, ed., *Ratio in een emotionele samenleving. Studium Generale 2006-2007*, Cultuurcahiers van de Hogeschool Gent XII, pages 95–108. Ghent, Belgium: Hogeschool Gent.

Zaenen, Annie, Daniel Bobrow, and Cleo Condoravdi. 2008. The encoding of lexical implications in VerbNet predicates of change of locations. In *LREC'08*. Marrakech, Morocco: ELRA.

Bobrow, Daniel, Cleo Condoravdi, and Annie Zaenen. 2009. Learning by reading: Normalizing complex linguistic structures onto a Knowledge Representation. In S. Nirenburg and T. Oates, eds., *Spring Symposium: Learning by Reading and Learning to Read*. AAAI, Palo Alto.

Zaenen, Annie and Richard Crouch. 2009. OBLs hobble computation. In M. Butt and T. King, eds., *Proceedings of the LFG'09 Conference*. Stanford, CA: CSLI Publications.

Bobrow, Daniel, Cleo Condoravdi, Raphael Hoffmann, and Annie Zaenen. 2010. Supporting rule-based representations with corpus-derived lexical information. In R. Mulkar-Mehta, J. Allen, J. Hobbs, E. Hovy, B. Magnini, and C. Manning, eds., *Formalisms and Methodology for Learning by Reading Workshop*. NAACL, Los Angeles.

Zaenen, Annie. 2010. Modeling the mapping from conceptual structure to syntax. In D. Gerdts, J. Moore, and M. Polinsky, eds., *Hypothesis A, Hypothesis B: Linguistic Explorations in Honor of David M. Perlmutter*, pages 215–239. Cambridge, MA: MIT Press.